MANOR HOUSES AND HISTORIC HOMES OF LONG ISLAND AND STATEN ISLAND

THE MANOR OF SHELTER ISLAND SHELTER ISLAND

MANOR HOUSES AND HISTORIC HOMES OF LONG ISLAND AND STATEN ISLAND

BY

HAROLD DONALDSON EBERLEIN

75 ILLUSTRATIONS

Kreuzer-Pelton House, West New Brighton

IRA J. FRIEDMAN, INC.

Port Washington, Long Island, N. Y.

MANOR HOUSES AND HISTORIC HOMES OF
LONG ISLAND AND STATEN ISLAND

Copyright 1928 by J. B. Lippincott Co.
Copyright renewed 1956 by Harold Donaldson Eberlein
This edition published in 1966 by arrangement with the
Estate of Harold Donaldson Eberlein

Library of Congress Catalog Card No: 66-21378

Manufactured in the United States of America

EMPIRE STATE HISTORICAL PUBLICATIONS SERIES XL

TO HIS FRIEND
REGINALD T. TOWNSEND
THE AUTHOR DEDICATES THIS
BOOK WITH MOST CORDIAL
REGARDS

FOREWORD

IN *The Manor Houses and Historic Homes of Long Island and Staten Island* are set forth the stories of the manorial and other ancient homes that are still standing in the insular portion of southeastern New York. As a part of the account of these houses, there are biographical and genealogical notes upon the personages who built or occupied them; likewise notes of the historical events associated with them.

Within the compass of a single volume, it was impossible to include *all* the houses, within the two islands, that deserve the attention of the antiquarian, the biographer or the historian; not a few were reluctantly omitted. It seemed better, however, to record, as fully as space would permit, the houses here dealt with, rather than to embrace a greater number at the expense of reducing the notices of those included to little more than a catalogue of names, dates and events.

For valuable assistance and for courtesies rendered, the author desires to thank Roger Wearne Ramsdell, Gordon S. Marvel, Lion Gardiner of Gardiner's Island, Miss Cornelia Horsford of Shelter Island, the late David Gardiner and Miss Gardiner of Sagtikos Manor, Reginald T. Townsend, Mr. and Mrs. William Floyd, Mr. and Miss Smith of St. George's Manor, Major J. H. Hasbrouck, Mr. Wall of the New York Historical Society, the Staff of the New York Public Library, the Staff of the Pennsylvania Historical Society, Miss McIntyre, E. S. Holloway and Mr. Eugene A. Armbruster for the use of a number of illustrations.

HAROLD DONALDSON EBERLEIN

Philadelphia
June, 1928

CONTENTS

LONG ISLAND

CONTENTS

STATEN ISLAND

ILLUSTRATIONS

LONG ISLAND

ILLUSTRATIONS

STATEN ISLAND

x

ILLUSTRATIONS

LONG ISLAND

LONG ISLAND

"ALL Gaul is quartered into three halves"—thus once did an Irish lad begin his translation of Caesar. A very expressive Hibernianism, to be sure, even though verbally not quite accurate.

Long Island, likewise, may be described as "quartered into three halves" of different sizes—English, Anglo-Dutch and Dutch. A Long Island map coloured to shew its Colonial make-up would look something like a block of Neapolitan ice cream. The eastern or largest "half" —the old East Riding that became Suffolk County—is English; the middle "half," comprising what is now a part of Nassau County, is English and Dutch together, the old boundary between the English and Dutch spheres of influence, before Dutch rule came to an end in New York, starting at Oyster Bay on the North Shore and running in a generally southerly direction across the island; and, finally, the western "half," containing the old Five Towns, is Dutch.

So it was in the beginning, and so essentially has it remained to the present day. So, in all likelihood, it will remain until the surging waves of polyglot and racially nondescript overflow of population from New York City, aided and abetted by local landboomers and speculative builders, completely submerge the ancient characteristics of one of the fairest spots on the Atlantic coast and carry a noxious deposit of "hot dog" booths and outdoor advertisement hoardings from Brooklyn to Montauk Point. Heaven avert that day as long as may be!

"Clams, ancestry and sand," promptly answered a local wag when a supercilious summer "foreigner" asked him one day what were the winter preoccupations of eastern Long Island. The clams are there in abundance, and superlatively good they are. The sand is there, enough to satisfy anyone, heaven knows. And there are hundreds of interesting things besides clams and sand, too. But the whole point of the laconic retort is that there was *ancestry,* even though it might be sandwiched in between clams and sand.

Ancestry on Long Island is a very vital force not to be overlooked. Not ancestry in the snobbish sense, as a fictitious and purchaseable sort of social varnish for parvenus who rely on trumped-up heraldic blasonings and wealthy ostentation to assure their position, but ancestry in the sense of close kinship and community of local standards and pride of hereditary possession of the same interests. The humblest fisherman can tell you whence he came for many generations back and to whom he is related, and he is proud of it. Likewise he is proud of his clams and sand and the bit of country that produces them, and he dearly loves that country. He feels, down in the bottom of his heart, that no one who has not been born and bred in the environment, and whose fathers have had the same privilege, can quite appreciate eastern Long Island. He habitually refers to anyone whose family has not been resident at least a century and an half as a "foreigner." He is not unkind nor churlish about it, but the distinction is there and has to be reckoned with.

This attitude all goes to make up the strong, ineradicable conservatism that is peculiarly characteristic of eastern Long Island. And this conservatism has kept a distinct type of architecture and a distinct type of social manners. The architecture of Long Island is based on the Connecticut "salt-box" type of house, and when houses have grown larger than the primitive type, the "salt-box" pattern has been expanded to meet the increased needs, but its dominating stamp is unmistakable. Eastern Long Island houses could not by any possible chance be mistaken for those found in the western end. They are as different, the one from the other, as day is from night.

Eastern Long Island architecture is of purely English derivation; western Long Island domestic architecture is Dutch in essence. The line of architectural cleavage comes about the middle of the island just where we find the line of racial cleavage. The Dutch houses at the western end of the island display more variety of treatment because the Dutch builder was something of an opportunist and very sensibly made use of whatever materials were readiest at hand. The eastern Long Island Englishman, however, was so entrenched in tradition that he would go to any amount of trouble to preserve the old ways and was not happy when he could not do so.

While we should be extremely foolish not to note with pleasure the diversified scenery of Long Island, the curious local customs that have prevailed time out of mind and still prevail, the highly fascinating history of the island with its witchcraft trials, its horse-racing fostered in the early days by the Provincial Governours, its fishing and whaling customs and all the romance of the sea that grew up around them, the peculiarities of its religious constitution, and its curious class distinctions that still obtain, nevertheless the real keynote to an understanding of everything pertaining to Long Island history and Long Island visible affairs is to be found in the old racial division between Dutch and English which has persisted in innumerable ways to this very day. The old domestic architecture shews it, the features of the people shew it, and little subtle peculiarities and mannerisms shew it at every turn.

The close affinity with New England, especially with Connecticut, is one of the most striking characteristics of eastern Long Island—all that part of the island comprised within the bounds of Suffolk. The domestic architecture is the outstanding, visible witness of that affinity—the sturdy central chimney; the short slope of the steep-pitched gabled roof in front, and the longer slope in the back, coming down to the tops of the ground floor windows and covering the kitchen in the lean-to, or else the roof of equal slopes, back and front, covering the oblong rectangle of the main body of the house, with a separate lean-to roof over the kitchen at the back; the windows with small panes and stout muntins; and the identity of plan, with the small, square entry, the stair winding up against the central chimney, the two large rooms one on each side of the entry, and the kitchen in the lean-to at the back. The only material difference was that the Connecticut houses were covered with weatherboarding while the eastern Long Island houses were commonly shingled with long shingles—sometimes as much as fourteen inches to the weather—because the shingles seem to have been locally easier to come by as a covering than the weather-boarding.

The similarity to New England is easy to account for when we remember that the people came, in the first place, from New England—Massachusetts and Connecticut; that their contacts in the early days were with New England rather than with the Colony of New Netherland and its successor, the Province of New York; that communication with Connecticut was easier and more natural than communication with Manhattan, particularly in the period when travel by road was difficult or well-nigh impossible and travel by water afforded the only convenient method of getting from place to place; that the eastern Long Island towns, for many years, by their own preference, were under the jurisdiction of Connecticut; that eastern Long Island for a long time bitterly resented and unanimously opposed incorporation with the Province of New York when the Duke's Government had supplanted Dutch control; and that it was a keen disappointment to the people when they finally had to surrender their Connecticut affiliation and accept the authority of the Provincial Governours of New York.

But similarity in domestic architecture is not the only visible link with the erstwhile New England association. The towns have gradually grown up after the New England pattern and they have faithfully preserved the New England atmosphere in their general aspect. There is the same stringing out of the houses along both sides of the high street, there is the same ample planting of elms and other broad-spreading shade trees, there is the same generous allowance of space for a village green and oftentimes a village pond as well, and there is the same universal air of order, trim tidiness and self-sufficient, imperturbable poise. Easthampton is one of the most characteristic villages of eastern Long Island, and Easthampton not only has an air of ripe distinction recalling the unruffled repose of some English village whose being is regulated by ancient tradition, but Easthampton also is thoroughly typical of a well-constituted Connecticut community. Its wide, elm-shaded high street, lined on both sides with old houses standing decorously aloof one from another and half-hidden by box bushes, rose vines and other intimate greenery; its broad green beginning, where the high street divides towards the south end of the town, and spreading out over an area large enough to embrace the old burying-ground and the duck pond— all these pleasant features have their counterparts in many a Connecticut or Massachusetts village.

In the constitution of their town government and in their ecclesiastical organisation, likewise, the people of Suffolk followed the pattern set them by their Connecticut neighbours and friends. The New England theocracy extended to Suffolk, though not in so virulent a phase, perhaps, as it shewed in Massachusetts. Persecution and meddlesome solicitude to regulate everyone's religious belief and practice may not have been cardinal features in eastern Long Island ecclesiastical polity, as they were in the citadel of Puritanism, but church membership in good standing was necessary before anyone could take part in civil affairs, even in the humblest capacity, and toleration was certainly not an enthusiastically cultivated virtue. Whatever hospitality and comfort itinerant

8

Quakers may have found at the Manor House on Shelter Island, elsewhere they got a very cold shoulder at best, while adherents of the Church of England met with unconcealed hostility and were looked upon with as much distrust and abhorrent animosity as were Roman Catholics.

However peaceable in behaviour many of their fellow Friends may have been, there is no disguising the fact that some of the seventeenth century Quakers were both aggressive and contentious and readily yielded to their impulse to "testify" in a manner that was highly distasteful to the Congregationalist majority of the East Riding of Yorkshire, as eastern Long Island was then designated. An echo of this we find in the record that, in 1677, the people of Huntington petitioned the Governour "that the Quakers may not be allowed to come into our meetinghouses in time of worship, to disturb us, as they frequently do, and that the Indians may not plant in the meadows we bought of them." To speak quite plainly, not a few of the early followers of George Fox were distinctly prone to raising a disturbance. If they had not shewn this awkward disposition, they would probably have suffered little inconvenience in New England beyond disability to vote or hold office.

Opposition to the Quakers was not always confined to protest merely for, in 1659, one Smith, of Southold, "for embracing the opinions of the Quakers, is ordered to be whipped and bound in a bond of £50 for his future good behaviour." Even more drastic as a measure for suppressing heresy and maintaining "liberty of conscience"—*i.e.,* liberty to acquiesce in the New England system of ecclesiastical polity—was what occurred, in 1660, in the case of Mary Wright, a poor, ignorant woman of Oyster Bay who had fallen under suspicion of witchcraft. It was unanimously agreed that a crime so enormous should undergo a rigid examination. In his *History of Long Island,* Thompson tells us that "there being no tribunal in this quarter competent, in the opinion of the people, to hear, try and determine a business of such magnitude, it was resolved to transport the accused to the General Court of Massachusetts, where charges of this sort were supposed to be better understood. She was arraigned there soon after, and although the evidence of the guilt of witchcraft failed, she was convicted of Quakerism, a crime, in the opinion of her judges, of about equal enormity, and therefore sentenced to banishment!" We ought to bear in mind, however, that most of the odium for this piece of intolerant savagery is to be put upon the Massachusetts General Court.

It is to the credit of the Suffolk people that they kept their heads, for the most part, on the subject of witchcraft and did not get hysterical like the people of the Massachusetts Bay Colony. Indeed, very few cases of witchcraft charges are recorded, and they seem to have been dismissed without creating any undue furore or resulting in flagrant cruelty and injustice. In 1658, Thomas Baker and John Hand, who were ordered to go from Easthampton to Connecticut "to bring us under their jurisdiction," were also to carry thither with them "the wife of Joseph Garlick to be tried for witchcraft." In 1665, "Ralph and Mary Hall are accused of witchcraft in that they practised sorcery on George Wood and

"THE HOLLYHOCKS," STREET FRONT, SOUTHAMPTON

OLD LAURENS HOUSE, SOUTHAMPTON

his infant child of Setauket, by which wicked and detestable acts they most dangerously and mortally sickened and languished." The responsibility of dealing with such cases was generally shifted to Connecticut or Massachusetts courts. There were no witch burnings, and a reasonable degree of common-sense was apparently exercised in handling such rare sorcery cases as did now and then crop up.

If they occasionally whipped erring fellow townsmen for expressing heterodox Quaker views, as they whipped Smith of Southold, whipping was by no means reserved as an agency of religious persecution. They were not sentimentally squeamish about administering bodily punishment. Their shrewd common-sense shewed them the wisdom and effectiveness of meting out prompt justice. They were convinced that chastisement worked repentance or, at least, put a deterrent and wholesome fear of God into the culprit and, if they gave the evil-doer stripes with one hand, with the other they were ever ready to help him back to the way of decent living. The offences punishable by whipping or setting in the stocks were various, but it is fair to say that in most cases the punishment was made to fit the crime and the results seem to have been salutary and direct, in sharp contrast to modern delay and red tape. In Southampton, youths and maidens who lied were to be spanked publicly, if their parents failed to administer the prescribed justice at home, and lack of veracity in those of riper years also called for castigation at the hands of the duly appointed town officer. In Easthampton a town ordinance gave the official who presided at the whipping-post three shillings for each whipping he performed.

The town whippers or spankers of the six original Suffolk towns were not kept unceasingly busy wielding the lash of correction, but under a paternalistic theocracy, armed with a fairly comprehensive equipment of "blue laws," they might readily have found more material for their attentions had the authorities been punctiliously rigid in their application of the town ordinances. The "Established Church" of Suffolk was the Congregational body and, just as membership in good standing was indispensable to any share in civil affairs, so the towns-people were collectively assessed and taxed for ecclesiastical maintenance. The Brookhaven town records, for example, shew us that "Sam Eburne and Rev. Mr. Phillip's sayllory" was to be levied "upon this Towne, Smithtowne & Collal Smith's manner." In addition to levying the parson's "sayllory" upon the people of Brook-haven, Smithtown and the Manor of Saint George, an entry of 1689 in the Brookhaven records states that "At a towne meeting, it was unanimously agreed that a house shall be built upon the land that was Goodman Moshier's, the same demensions of Jonathan Smith's to remain a personedge house to perpetuity. The Towne have also agreed yt 65 pound shall be given for ye Land."

From the paramount position of the Congregational hierarchy indicated by many such entries as the foregoing, we can well understand the enactment of all sorts of town ordinances regulating personal conduct in conformity with the accepted theocratical standards. To quote the Brookhaven Town Records once more in illustration, in 1674 there was set forth, in behalf of the good manners and morals of the people dwelling within the town limits, a schedule of "Orders and Constatutions maed by the Athoaty of this towne, 8th. July, to be duly cept and obsarved :—

(1) Whereas, there have beane much abuese and prophaneing of the Lord's day, by the younger sort of people in discouresing of vaine things and runing of Raesses, Therefore, we make an order, that whoesoever shall doe the licke againe, notis shall be taken of them and be presented to the nex court, there to answer for ther falts and to Reseve such punishment as they desarve.

(2) Whereas, It have bene two coman in this towne for young men and maieds to be out of ther father's and mother's house at unseasonable tiems of niete, It is therefore ordered that whoesoever of the younger sort shall be out of ther father's or mother's house past nien of the clock, at niet, shall be sumonsed into the next court, and ther to pay court charges, with what punishment the cort shall se cause to lay upon them, ecksept they can give sufficient Reson of there being out late."

The penalties for violations of the curfew ordinance and the ordinance against Sunday "Raessing" and "discouresing of vaine things" were apparently left to the discretion of the "cort" which may occasionally have seen fit to call in the town whipper. As a rule, however, moderate counsels and common-sense seem to have prevailed and, considering the touchiness and proneness of some of the plainer sort to contention and petty litigation, a goodly number of cases were arbitrated and differences composed out of court. Witness the following, in 1673 :—

13

"These presents testifieth there was a controversy betweene Elizabeth, wife of John Daves and Sarah, wife of William Sallyer, and Jonathan Daves and Sarah, his wife, and all these women, with the consents of there husbands, and the former arbetrators, have chosen John Tooker and Andrew Miller, to arbitrate all differences betweene them from the beginning of the world to this day."

All the same, notwithstanding willingness to arbitrate petty squabbles and the usual prevalence of common-sense in the awarding of judicial sentence, "sabbath-breaking and profanity were crimes for which most of the towns prescribed punishment" more or less severe, while lying, slander and drunkenness were liable to heavy penalties. Extreme constructions were sometimes put on the ordinances, and one case is recorded of a man being roundly fined for bringing home a lost ox on Sunday.

Of two more of the 1674 Brookhaven ordinances respecting orderly behaviour in the town, one informs us that

(3) "Whereas, god have bene much dishonored, much pressious tyme misspent and men Impovershed by drinking and tiffling ether in ordnery or other privet houses; therefore, we maek this order that whosoever shall thus transgress or sett drinking above two hours, shall pay 5s., and the man of the house for letting of them have it after the tyme perfixed, shall pay 10s., exsept strangers onely."

The other ordinance prescribes

(4) "That whosoever shall Run any Rases, or Run otherwise a hors back in the streetes of within the town platt, shall furfeit 10s. to the use of the town."

The town fathers were evidently as solicitous about speed

limits as some of their modern successors. Their discouraging attitude towards racing was not in accord with the Governour's efforts to promote racing on Long Island, but then the Governour was the Governour of *New York,* and Suffolk, at this time, was more or less under the wing of Connecticut.

While the people of Suffolk were quite ready to *regulate* the drinking habits of their communities, *prohibition* was a thing neither desired nor even thought of. The trustees of one Suffolk town, early in the eighteenth century, to ensure a full and punctual attendance at their meeting by imposing for non-attendance a penalty that would hurt, ordered "from this time forward, that, if any one of ye Trustes after worning givin Doth not appeare at ye time and place, shall forfit a pinte of Rum." This order, if we may judge from other entries of the period, had the desired effect. Rum, or something else equally alcoholic, figured as a perfectly legitimate agency in the local diplomacy to which no "conscientious objector" could possibly take exception. At a general Brookhaven "towne meeting" holden 22 August, 1671, "it was voeted and agreed upon, that John Tooker, henery pering, Mr. Bayles and Samuell daiton to goe and vew the medoes at Unkechaege and treete with sachem about the purchas of the medows, they caring some likers with them to the Indians upon the towne's account."

Query, according to the moral standards of a later date, were the "likers upon the towne's account" to be reckoned as bribery and corruption, as a courteous incident of diplomacy, or merely as a token of the town's good will? At any rate, we can rest assured that these seventeenth century sons of Brookhaven were wise in their generation.

The wording of the last quoted ordinance, in which only one man is given the title "Mr.", was not the result of chance. "Mr." and "Mrs." were really titles of respect, not used indiscriminately for everyone, but given only to persons of consequence and pre-eminent standing. In the town of Southampton, for thirty years after its settlement, there were only five persons dignified by having "Mr." placed before their names. Other people were "Goodman" and "Goodwife" or "Goody"—"Goodman Moshier," for example, in one of the resolutions previously mentioned.

That "Mr." was not an empty honour devoid of material privileges may be gathered from the following characteristic incident. In the early days, as a communal affair the Town of Southampton regularly pursued the business of "killing Whales at the South side of the town in the Atlantic Ocean" and the "profitts of the Whale [were] divided among the Inhabitants in proportion to their rights in the town as Original Purchasers." Everyone had to help in this business "excepting Mr. James & Mr. Lyon Gardiner who were excused by the town on condition of paying so much strong liquor."

The exemption enjoyed by Mr. James and Mr. Lyon Gardiner from a manual share in the operations of whaling and rendering the oil was not, perhaps, to be reckoned altogether a social distinction, although social distinctions were fully recognised and appeared in the perplexing task of "seating the meeting" in the Congregational and "Prisbeterin" meeting-houses, an occasion that invariably gave rise to not a little envy and heart-burning, for the people were exceeding jealous of their social prerogatives as established by their seats in meeting. It was easy enough to settle the status of the Lord and Lady of the Manor and their family and to seat them most honourably according to their rank, but it demanded the utmost tact and discrimination to place the rank and file of the people with the minimum of discontent. Whatever resentments the "seating" may have kindled in the breasts of individuals, nevertheless they abode by the decisions of those who had charge of the matter, and whatever petty internal irritations might exist, the people of each town displayed a singularly united front to all outside their own town boundaries.

There were—there still are—*clans* as well as clams. To a dweller in Southampton or in Easthampton, a man from Southold or Sag Harbour was a foreigner. To this very day, anyone whose family has not lived in his particular community for at least three generations is looked upon as an outsider, a "foreigner," and is spoken of as such. The folk of each community were mightily jealous of their community rights and privileges in which "foreigners" had neither part nor lot, and they were not slow to let this be plainly understood. Time and again can be found resolutions in the old town records directing that shell fish are not to be "catched by fourigners" or that "No furener Shall Chase within this Towne with Howns." And to ensure that their whaling rights were not invaded by outsiders, there were wards and wardens for the beaches.

Despite clannishness, blue laws and a somewhat austere

and generally Puritanical outlook, life in early Long Island was by no means such a drab affair as some might be inclined to imagine. There were divers amusements from horse-racing and fox-hunting down to village husking-bees. Court records can hardly be considered a promising source for light on local merry-makings. Yet, to quote a single instance, the Huntington Town Records give us an amusing glimpse of some rustic doings in the seventeenth century quite typical of the countryside at that time. The horseplay got too much on the nerves of some touchy people and so the matter got into court. We read that:—

"Rachell Turner sayth, that being husking at Thomas Powell's, James Chichester found a red ear, and then said he must kiss Bette Scudder; Bette sayd she would whip his brick, and they too scufeling fell by her side; that this deponent and Tho. Scudder being tracing, and having ended his trace, rose up and took howld of James Chichester, and gave him a box on the ear."

But aside from bucolic gatherings where amorous swains and coy lasses fell to "scufeling" by way of diversion; funerals, weddings, town meetings and other occasions of general assemblage of a more or less festive nature, with a consequent opportunity of tongue-wagging for the elders, and courting for the younger element; impromptu horse-racing, thoroughly enjoyed by all, but outwardly rather frowned upon by the more staid members of the community; and gunning for the game that was everywhere plentiful, there were other causes of excitement that kept seventeenth and eighteenth century Long Islanders from mental stagnation.

OLD MACKAY HOUSE, SOUTHAMPTON

THE SQUAIR-FOSTER HOUSE, SOUTHAMPTON

SCORING,—COMING UP FOR THE WORD.

LITTLE FRED, NEEDLE GUN, JESSE WALES, BELLE OF SARATOGA, OLD PUT, AND LADY WHITMAN

TIME 2:20   2:23½   2:23½.

One source of periodic commotion was provided by runaway slaves. Judging from the advertisements describing them, they must have been an highly diverting lot. One of these negro truants who took French leave of his master, in 1764, is recorded as "wearing a Scottish bonnet and speaking many languages." One of John Sloss Hobart's blacks departed unceremoniously from Eaton Manor, and the advertised description tells the public that the runaway had thick lips, bandy legs and "speaks very bad English," so he could scarcely have been regarded as an ebony Adonis. A much tonier nigger ran away from Thomas Robinson, of Brookhaven. His name was Ned, he could read and write and, it was presumed, had written himself a pass. He had on "a new grey Kersey coat and new pair of pumps." He was also enterprising, for "he stole a barge and was seen off Lloyd's Nack, steering west. Red jackets, beaver hats, "speckled trowsers," and similar nondescript habiliments figured largely as marks of identification for these errant Africans. Sometimes they were desperate characters and indulged in murder, arson and robbery.

The desperate and dangerous characters, however, seem to have been the exception rather than the rule. Indeed, for the most part, the Long Island blacks were apparently a contented and amiable lot and also valuable workers. The desire to make off and try their experience in the great outside world was by no means universal. David Colden, on one occasion, advertised for sale a healthy man and woman "neither in the least infatuated with a desire to obtain freedom by flight."

When the blacks were ill, they were looked after by

their masters and mistresses with the utmost solicitude. In the Lloyd family papers, for example, can be found a number of allusions to medical attention for the slaves, and there are letters from the family doctor giving directions for remedies and for nursing ailing negroes at the Manor of Queen's Village.

Peddlers and itinerant quacks made their appearance from time to time and always proved a source of local interest. Sometimes the quack doctors combined their business with other occupations and advertised their nostrums, when newspapers came to have sufficient circulation to be a useful medium of publicity. One modest healer with a panacea to sell, informs the public that

"It has pleased Almighty God to give me the wisdom to find out the *Golden Mother Tincture* and such a *Universal Pill* as will cure most diseases. I have studied European physicians in four different languages. I Don't take much money as I want no more than a small living, whereto God will give us his blessing.

Johannes Casparus Rubell
Flat bush
Minister of the Gospel and Chymicus."

The quack, "minister of the gospel," chymicus, yearning to cure all the ills of humanity with cheap pills, was not the only sort of clerical itinerant of doubtful value to the community. In 1764 a reward of £5 was offered for the recovery of an horse. The advertisement says that on

"August 18, came to the house of Thomas Emmans, Yonkers, one Moses Pierce, who said he was a Presbyterian minister of Huntington, born at Sag Harbour, and married a Glassenburgh, back of Middletown, Connecticut. He had on a white wig and full suit of black clothes. He hired a mare, saddle, bridle and horsewhip, and crossed Dobb's Ferry, and it is supposed he has gone off with her."

The inference was, no doubt, correct as it was October when the owner advertised. This glibly specious impostor, who kidnapped the Yonkers mare, was probably one of the crop of humbugs that sprang up on the trail of Whitefield's evangelical tour and preyed on the reawakened religious zeal of the people. The *New York Mercury* of October, 1764, notes, "Very great changes have been wrought on many persons of late in the neighbouring Provinces and especially on Long Island, by Whitefield's preaching."

Country fairs, too, supplied an occasional source of diversion. By Act of Assembly, in 1774, two annual fairs were to be held in Suffolk; the first at Southampton, the first Tuesday in July, and the second at Southold, the second Tuesday in September. Each was to last for four days. By this time the road system had become sufficiently well organised to make the successful holding of fairs possible. In earlier times, the lack of roads, and the precarious condition of those that did exist, would have proved a serious obstacle. Communication by water, as already pointed out, was for a long time far more convenient and natural.

Only two years before the establishment of these Suffolk fairs, the *New York Gazette* contained an announcement of a new transportation venture:—

"Samuel Nicolls, Benj. Havens and Nathan Fordham propose to erect a stage waggon to drive from Sag Harbour to Brooklyn ferry once every week in summer and once a fortnight in winter. The stage will set out from the Ferry at 10 A.M., Monday and that night will put up at Samuel Nicoll's in Hempstead plains, where a waggon will be ready for their reception on Tuesday morning to carry them thence to Epnetus Smith's, Smithtown, and there exchange passengers and then proceed to Benj. Haven's at St. George Manor, and on Wednesday morning set out for Nathan Fordham's at Sag Harbour, where a passage boat will be ready to carry all passengers to New London. Goods per hundred, one penny a mile, and baggage as usual.

Thus a passenger may in three days be conveyed 120 miles on a pleasant road for 18s. in a convenient waggon, and meet with the best entertainment. It is intended that the waggon shall come once a fortnight by Islip."

This marked a signal advance in the development of Long Island road travel, and was a far cry from that day, in 1674, when Isaac Platt, constable of Huntington, was "cited befor the Governour for neglecting to attend the Sessions at Jamaica, and not furnishing Captain Salisbury with post horses, when he was riding express."

As early as 1724 the General Assembly appointed commissioners to lay out three roads running the length of the island. By 1733 these roads were laid out and called the North, Middle and South Country Roads, and along them the mails and the travelling public were carried by stage lines. The service, however, was anything but expeditious or comfortable for many years afterward, and the condition of the roads was often thoroughly discouraging to travel.

The roads, perhaps, might have experienced more rapid improvement had horse-racing and horse-breeding got the same official encouragement in the middle and at the eastern end of the island as they had from an early date at the western. In 1665 Governour Nicoll established horse racing on Hempstead Plains and gave a plate to be run for. The races were run on the site of the old Newmarket course, near the Little Plains. In 1669 Governour Lovelace, so we are told, derived great amusement and pleasure from the "general training" and the race-course set up by Nicoll's fiat at Hempstead. It was Lovelace, indeed, who named the course Newmarket. He likewise ordered the justices of Hempstead to receive subscriptions "from all such as were disposed to run for a *crown of silver,* or the value thereof in good wheat, 'for the purpose of improving and encouraging a good breed of horses.' " Right down to the end of the Colonial period and, indeed, afterwards we find frequent allusion both to racing and fox-hunting on Long Island, especially from the middle westward.

The western part of Long Island was radically different from the middle and the east not only in the character of its people and the architecture of the houses they lived in, but also in the face of the country. In the middle and east we find hills and rolling downs as well as plains and heavily wooded tracts. Along the south shore, towards the east, the heavy growth of oaks and the lush vegetation are reminiscent of the southern parts of Hampshire and Wiltshire. In the west, the ditches and dykes and the prevailingly level lands recall the Low Countries and the fen tracts of East Anglia.

Queens County was divided into six towns or townships—Newtown, Flushing, Jamaica, North Hempstead,

Hempstead and Oyster Bay. Kings County, the most distinctly Dutch in its origin and characteristics, had its Five Dutch Towns, increased by the addition of two more at a subsequent date, so that there were in all seven town corporations—Gravesend, Flatlands, New Utrecht, Flatbush, Brooklyn, Bushwyck and Williamsburgh.

The external character of the houses in the Dutch west end of Long Island is discussed in connexion with the several homes described. Inside they were devoid of any architectural pretensions save, perhaps, biblical blue and white tiles around some of the fireplaces. Stress was laid upon solid domestic comfort rather than stately aspect. Low ceilings with heavy, hewn beams; broad generous fireplaces with polished brass fire irons; dressers with a shining array of pewter, copper and tin; and substantial furniture, with capacious chests and the decorated *kas* or wardrobe—these were the outstanding features of the spacious interiors.

Life was orderly, industrious, full of substantial comfort and, in the main, uneventful. The punctuation points of existence, so to speak, were tea parties, quilting-bees, weddings, christenings and funerals, along with the regularly recurring church-goings on Sundays and festivals. Quilting-bees, husking-bees and other forms of corporate work were invariably followed by a generous feast and games or dancing. Drones and idlers had no place in the Dutch scheme of life. Everyone was expected to do his or her fair share of labour. Sinecures amongst public servants were unknown. No better instance of what duties the townsmen looked to their employees to fulfill can be given than a summary of requirements laid down for one of the early schoolmasters of Flatbush. Five days in the week school began with prayer at eight in the morning and ended at eleven with prayer for dinner; at two the afternoon session began with prayer after meat and ended at four with evening prayer; besides giving instruction in the regular curriculum, the schoolmaster was to catechise the pupils once a week; he was also to act as clerk at the church services on Sunday and be responsible for the reading and singing in church; likewise, he was to take charge of the interment of the dead at a stipulated scale of prices and part of his duty, in this connexion, was to go about and deliver invitations to attend funerals, a function for which there was extra compensation if he had to go beyond the limits of the town!

At the time of the Revolutionary War political sentiment was divided in the west, as it was in the middle and the east. This diversity of conviction was to be found amongst both the English and Dutch elements. Ambrose Serle, writing to the Earl of Dartmouth, in April, 1777, says:—

"Long Island (from the Tour of which I am just returned) is the only peaceful and happy spot in this part of America. The Inhabitants are exceedingly benefitted by supplying the Army, and are, excepting a few Presbyterians to the Eastward, eminent for their Loyalty, on which Account they suffered much while under the Terror of the Rebels."

A few months before this, a letter written by one of the Hessian officers expresses appreciation at the pleasant aspect of Long Island as well as noting the attitude of the Quakers in and near Flushing.

MANORS AND HOMES OF LONG ISLAND

"Long Island is a beautiful island," he says. "It has a great number of meadows, orchards, fruit trees of all descriptions, and fine houses. . . . The Quakers are not rebels; on the contrary they have publicly proclaimed in all their gatherings and churches that whosoever went armed would lose their membership." And then he continues, "The whole island forms an exquisite picture. . . . The ladies on this island are not ugly, and upon the mainland are even said to be pretty!"

THE MANOR OF GARDINER'S ISLAND
TOWN OF EASTHAMPTON, SUFFOLK
MARCH 10, 1639: ERECTED A MANOR, 1686

"In the year of our Lord 1635, July the 10th., came I Lion Gardiner, and Mary my wife, from Worden, a towne in Holland, where my wife was borne, being the daughter of one Derike Willemson deurant. Her mother's name was Hachin, and her aunt, sister of her mother, was the wife of Wouter Leonardson, old burgermeester. We came from Worden to London and from there to New England, and dwelt at Saybrook fort 4 years (it is at the mouth of Connecticut River), of which I was commander; and there was born to me a son named David, 1636, the 29th. of April, the first born in that place; and in 1638 a daughter was born to me, called Mary, the 30th. of August; and then I went to an island of my own, which I bought of the Indians, called by them Manchonake, by us the Isle of Wight; and there was born another daughter, named Elisebeth, the 14th. of Sept., 1641, she being the first child of English parents that was born there."

THUS, in his own words, entered in his family Bible, we have the first Lyon Gardiner's account of his migration to America and of his purchase and settlement on Gardiner's Island. Complementing this narration is Governour Winthrop's record:—

"Nov. 28, 1635, there arrived a small Norsey barque of 25 tons, sent by the Lords Say and Brooke, with one Gardiner, an expert engineer, and work base, and provisions of all sorts, to begin a fort at the mouth of the Connecticut River. She came through many great tempests, but through the Lord's great providence her passengers and goods all safe."

Lyon Gardiner, the first of his line in America, came of a well-known East Anglian family and was born in Norfolk in 1599. He held a lieutenancy in a regiment under Lord Vere that went to serve in the Low Countries. His marked ability as a civil and military engineer both won the recognition of his own superior officers and likewise attracted the favourable notice of the Prince of Orange who appointed him Master of Works and Fortifications of the camps in the Netherlands. Thus, it must have been a deserved honour, when an Englishman was placed at the helm of defence in Holland, by a great general, bred to the science of war, and commanding a contest like that against Philip of Spain.

While stationed in the neighbourhood of Worden, Lyon Gardiner not only met Mary Williamson Durcant, who became his wife, but was also much in the company of such men as Hugh Peters, John Davenport and other early Puritans who had sought asylum in Rotterdam. At their instance, it is said, Gardiner accepted a post offered him by the company of adventurers who were minded to establish what was afterwards known as the Saybrook Colony in Connecticut. The most conspicuous promoters of this venture included Lord Say and Sele, Lord Brook, afterwards Earl of Warwick, Sir Richard Saltonstall, John Hamden, Oliver Cromwell, Sir Matthew Boynton, Colonel George Fenwick and Sir Arthur Heslerigge.

In the capacity of engineer, architect, builder and general factor or commander, Lyon Gardiner was to precede them to America "for drawing, ordering and making of a city, towns and forts of defence," besides rendering "suitable for the reception of men of quality" "the site of a city, and castles, and palaces" that had already been chosen at the mouth of the Connecticut River. Three hundred able-bodied men were to be under his immediate control. Fifty of them were to till the soil, fifty were to rear the buildings, and the remaining two hundred were to garrison the forts. This responsible and onerous post Gardiner was to fill for four years, and the needful supplies were to be forwarded from England as the work progressed.

On landing at Boston, after a trying voyage that had lasted from the beginning of August to the end of November, Gardiner, who had long been expected, met with a warm welcome from Governour Thomas Dudley and from John Endicott, Simon Bradstreet, Sir Henry Vane, John Haynes, Richard Bellingham, Roger Ludlow and both the elder and the younger John Winthrop. Up to the time of Gardiner's arrival, Boston had been altogether without fortifications and his presence there moved the leaders to take advantage of his experience and engage him to construct for them the much needed defences. The men of Boston gave their services for the labour and, under Gardiner's direction, built the fort on Fort Hill that continued in use until after the Revolutionary War.

While this work was going forward, twenty men had been sent to break ground at the mouth of the Connecticut River and build a suitable dwelling and other buildings for Gardiner and his wife. The first winter was so bitterly cold and stormy that no work could be done to prepare for "the reception of men of quality" and, at last, when spring came, there arrived not an imposing array of notables, nobles, labourers and soldiers to rear and occupy the projected "castles and palaces" in the "city, towns and forts of defence," but only Colonel Fenwick and a manservant.

Despite the manifold disappointments, the anxieties and dangers, the hostilities with the neighbouring Indians, and the long-delayed arrival or absolute non-appearance of eagerly expected men and supplies, Lyon Gardiner stuck resolutely to his post. Then, at the end of his engagement with the "Lords and gentlemen" of the Saybrook Colony, he bought from the Indians the island now known as Gardiner's Island and there established himself.

Gardiner's Island was part of that vast and princely tract previously granted to William Alexander, Earl of Stirling, and on the 10th. of March, 1639, he had from James Farrett, the Earl of Stirling's agent, a grant confirming "to Lion Gardiner, his heirs and assigns forever the island he hath now in his possession." There was a stipulated quit-rent of £5 to be paid yearly. From the very outset, Gardiner's Island was an independent domain, wholly free from any town relation or interference, and it was not until after the Revolutionary War, in 1788, that it was placed within the jurisdiction of East Hampton.

Until 1653 Lyon Gardiner dwelt on his island with no neighbours but the Indians. He then removed to East Hampton, leaving his son David in possession. David continued on the island till 1657, when he left to spend several years in England. In 1663 Lyon Gardiner died, his wife, son and daughter surviving him. In his will, dated the 13th. of August, 1658, he left all his real estate to his wife "to dispose of it before her death as God shall put it into her mind, only this I put her in mind of, that, whereas my son David, after hee was at liberty to provide for himself, by his owne engagement hath forced me to part with a great part of my estate to save his credit, soe that I cannot at present give to my daughter and grandchild that which is fitting for them to have."

Notwithstanding the testator's memorandum implying substantial advances to his son, the inventory of his property shews that he was still a very wealthy man for his day. Besides an estate of about half the value at East Hampton, the island inventory alone indicates possessions far above the ordinary. By reading between the lines of it we can gather not a little light on the conditions of life on the island at this early period. The island itself is valued at £700;

"ye great house and long, £100; the new house, £30; ye new barne, £40; ye old barne, £10; the house Simons lives in, £20; ye bake house and cellar, £10; ye old mare, £15; gelding 2 years old, £8; a yearling colt, £6; 6 oxen, £40; 7 cowes and some calvs, £35; 1 steer, 4 years old, £6; 3 3 years old, £13; 6 2 years old, £18; 5 yearlings, £7 10s; 1 great Bull, £5; ewe sheep 114, £57; of wethers & rams 66, £49 10s; a jack, £1; 4 boxes for wheels, 10s; 1 broad ax, 2 narrow axes, 16s; 2 adzes, 8s; a bung borer, 2s; 2 wedges, 6s; a tennon saw, 8s; 2 pair fork tines, 2s; stilliards, £1 10s; 5 sicles, 4s; a chest, 8s; a feather bed and bolsters and two old blankets, £3; a hogs head & 6 bushels of salt, £1 10s; 4 barrels of pork, £14; a grindstone and irons to it, £1 10s; 1 hammer, 1s; a punch for hop poles, 3s; 2 great bookes, £2 5s; part of a corslet, 10s; cross staff and compass, £4 10s; steel mill, £2; 4 chairs, £2 10s; 2 shares and 2 coulters, £1 16s; 2 pair clevises, 10s; 2 setts of hoops for a cart, £1 10s; hooks and staples for 4 yokes, £1; 2 bolts and collar, 6s; axle tree pins, linch pins 8, and 3 washers, 14s; 11 harrow teeth, 5s; total £511 7s."

The bucolic tone is clearly dominant and the enumeration of flocks and herds has a patriarchal ring very comfortable and satisfactory to think of, but there is one thing we would gladly know more about—"ye great house and long," which was presumably Lyon Gardiner's first permanent home on the island. We should like to know, too, what "the new house," rated at the worth of £30, looked like and likewise "ye bake house and cellar." Furthermore, amidst the pastoral company of ewes and rams, oxen and yearlings, "7 cowes and some calvs," there crops up mention of "2 great bookes," "part of a corslet" and of a "cross staff and compass," all of which help us to envision the first master of the island, in buff coat and baldrick, corselet and helme, in the days when he was ordering the military and civil affairs of Saybrook, warding off the attacks of wily Pequots, or laying out the sites of a "city, towns and forts of defence."

At every point where Lyon Gardiner appears in the early annals of Connecticut or of Long Island—and his appearances are many—we descry an outstanding, forceful figure, conspicuous alike for many-sided capability and resourcefulness as well as for tactful common-sense, probity and fair dealing with all men, red or white. He was pre-eminently a man fit for the task of hewing out a new country, and he was a man respected by the Indians. His "History of the Pequot War," an episode in which he played an active rôle, is an invaluable document telling the plain, unvarnished truth in a way that shews in no very favourable light the folly of ungrateful and sometimes malapert colonists, who sadly vexed Lyon Gardiner, refused to heed his warnings and scoffed at his wise precautions when he was trying to do them a service. Had they been more willing to hearken to his counsels, more of them would have escaped with whole skins. He truly gauged the treachery of the Pequots, with whom he well knew how to deal, and he likewise rightly judged the honesty and fidelity of Wayandance, the Sachem of Long Island, from whom he bought his island domain.

Besides being a document of the first importance, the "History of the Pequot War" is a bit of straightforward, vigorous writing, instinct with that refreshing combination of simplicity, and pithy, vivid imagery to which much of the prose of the period owes not a little of its compelling charm. Witness the prefatory letter, attached to the History, addressed to his "Loving Friends, Robert Chapman and Thomas Hurlburt," and dated from East Hampton the 12th. of June, 1660. After alluding to their request for his account, he continues:—

"I have now endeavoured to answer your Desires and having rumaged and found some old papers then written it was a great help to my memory. You know that when I came to you I was an engineer or architect, whereof carpentry is a little part, but you know I could never use all the tools, for although by necessity I was forced sometimes to use my shifting chissel and my holdfast, yet you know I could never endure nor abide the smoothing plane; I have sent you a piece of timber scored and forehewed unfit to join to any handsome piece of work, but seeing I have done the hardest work, you must get somebody to chip it and to smooth it lest the splinters should prick some men's fingers, for the truth must not be spoken at all times, though to my knowledge I have written nothing but truth, and you may take out or put in what you please, or if you will, may throw it all into the fire; but I think you may let the Governour and Major Mason see it."

Parts of the narration are rich with Gardiner's good sense tersely put in a few forceful words or else as quaint conceits clothed in similes and metaphors; parts carry the story rapidly forward with a minimum of broad strokes barely essential to the dramatic sharpness of the picture. When some headstrong colonists, spurning his advice, set forth against a Pequot village where the harvest has just been garnered, he bursts out: "Sirs, Seeing you will go, I pray you, if you don't load your Barques with Pequots, load them with corn." When the Boston worthies solicited him about their defences, he writes "these entreated me to go with Mr. Humfry and Mr. Peters to view the country, to see how fit it was for fortification. And I told them that Nature had done more than half the work already, and I thought no foreign potent enemy would do them any hurt, but one that was near. They asked me who that was, and I said it was Captain Hunger that threatened them most, for (said I,) War is like a three-footed Stool, want one foot and down comes all, and these three feet are men, victuals and munition."

Lyon Gardiner's death, in 1663, left his wife mistress of a very substantial estate both in lands and chattels, as

THE MANOR HOUSE, WEST FRONT, GARDINER'S ISLAND

we have already seen. Tradition has it that the price Lyon Gardiner paid the Indians for his island domain consisted of "one large black dog, one gun, a quantity of powder and shot, some rum, and a few Dutch blankets." To James Farrett, the agent of the Earl of Stirling, he paid somewhat more along with a quit-rent of £5 to Lord Stirling if it were demanded. In 1665 Governour Nicoll issued a confirmation of the patent to Gardiner's Island, stipulating an annual payment of £5. Governour Lovelace commuted this annual payment, reserving in lieu of it, as an acknowledgement to His Royal Highness, "one lamb, to be paid the first day of May, yearly."

After the death of Mistress Gardiner, in 1665, the island and all its possessions descended to David Gardiner. David, born in 1636 while his father commanded Saybrook Fort and thus the first English child born in Connecticut, had married Mary Lerringham while he was in England. It was during his proprietorship, in 1686, that the estate was erected into a manor. The letters patent issued by Governour Dongan establish the "Lordship and Manor of Gardiner's Island" and empower the Lord of the Manor to hold Court Leet and Court Baron, besides investing him with the "Advowson and right of Patronage of all churches" within the Manor precincts, as well as with divers other rights and privileges wont to be accorded in similar cases.

Both Lyon Gardiner and his son David maintained the most friendly relations with their close neighbours, the Montauk Indians. As a matter of fact, Lyon Gardiner was chiefly instrumental in restoring to Wayandance, the Sachem of Montauk, his daughter who had been captured and held for ransom by the Narragansett Nini-craft and his men. In gratitude for his good offices the Sachem deeded his benefactor a part of the territory now comprised within the boundaries of Smithtown. In his deed to Lyon Gardiner, Wayandance reserved to himself and his people "whales that shall be cast upon this beach," and likewise "liberty to cut, in the summertime, flags, bullrushes, and such things as they make mats of, provided they doe noe hurt to the horses that is thereon." When Wayandance died he "left his son, the young Wyonkombone, in the care of his good friends Lieutenant Lyon Gardiner and David Gardiner of the Isle of Wight who were appointed Guardians to the Young Prince." Friendship with the Indians of Montauk seems to have been a family tradition, descending from father to son; and this cordiality more than once simplified the question of labour on the island for, so the family historian tells us, "during the lives of Lion, David and John Gardiner the first three Proprietors of this Island, the Indians . . . . . . were hired . . . to plant and till the Indian corn; being thought good hands for that business."

During the lifetime of David Gardiner, the second master of the island and the first Lord of the Manor, the eastern end of Suffolk continued to increase rapidly in prosperity and in the number of colonists but the contacts of the people, notwithstanding their proper Provincial affiliations and allegiance, were with Connecticut rather than with Manhattan. David Gardiner, being a man of affairs as well as a great land owner, was much in Connecticut, the Colony of his birth, and it was there that he died suddenly at Hartford, in July, 1689. The inscription on his tombstone quaintly states that he was "well, sick, dead in one hour's space."

John Gardiner, his eldest son, succeeded as second Lord of the Manor. His period of ownership was marked by the famous and unwelcome visit of Captain Kidd to the island in the summer of 1699. Captain Kidd's name is attached to such varied stories, many of them of questionable probability and still more of them indubitably apocryphal, that it is really a relief when we can past all peradventure link him with actual facts and dates. Captain Kidd, in his very own person, did really visit Gardiner's Island in the summer of 1699 and treasure, that could be seen with the eyes and handled with the hands, he did really leave buried there.

Of the manner of his coming, and of his behaviour while there, two somewhat different accounts exist by members of the Gardiner family. John Lyon Gardiner, the sixth Lord of the Manor, in his historical sketch written in 1798, referring to Kidd's visit, says that "he took what fresh provisions he wanted; came in the night and cut the old gentleman's hands in the dark with their cutlasses; destroyed feather beds; scattered the paper money about the house; staid several days and lived well; tied the old gentleman up to the mulberry tree, which is now standing at the north house; left money etc. with him. It was hid in a swampy place at Cherry Harbour. He shewed Mr. John where he put it, told him if he never called for it he might have it, but if he called for it and it was gone, *would take his or his son's head.*" Needless to say, with this understanding, the deposit was much

safer than it would be in some modern banking institutions.

Sarah Gardiner Tyler's version is that "Captain Kidd
landed upon the island, and buried a large chest of treasure. Fearing the açt had been discovered, Kidd went to
the proprietor and told him what he had done; he knew
his presence was a threat, in this isolated abode, and
demanded refreshment for himself and his vicious looking crew. Among the things provided was a roast pig.
Kidd was so pleased with his repast that he took courteous
leave of his host and hostess, and upon so doing presented
Mrs. Gardiner with a cloth of gold of exquisite beauty,
which has been carefully preserved and handed along
from generation to generation. Not quite satisfied with
having placed himself in the position of a beggar before
a gentleman and his family, Kidd is said to have left a
costly diamond in the well bucket, where he pretended
to drink, just before quitting the island. The diamond
was found, whether in the well bucket or elsewhere,
and has ever since been treasured by the members of the
Gardiner family."

So far as Kidd's deportment is concerned, the two ver-
sions are contradictory, although in most of the main
incidents they are by no means irreconcilable. The slash-
ing of Mr. Gardiner's hands with cutlasses occurred at a
much later date, when an wholly different band of pirates
descended upon the island and carried off everything of
value they could lay their hands on; for this particular
bit of the narrative John Lyon Gardiner obviously got his
facts jumbled, for that identical piece of personal violence towards the Lord of the Manor is unmistakably

chronicled in connexion with the subsequent piratical foray, years after Kidd had paid the final score for his misdeeds. Although Captain Kidd's manners may not have been tinctured with Chesterfieldian grace, and though his call for food may have been a bit abrupt, there is nothing in the least improbable in his telling Mr. Gardiner the whereabouts of his treasure, with a pointed hint to let it severely alone. Neither is there the least improbability in the story that the roast pig tickled Captain Kidd's palate and that he gallantly gave his hostess an handsome present as a souvenir of his visit. That was the way of seventeenth century buccaneers when they were pleased and felt disposd to be gracious. The cloth of gold and the jewel are still in the possession of the family to witness the accuracy of Mrs. Tyler's story.

At all events, treasure was buried on the island and, not long afterwards, when Captain Kidd shewed himself in Boston he was placed under arrest. From his papers it was known what he had left on Gardiner's Island, and the Earl of Bellomont straightway sent an express to John Gardiner bidding him carry to Boston the property Kidd had left in his custody. Agreeably to Bellomont's orders, Gardiner carried the treasure to Boston. According to one account he gave it into the hands of Kidd himself; it was on his return home that he found the ring sticking in the lining of the bag in which he had carried the jewels. The other version of the story has it that Gardiner delivered the valuables to Samuel Sewall, Nathaniel Byfield, Jeremiah Dummer and Andrew Belcher, who had been appointed the "Commissioners to receive and secure the Treasure, Goods and Merchandise imported in the sloop Antonio, Captain William Kidd, Late Commander."

A manuscript, or rather a receipt, still in the possession of the family, after enumerating various articles of treasure such as "Gold, Silver, precious Stones, Silver candlesticks, pieces of Silk &c., &c. received of Duncan Campbell," goes on to mention sundry items received of Mr. John Gardiner on the 17th. of July, 1699, viz: "747¾ ounces of Gold Bars and gold dust, 817½ ounces of Silver and 4⅞ ounces of precious Stones, 12½ ounces of unpolished stones, one piece of Cristal and beazer Stones, etc."

Kidd's fate, after his capture in Boston is well known. He was kept in prison for some months in Boston and then, in the summer of 1700, he was sent to England in a man-of-war sent out to fetch him. In England he was kept in confinement for another year while agents of the government dug up all the evidence they could find against him in the East Indies. During all this time his case had stirred up so much discussion that there was danger of even His Majesty himself being dragged into the scandal. Although the evidence was, in many ways, insufficient to convict Kidd, it seemed expedient that he should be made an example and he was accordingly executed. Whether Kidd was a gallant and misjudged gentleman, the victim of untoward circumstances and the scapegoat for more influential but equally culpable associates, or whether he was a rogue and richly deserved his fate, will probably always be more or less of a moot question. Fair judgment, however, seems to point to the former conclusion.

THE MANOR OF GARDINER'S ISLAND

He was convicted and sentenced to death, not on the charges of piracy—which would have implicated too many powerful and highly "respectable" personages—but on the charge of murder. As a matter of fact, the "murder" was the slaying of a mutinous seaman and was a justifiable act of discipline. Everything points to the fact that he was forced into piracy against his will. Having less powerful connexions than any of those associates who egged him on, and then ran to cover and deserted him in his hour of need, the Kidd was made the Goat.

The distinction between piracy and privateering at the end of the seventeenth century was very hazy and conveniently elastic. Piracy was

"the logical outcome of the system of privateering which the maritime nations of that period had adopted as a legitimate arm of war. King William's War drew out from the colonial ports scores of swift-sailing combatants, armed with the King's commission to capture and destroy enemies' ships. Many of them, once at sea, were unable to resist the temptation to take and plunder indiscriminately, and thus became pirates of full import. This guild flourished at New York under Fletcher as never before, simply because the war gave it cloak and opportunity. Most of the principal merchants connived at it, and profitted by it.

The method of procedure was as follows:—Putting to sea as a privateer, under the aegis of his commission, the pirates bore away for the Arabian Gulf, the Red Sea and that part of the Indian Ocean bordering the southern shore of Asia. These seas were then traversed by the rich galleons of the British and Dutch East India Companies, bearing precious fabrics, spices, gold and gems from the opulent cities of the Orient. These argosies fell an easy prey to the corsairs, who, after capturing them, would send their booty to New

York, and, in their character of privateers, enter it in the Admiralty Court there as lawful spoil of war.

This was one method. The more popular plan, however, was to carry the prize to a pirates' stronghold on Madagascar Island, where they usually found a merchant ship waiting, having been sent out by the merchants of New York with supplies, such as the freebooters required, and which would then load with the corsair's booty and return to New York as an honest merchantman, the pirates not appearing in the transaction."—*Memorial History of the City of New York.*

Kidd was launched on his career as a privateer and sponsored by Robert Livingston, Lord Bellomont and Robert Livingston financing the scheme. The King was made a partner to the enterprise. In 1695, when certain events had taken place that made it imperative to suppress piracy in the Indian Ocean and protect the East India Company's ships, Robert Livingston proposed to Bellomont "to fit out a private expedition against the pirates, the reward for the risk incurred to be the spoil of the pirates taken." Kidd was recommended as a fit person to put in command.

Kidd being approached, announced his terms:—One of the King's ships, of about thirty guns, and an hundred and fifty men. Somers, the Lord Chancellor, the Duke of Shrewsbury, Lord Bellomont, the Earl of Romney and Lord Oxford considered this project in consultation with the King and

"it was agreed to furnish Kidd with ship and crew in return for a certain share of the booty he should take. The agreement was made by Bellomont acting for his colleagues, and was dated at London, February 20, 1695-6. By its terms the

Earl [Bellomont] agreed to provide a good and sufficient ship, to pay four-fifths of her cost, victualling and equipment, to procure a commission from the King empowering Kidd to fight against the King's enemies and take prizes from them as a private man-of-war, and to conquer and subdue pirates, and to capture them and their goods." With these prizes he was to proceed to "Boston in New England. In case he captured no pirates or prizes, he and Livingston were to refund the money advanced amounting to £6000. The prize-money was to be divided—one fourth to the ship's crew, the other three-fourths into five equal parts, four of which were to go to the Earl, and the other fifth to be divided between Kidd and Livingston, who were also to pay one fifth of the entire expedition. If, however, Kidd captured and turned over to Bellomont prizes to the value of one hundred thousand pounds, the ship should remain his as a reward for his services. . . . It only remains to add that King William himself was a partner in this strange enterprise, and a prospective sharer in its spoils"—*Memorial History of the City of New York*.

The whole undertaking was nothing more nor less than *piracy under royal patronage*. With perfect propriety Kidd might have styled himself "Pirate by Appointment to His Majesty King William III." And he could have displayed the Royal Arms above the "jolly Roger." Before judging Kidd too harshly, it would be just as well to take into account all the extenuating circumstances.

John Gardiner, the third proprietor and second Lord of the Manor, who had the experience with Captain Kidd, died in 1738 and was followed by his eldest son, David, as third Lord. David, born in 1691, was the last owner who could speak the Montaukett Indian language. Dying in 1751, he was succeeded by his eldest son, John, born in 1714, as fourth Lord. John died in 1764, being succeeded by David, the fifth Lord, who built the present Manor House and lived till 1774. David was followed by his eldest son, John Lyon, the sixth Lord, who lived till 1816.

This brings the succession down well past the turn of the century. It is a curious thing that from the time of the first David Gardiner, the Manor has descended through a regular alternation of Davids and Johns. In the will of David Gardiner, the third Lord, there is the following clause:—

"I leave to my eldest son, John, my island called Gardiner's Island, and after his decease to his eldest son, and after his decease to the eldest son of the said eldest son, and in that manner to descend to the male line of my family to the end of time."

Although the abolishment of perpetual entails at the time of the Revolutionary War made the intention of this will of no legal force, the custom of descent has always been maintained by the family in accordance with the desire of the testator.

During the Revolutionary War Gardiner's Island suffered not a little depredation and damage at the hands of the British army and navy. On one occasion a fleet of thirteen British ships came to anchor in Gardiner's Bay and a landing party came ashore to levy on what supplies they could for famished troops in Boston. They took 1200 sheep, a cargo of hogs, fowls, cheese and hay worth several thousand dollars, without payment, and went off. At another time Vice Admiral Arbuthnot, with eleven ships, stayed for a summer and winter in Gardiner's Bay, making constant draughts on the resources of the island, taking horses for the use of the officers on shore, and doing great damage to the timber.

A number of British officers were billetted on Colonel Abraham Gardiner at East Hampton, much to his annoyance, although they were always courteously treated by their involuntary host. Sir William Erskine, Lord Percy, afterwards the Duke of Northumberland, Governour Tryon and Sir Henry Clinton were all quartered there at one time or another. All of them made frequent trips to Gardiner's Island which proved a most inviting hunting ground. In stormy weather they took possession of the Manor House and played quoits in the dining room whose oaken floor still shews traces of their sport.

Major André, too, was quartered with Colonel Gardiner at a time when Dr. Nathaniel Gardiner, the Colonel's son and a surgeon in the New Hampshire Continental Infantry, came home on leave of absence. Dr. Gardiner's presence in the house was carefully concealed, but after he had left, André told the family that he had known the doctor was there all along and that he would have liked to meet him, but that his duty as a British officer would have obliged him to arrest Dr. Gardiner as a spy. Curiously enough, Dr. Gardiner was ordered to attend André on the night before his execution.

When André was leaving East Hampton he exchanged wine glasses with his host, leaving two of his own from his camp chest. Needless to say, these are still carefully treasured.

In 1812, when America was again at war with the

Mother Country, a fleet of seven British battleships of the line, several frigates and other vessels as well, came to anchor in Gardiner's Bay. They all got supplies chiefly from Gardiner's Island. Oxen were even taken from the plough to be slaughtered. Admiral Sir Thomas Harvey, who was in command, tried to keep his men from being disrespectful to the proprietor and his family, but it was a difficult undertaking, especially as some of the younger officers did not set a particularly good example. A few weeks later Captain Sir Hugh Pigott came on shore with some of his men and behaved in a most insolent manner so that the family and servants were sent to the cellar for safety. A little afterwards came a letter of apology for Pigott's conduct from the Commander-in-Chief.

The Manor House now standing was built by David Gardiner in 1774 to replace a former dwelling. Though exceedingly simple in its exterior architecture, it has the poise that comes only from well-studied proportions. It is a distinguished specimen of that pleasant and satisfying eastern Long Island manner resulting from a combination of Georgian elements with the early Colonial type.

THE MULFORD HOUSE
EASTHAMPTON
c. 1655–1660

IN ALL of East Hampton, visibly reminiscent as the town is of its past, there is no more thoroughly characteristic link with the days of early settlement than the Mulford house, standing on the east side of the High Street just south of the point where the village green cleaves the broad thoroughfare into two divergent roadways which come together again after bounding the old burying-ground and the pond.

Its gable end to the street and its longer front facing south, the Mulford dwelling is a typical seventeenth century example of the "salt-box" house built about a central chimney which both anchors it, so to speak, and gives it poise. The chimney-top rising midway the ridge of the roof and the long slope of the roof at the back, together emphasise the likeness of the building's contour to that of the old-fashioned salt-boxes that used to hang in farm-house kitchens. Hence the name "salt-box" house, a type commonly found amongst early Connecticut dwellings which the first Colonists had been familiar with in the Mother Country and quite naturally continued to use in the new land to which they had come. As eastern Long Island, or at any rate that part of Suffolk comprised within the towns of East Hampton, Southampton and Southold, was to all intents a part of Connecticut for a number of years after its first settlement, it was to be expected that the same manner of architecture should obtain.

The Mulford house is singularly unspoiled by those tamperings, repairs and "improvements" that have gone far to obliterate the pristine character of so many old houses and destroy the charm that only the unmolested mellowing process of age can give. When it was first built it was doubtless far less appealing to the eye, but with the lapse of years its lines have inevitably softened, its timbers have accommodated themselves to the wonted strains, the roof contours have assumed a fluid quality, and the unpainted shingles of its walls—only the doors, window frames and sashes were ever painted—have taken on an elusive silvery grey-brown hue that is peculiarly agreeable. Then, besides, there is the grateful foliage of old, overarching trees and there is the caressing companionship of ancient box bushes, altheas, rosevines and dense-clustering clematis.

East Hampton was settled in 1648 and this house was built somewhere about 1655 or 1660—there is no remaining record of the precise year. At all events, it was beyond doubt one of the first *permanent* dwellings to be erected. The earliest abodes of the Colonists were mere temporary shelters that could not have lasted more than a very few years at most. As Thompson tells us in his *History of Long Island,* their dwellings were "of the rudest construction with straw roofs and wooden chimneys plastered on the inside." There was no glass in the windows, and they were utterly devoid of almost every feature of either comfort or convenience. As the thatched roofs were always an especial source of danger in winter

MULFORD HOUSE, EASTHAMPTON

MULFORD HOUSE, WEST FRONT AND DOORWAY, EASTHAMPTON

when roaring fires blazed on the hearths, the law obliged every man to have a ladder that reached to the top of his roof, and one man was appointed to see that all the chimneys of the town were well plastered and swept. These flimsy structures soon gave place to staunchly framed, well built and comfortable houses some of which, like the Mulford house, still remain as eloquent memorials.

It seems probable that this house was at first the home of Josiah Hobart, High Sheriff of Suffolk County, but it soon passed into the hands of the Mulford family and has been known as the Mulford house ever since. John Mulford, who came amongst the first settlers of East Hampton, played a conspicuous part in the annals of the town's infancy. He, along with Thomas Baker and Robert Bond, likewise Justices of the Peace, served in the court of three justices, called the "Court of Three Men." By a provision of the General Court the "Three Men" were instructed to "meet the first second Day of the Week of every month for the tryall of any cause according to the publick good of the people & whosoever of those three Men doe not attend the Day at 8 o'clock in the morning shall be liable to pay 5s." Justices of the present generation would probably utter vigorous protest against performing official duties at that hour of the morning.

Captain Samuel Mulford, son of the first John Mulford, "was a man of an original genius, of good judgment but of an odd turn." He had very decided opinions and was outspoken. Consequently his "original genius and odd turn" succeeded in stirring things up time and again in a distinctly lively fashion. He was universally esteemed, however, by the people of the whole of Suffolk and, when representing his county, by hook or by crook he usually managed to get what he set out to get. Born in 1644 or 1645, he was commissioned a Captain of Militia at a very early age. For many years he was the Recorder and always occupied a conspicuous position in town affairs. In 1705 he was elected a member of the Provincial Assembly for Suffolk and from that time until 1720 was continuously re-elected.

He never hesitated to denounce roundly what he conceived to be abuses in the Colonial government and had an uncomfortable way of putting his finger directly on the sorest points, a course which did not at all endear him to his political opponents. In 1714 he made a speech in the Assembly that brought down upon his head the wrath of the Governour and his party. The speech was ordered to be put into the hands of the speaker for summary action. Mulford's rejoinder to this order was to have the speech published and circulated. For this contumacious behaviour the Governour retaliated by having a suit instituted in the Supreme Court against the member from Suffolk. As it was in the Governour's power to prolong the proceedings, Mulford was being kept away from his home unduly long and was unable to attend to his personal affairs. Finally, the other members of the Assembly, recognising the injustice of the situation, united in petitioning that the case might be dropped and Captain Mulford allowed to go back to East Hampton.

East Hampton, along with other Suffolk towns, derived no small profit from whaling. These towns regarded it as a piece of unwarrantable oppression when the Governour levied a tax of one tenth of the oil and bone for the King's use. Not only did Mulford vigorously oppose this tax but even advocated a bounty for the whalers. Failing to win his point in the Provincial Assembly, he determined to go to England and lay his case before the King and Council, although he was then seventy years old or a little more.

Without saying anything about his purpose, he secretly embarked from the eastern end of Long Island for Boston and there took ship for England. On his arrival in London an incident occurred that shewed Mulford's readiness of wit in taking care of himself in an highly original way. The account given by Bayles, the historian of Suffolk, tells us:

"Unaccustomed to the sights and sounds of crowded cities, and with none to urge his case or assist his claim, Samuel Mulford stood in England's capital, unknowing and unknown" and without any attention from the great. . . . "At length by singular accident he became the object of public attention and ultimately gained the ear that brought a just decision to his cause."

"His unsophisticated appearance rendered him a conspicuous and suitable subject for the operations of the light-fingered gentry, and the contents of his pockets were quickly transferred to their own. It would seem as if the proverbial Yankee sharpness must have been early developed in this clime and prompted him to have several fishhooks sewn into his garments in such a manner that the next hand that was introduced into his pocket received an invitation to remain that it was found impossible to decline."

"This amusing affair was quickly noised abroad; it was mentioned in the newspapers at this time, and from an unknown individual he became the topic of the hour. His case was examined before the Council, his information duly appreciated, the tax on oil ordered to be taken off, and he returned to his constituents with his efforts crowned with well merited success."

Back once more in America with his object accomplished, he took his seat in the Assembly only to be met by the active hostility of the Governour whose temper apparently had not cooled. The old matter of the obnoxious speech was revived and, thanks to the vote of an house completely subservient to the Governour's bidding, Mulford was expelled from his seat. The people of Suffolk promptly re-elected him, and continued to re-elect him till October, 1720; then he was finally expelled for protesting against the legality of the house and refusing to unite in an address to the Governour.

Captain Mulford's ready tongue and abruptly expressed opinions always kept him more or less in hot water during his legislative career. One of his sundry expulsions from the Provincial Assembly appears to have come about primarily from his saying that the "house was governed by the devil." A number of the members seriously objected to the imputation. He was readmitted to his seat, however, on explaining that he meant that "the house was directed by the Albany members, they by Colonel Schulyer, he by the Mohawk Indians, and they by the devil!"

Samuel Mulford died in 1725, full of years and honours and sincerely respected and esteemed by all the people of Suffolk County whose interests he had so long a time faithfully served.

"HOME, SWEET HOME" HOUSE
EASTHAMPTON

VERY like its next door neighbour, the Mulford House, is the so-called "Home, Sweet Home" House in Easthampton. It stands on the east side of the high street, just where that thoroughfare broadens out and splits in two to enclose the ancient village green, the cemetery, and the duck pond. This erstwhile home of the Payne family, like the Mulford house, is of the familiar Connecticut "salt-box" type. Its gable end is towards the street, and the whole structure is covered with long, unpainted shingles. It is now so embowered amongst trees, and covered with trailing vines that its architectural identity is almost completely hidden from view. The trees, the rose-vines, the clematis, the trumpet-creepers, and the other growths that lovingly clothe this old dwelling lend a certain charm, however, that would not exist were the outward environment more austere.

The Town of Easthampton has recently acquired this old house, and it will be carefully preserved as a literary shrine. There has long been much acrimonious discussion as to whether John Howard Payne, the author of "Home, Sweet Home", ever lived in this house or not. The proability is that he did spend several years of his early youth there, but it really matters very little whether he did or did not. The house has become a symbol of certain things, and as such is regarded with affection not only from one end of this country to the other, but even across the water, for the sake of those verses which Payne wrote, and which were supposed to allude to this little dwelling. As a symbol, therefore, the Town of East-hampton has done well to preserve and cherish the build-ing. Let the critics and acrid antiquarians fight it out amongst themselves as to the issue of Payne's actual residence, but while they fight let us enjoy the beauty that it holds.

The house is very old, but its history before the Payne family came for a brief sojourn in Easthampton seems to have been uneventful, so that there is little to record. Our history of it, therefore, may begin with the coming of the family, whose connexion with it has made it known wherever the English language is spoken.

John Howard Payne, a son of William and Sarah Isaacs Payne, and a descendant of Thomas Paine, who emigrated from England in 1622 and settled in Yar-mouth, was born in New York City the 9th of June, 1791. His father, William Payne, was one of those brilliant and sensitive men who seem destined from the cradle, if not to actual misfortune, at least to the disap-pointment of never realising their ambitions, or filling the place they are really capable of filling. His wife, Sarah Isaacs, was from Easthampton, and has always been reputed a woman of singularly sweet and lofty dis-position. Her father was a Hebrew and a man of most estimable character. In early life Mr. Isaacs had been converted to Christianity, and his sincerity was such that he won the respect and affection of all his neighbours. How he was respected by them may be seen by the inscription which they caused to be put on his tombstone

PAYNE HOUSE ("HOME, SWEET HOME"), WEST FRONT, EASTHAMPTON

PAYNE HOUSE ("HOME, SWEET HOME"), NORTH GABLE END, EASTHAMPTON

PAYNE HOUSE ("HOME, SWEET HOME"), DOORWAY, EASTHAMPTON

PAYNE HOUSE ("HOME, SWEET HOME"), OLD MILL, EASTHAMPTON

in the old burying-ground at Easthampton—"An Israelite indeed in whom is no guile".

William Payne, the father of John Howard, after his marriage with Sarah Isaacs, lived for a time at Easthampton and taught in the Clinton Academy, which faces on the high street a little distance north of the "Home, Sweet Home" House. The claim for John Howard Payne's residence in the "Home, Sweet Home" House is based on the probability of his having lived there as a very small child, while his father was teaching at the academy over the way. That he lived in the house when from three to four years old was not only possible but quite probable, but there can be no question that he did not live there at a later date. He may have entertained some very early recollections of the house, or he may have received descriptions of it from his family, or might even have seen sketches of it, so that it is not impossible that he had a reasonable familiarity with its appearance when years afterwards he wrote his famous song in Paris.

As a matter of actual history, wherever Payne's infant years may have been passed—in New York City or in Easthampton—he was in Boston when old enough to go to school, and there he was educated. The circumstances of the family had become more and more straitened, especially after his mother's death, and it was necessary for Payne's older brother to do what he could to support the failing years of their father, who had been grievously broken by the death of his wife. This elder brother had a position as clerk in a counting house in New York, but died at an early age. John Howard, realizing how much his father needed assistance, applied for the position which the death of his brother had made vacant, and it was given to him. While working by day in the counting house, by night he was studying and editing a little paper, called the Thespian Mirror, which dealt with dramatic criticism. His writing was so brilliant that he soon drew attention to himself and gained friend after friend, all of whom were eager to lend their influence to assist so engaging and clever a lad.

His dramatic criticisms brought him continually in contact with actors and the stage, and it was not long before he developed great ability as an actor. Owing to his father's scruples, however, he forebore to appear in public, until finally the old gentleman, realising that he was standing in the boy's light by his insistent objections, withdrew his opposition, and thereupon Payne went upon the stage and won for himself a distinguished reputation.

Payne's later life was largely made up of travelling, acting, and writing plays. His successes on the stage in England were most flattering, and wherever he played crowded audiences hailed him with delight. In addition to his conquests on the boards, he found time to write and edit plays, and compose the verses of many songs, some of which enjoyed great popularity. "Home, Sweet Home" was a product of this dramatic-literary activity of Payne's. The music is adapted from an Italian song; the words are taken from a play which he wrote, entitled Clari, or the Maid of Milan.

It took at once as soon as it was produced, and its popularity spread like wildfire over England and America. It was written while Payne was living in France. As a

CLINTON ACADEMY, SOUTH FRONT AND EAST END, EASTHAMPTON

confirmed traveller, Payne had an admirable opportunity to become conversant with the various requirements of foreign consular representatives and this qualification was recognised when, in 1841, he was appointed United States Consul to Tunis. From this post he was recalled in 1845. He then lived in Italy, Paris, and London until 1847, when he returned to America and went to Washington, living there until 1851. At that time he was reappointed Consul to Tunis, whither he went and served until his death in April, 1852.

THE MANOR OF SHELTER ISLAND

BETWEEN the horns of the easternmost end of Long Island that taper off to Orient Point on the north side, and Montauk Point on the south side, and between the Great Peconic Bay to the west, and Gardiners' Bay to the east, lies Shelter Island, a spot of rare beauty richly favoured by nature.

When King Charles I, in 1636, caused the Plymouth Company to issue to William Alexander, Earl of Stirling, a patent for Long Island and the smaller neighbouring islands, the whole insular area was still in the hands of its aboriginal Indian occupants. The acquisition of a domain of such extent required the services of a reliable agent who could be on the ground and direct the moves looking to its development.

As such a fully-empowered agent for the Earl of Stirling, James Farrett sailed for the Colonies early in 1638. On his arrival here, his first duty was to examine all the territory covered by Lord Stirling's patent. In return for his services, he was to have the right of choosing ten thousand acres of the best land in the whole domain for himself. Farrett, as one historian has aptly said, "with unerring judgement chose Shelter Island together with its little neighbour, Robbins Island, as his portion." Hence the place was known for a time amongst the English colonists as "Mr. Farrett's Island" or "Mr. Farrett's Patent." Shelter Island contains about nine thousand acres; its shape is irregular with a maximum

SHELTER ISLAND MANOR HOUSE, SOUTH AND EAST FRONTS, 1735. SHELTER ISLAND

SHELTER ISLAND MANOR HOUSE, EAST SIDE AND GARDEN DOOR
SHELTER ISLAND

length of about six miles and a maximum width of about four.

Farrett seems to have attempted no settlement on the island and, in 1641, sold it to a substantial merchant in the New Haven Colony, Mr. Stephen Goodyear, who soon afterwards became the Deputy Governour. Three or four months after his purchase, Goodyear tried to sell the island to the New Haven Company but, upon mature consideration, they decided not to avail themselves of the Deputy Governour's offer. Without making any move to colonisation there, Mr. Goodyear remained in sole possession till ten years later, 1651, when he sold the island to a company of four associates—Thomas Middleton, Thomas Rouse, and Nathaniel and Constant Sylvester, for sixteen hundred pounds "of good merchantable muscovado sugar."

All four of these associates were engaged in the West Indian sugar industry. Rouse went to Barbadoes and became a wealthy sugar planter. It is said that there he united with the Quakers. The two Sylvester brothers were the sons of Giles Sylvester. They also had interests in sugar planting in Barbadoes. First, however, before coming to the West Indies, they went to Holland with their father, Giles Sylvester, where he died. His family, after that, went to Barbadoes, and Nathaniel and Constant became merchants. Constant remaining in Barbadoes and becoming one of the Governour's Council, lived there till his death in 1671. Nathaniel Sylvester did not remain long in Barbadoes, but came to Shelter Island, being the only one of the four associates who did so. His brothers Giles and Joshua followed him to

Shelter Island a little later. Giles, soon after this, went back to England, while Joshua, after living with his brother Nathaniel on Shelter Island for a few years, moved to Southold.

The Sylvester brothers came in the "Golden Parrot" in 1652. Accompanying Nathaniel was his wife, a girl of sixteen, Grissell Brinley by name, a daughter of Thomas Brinley, Esquire, of Datchett, Bucks, who was Auditor General of the Revenues to both King Charles I and King Charles II.

Their wedding trip, which was really their journey to their new home, brought Nathaniel and his wife by way of Barbadoes, where they stayed as guests for a time at the home of Constant Sylvester. Then, leaving Barbadoes, they sailed towards the coast of New England but, by ill chance, just as they neared the end of their journey they were shipwrecked and many of the goods they had brought with them for their new home were lost. It is said that Nathaniel Sylvester also shipped to Shelter Island from England a quantity of building materials, along with sundry domestic articles and a force of workmen who were instructed to prepare a house for him against his arrival. Just how much these workmen accomplished before the arrival of Nathaniel Sylvester and his bride it is impossible to say, but probably not a great deal was done.

Accompanying Captain Sylvester and his wife were several slaves from Barbadoes along with other servants. The Sylvester family and their retainers were the first white settlers on the Island. Their first child was born about the middle of August 1654.

THE MANOR OF SHELTER ISLAND

It was very soon after their arrival at their new home that Shelter Island became indeed a shelter, for not a few of the persecuted Quakers found an asylum there and were comforted and helped by Captain Nathaniel Sylvester and his family. Lawrence and Cassandra Southwick, amongst others, found sanctuary in this place. They were both well advanced in years, and after they had been put in prison in Boston, starved and flogged, they were banished from New England and threatened that if they ever came back they would surely be put to death.

New England was rigorously zealous for religious liberty, but it was religious liberty of one particular brand, and freedom to practise one sort of religious education. Those who did not agree with that one form might stay away or suffer such ill treatment as might befall them. After their charitable reception in religiously free New England, the Southwicks died and were buried on Shelter Island. Mary Dyer, who afterwards was hanged on Boston Common, had previously been a guest on Shelter Island and experienced the kind of treatment that Nathaniel and Grissell Sylvester always bestowed on the poor and distressed. William Leddra, and Joseph Nicholson and his wife, tasted the gracious hospitality of the Sylvesters. Their wounds were dressed and healed, as well as their spirits strengthened and cheered.

It would be too long to enter into a detailed catalogue of all the Friends who visited the Island and always experienced a cordial reception, but we may mention that John Taylor of York and William Robinson and George Fox, the great apostle of the Friends, either came first to

Shelter Island on their American journeys or at some time stayed there. It was well known amongst Friends that, except in this Island and the Colony of Rhode Island, there was not at that time a spot in any of the Colonies of North America on which a Friend could set his foot without immediately exposing himself at least to suffering and inconvenience and possibly to actual martyrdom.

Although Nathaniel Sylvester and Grissell Brinley, his wife, were not of the Society of Friends when they left England, it seems that within a few years after his settlement at Shelter Island Nathaniel became a professed Friend and his wife probably followed his example. It is recorded that as early as March, 1659, Nathaniel Sylverter is alluded to as a friend of Quakerism.

Nathaniel's brother Giles Sylvester, who lived for a time in Southold, apparently got himself into hot water by his Anti-Puritan sentiments, which at first he made no pains to conceal. In the Southold records, a paper dated the 28th of November 1657 contains a sort of recantation by Giles Sylvester of words inadvisedly spoken, words which gave offence to the Puritan Authorities of the little town. It says:

"Whereas I am accused to say that all the ministers in New England were worse than witches, I owne I said soe for which I am heartily sorrowful and owne to bee very inconsiderately spoken and to my folly and wickedness . . . and hope the Lord shall guide my wayes and words to be more circumspect and like to Himselfe. Then the parties that heard them finding themselves grieved, I told them that I meane noe other

than those that were formall and not spirituall, such was my
meaning, though not expressed till exception was made; therefore, I say, as I sayed, it is very evill in me or in any man to
say such thing, for we ought not to speak evill of any man."

GILES SYLVESTER

The first Manor House on Shelter Island was begun
in 1652 and, as it was not a large mansion, although very
substantially built, it was probably finished not a great
while afterwards. From the very outset, the manor seems
to have been possessed of that atmosphere of home which
the owners had brought with them from the Mother
Country. Their love of plants and flowers had impelled
them to bring across the sea not only roots, bulbs and
seeds, but the actual plants, in many instances, that they
loved to have around them. A witness of this love and
foresight may be found today in the ancient box bushes,
or rather boxwood trees, that grow close to the site of
the original Manor House. They were planted by their
loving owners two hundred and seventy-five years ago,
and their beauty and grace at the present day, as well as
the sincere pleasure they give to all who look at them,
justify the pains of the original settlers who brought
them overseas.

The old or first Manor House sheltered the family of
Nathaniel Sylvester, and his children who succeeded
him, until 1735. At that time Brinley Sylvester, then the
Lord of the Manor, thought that the old house was inade-
quate. After building the present Manor House, in
which by the way he incorporated some of the material
that could be taken from the old house before its demolition, he razed the first home of the family to the ground.

A stone marks the spot to-day where the old house stood, and the lines of its foundations can still be traced in the turf.

In the two hundred years that the present Manor House has been standing, an ineffable mellowness has settled upon the whole place. One instinctively feels, on approaching the house and gazing on its gardens, that the whole establishment has always had the loving care of gentle folk. In a property which has often changed hands, there is always a lack of an indefinable something. One feels it, but cannot capture it and express it in definite words. On the other hand, a place like the manor of Shelter Island seems to have absorbed in some subtle and curious manner the personality of the family that has always lived there. Not only have all the old English domestic traditions been faithfully preserved inside the house and in its immediate surroundings, but the traditional spirit has permeated the gardens as well. Quaint old flowers, not found in most places, are there to be met flourishing in kindly soil. Everywhere there are traces of the old English manner of garden lay-out that existed before the idiosyncrasies of "Capability" Brown and Horace Walpole wrought havoc in English garden ideals. There are the geometrical paterres, edged with ancient boxwood. There are the gravel paths over whose hard beaten surface velvety moss is softly creeping. There, too, are the arbours and borders of flowers, whose homely aspect possesses also a certain patrician quality, flowers usually despised and thrust aside in favour of more highly cultivated and specialised competitors, flowers such as the old fashioned spice pinks, humble portulaccas and gentle forget-me-nots, flowers that our grandmothers cherished, which call up reminiscences of those gracious ladies whose lace caps exhaled the dainty aroma of lavender.

As one enters the estate and, after winding through woodland roads, comes out into the opening where the house stands, there comes a strong feeling that the peace of God is upon the place. It is so absolutely apart from the rush and bustle of the everyday world, so self-contained and self-sufficient of mien, so calm and composed in its assurance and dignity that entrance within its enclosure is like stepping into another world or going back to the England of several centuries ago.

Near the head of the inlet, back of the Manor House, is a stone bridge generally called the water-gate. Moss-covered steps descend to a landing stage, and from here the barges, rowed by lusty slaves, were wont to put off for the mainland, or out to ships waiting in the bay to take those who were going away. The sight of these old worn steps calls to mind the worthies of past time who have trod them in their goings and comings. There was scarcely a person of note in the Province of New York, or in any of the neighbouring Provinces, who had not gone up and down them.

There are, naturally, many stories connected with the Manor House, and the steps recall one of these. One of the daughters of the house, having gone over to the mainland, was sitting under a canopy in the barge driven by the arms of six stalwart slaves. A stranger, young and handsome, standing on the shore and seeing her approach, was so struck by her grace and beauty that he could not rest till he had succeeded in getting an introduction. He was completely captivated and in due time became her husband.

Another daughter of the house, on being asked one time if she was not proud of her father's estate and possessions, promptly replied: "No, I'm not proud of my father's ships, nor of our fine linen, nor of our silverware and fine clothes; I'm proud of just one thing—that I know how to spin!"

Some of the legends belonging to the place are not pleasant, but all have a picturesque flavour. One story tells of the spectre that announces the coming death of the Lady of the Manor. A tall, white-robed figure appears far down an avenue of cherry trees leading up to the house. "The figure walks with a stately tread and bows to the ground three times, raises itself, steps forward a short space and bows again; rising a third time, and stepping forward once more, it reaches the lawn before the entrance door. Here the spectre stops and bows deliberately, only to disappear as mysteriously as it came."

There are other ghosts, too, who are less sinister in their aspect and manner of coming and one, indeed, is quite gentle and reassuring. But one of the most engaging tales has to do with that exceedingly picturesque gentleman, Captain Kidd. It seems that while sailing along the shores of Long Island, on one of his expeditions, the free-booting captain was short of fresh meat and landed on Shelter Island, near the Manor House, with some of his crew, to see what they could find to satisfy their want in the larder. It so happened that

SHELTER ISLAND MANOR HOUSE, THE SOUTH DOORWAY, SHELTER ISLAND

SHELTER ISLAND MANOR HOUSE, THE FOUNTAIN PARTERRE
SHELTER ISLAND

there were two pigs in the yard of the Manor House, and these Kidd nonchalantly ordered his men to take. The pigs, however, had other plans and raised an hideous din of objection. The uproar brought out a maidservant of most undaunted and determined aspect, who defied the whole crew, and bade them let the pigs alone and be off.

Kidd decided this was a case for gentle diplomacy. In his blandest manner he explained to the irate domestic how badly he needed the meat, and tore several links from a gold chain about his neck which he offered in payment. This smoothed the situation and the pigs forthwith went aboard Kidd's ship. The links are still treasured at the Manor House and, to judge from their weight, they are worth decidedly more than the value of the pigs.

Although parts of the original grant have been alienated by sale, the Manor as an whole has never passed out of the family. The Sylvester family, in the male line, became extinct but through descent in the female line the Manor passed to the Gardiners, and from the Gardiners, through the same channel of inheritance in the female line, it has passed to the Horsford family.

THE MANOR OF FISHER'S ISLAND

GRANTED 1640: ERECTED 1664

JOHN WINTHROP the Younger, son of the Governour of Massachusetts and himself subsequently the Governour of Connecticut, obtained a grant of Fisher's Island from Massachusetts the 7th. of October, 1640. The General Court, not feeling quite certain of its territorial jurisdiction, inserted a proviso in the grant. Thereupon Winthrop applied to the Connecticut General Court for a confirmation of the grant. To his application the Court replied, April 9th. 1641; "Uppon Mr. Wyntrops motion to the Courte for Fyshers Iland, It is the mynd of the Courte, that so farre as yt hinders not the publike good of the Country, either for fortifieing for defence, or setting uppe a trade of fisheing or salt & such like, he shall haue liberty to prceed therein."

Winthrop did not settle on the grant until the spring of 1644, when he is said to have begun building and planting there. In 1644 he received from Massachusetts the grant of a plantation at New London and began clearing the land the following year. When he brought his family from Boston in October, 1646, making the journey by water, he met a violent storm and turned aside to Fisher's Island where he settled them and spent the winter.

In 1664 Fisher's Island was detached from New England and included in the King's grant to his brother, James, Duke of York. Thus began the bitter contention

68

that lasted for many years as to whether Fisher's Island, along with other adjacent islands and the eastern end of Long Island, fell under the jurisdiction of New York or Connecticut.

In view of the disputed jurisdiction, Winthrop applied to Governour Nicoll of New York for confirmation of his rights, and from Governour Nicoll, in 1664, he received a manorial grant establishing him and his heirs as Lords of the Manor, and conveying the said Island with all privileges of fishing, hawking, hunting, and fowling pertaining thereto, as well as all other profits, commodities, emoluments, and hereditaments. In the patent it was also expressly set forth that "this Island domain shall be held deemed reputed taken & be an Intire Enfranchised Towneship Mannor & Place of itself & shall always from tyme to tyme & at all tymes hereafter have hould and injoye like & Equall privileges & Immunityes with any Towne Infranchis'd Place or Mannour within this Goverm.t . . . only yielding Rendring & Paying yearely & every yeare unto his Royall Highnesse ye Duke of Yorke & his Heires or to such Governour or Governours as from tyme to tyme shall be by him Constituted & appointed as an Acknowledgm.t ONE LAMB upon ye first day of May if ye same shall be demanded."

Whether this payment in kind was ever required and discharged is not recorded, but a gift of live stock was essayed during the reign of Queen Anne, when the Lord of the Manor at that time endeavoured to present Her Majesty with a pair of moose deer as products of the estate. One of the deer died, however, and the leg of the other was broken in trying to capture it, so that Her Majesty got only the horns of the noble stag.

John Winthrop the Younger, the grantee and first Lord of the Manor, was born in February, 1606, at the Manor of Groton, near Lavenham in Suffolk. This manor had been acquired in 1544 by Adam Winthrop, the grandfather of John Winthrop the *Emigré* and great-grandfather of John Winthrop the Younger. John the Younger received his education in England and was an early member of the Royal Society. That he should have become a member of the Royal Society at his age— he was only twenty-four when the family migrated to America—is sufficient testimony to the manner of man he was. Arrived in America, he shewed his genius for leadership by founding the Town of Ipswich in Massachusetts and New London in Connecticut. After labouring to build up the Massachusetts Colony, he obtained by grant and purchase large holdings of land in Connecticut and Long Island. In view of the close connexion existing at that time between Connecticut and eastern Long Island, it was the most natural thing in the world that Winthrop should extend his settlement projects as he did. For nearly twenty years he was Governour of Connecticut and was instrumental in procuring the Connecticut charter from Charles II. In the intervals of public duty he lived either at New London or at his Manor of Fisher's Island. He died in Boston, full of years and honours, in 1676.

Upon the death of the Governour, John Winthrop of Connecticut, the first Lord of the Manor of Fisher's Island, the estate descended to his eldest son, Fitz-John

Winthrop, born in 1638. Keeping up a close connexion with the Mother Country, as was the habit of the family, Fitz-John Winthrop served as a General in the Cromwellian army under Monk in Scotland and elsewhere until the Restoration, and he was also sometime Governour of Stirling Castle. After the Restoration, returning to New England, he was a conspicuous figure in the Indian wars and, in 1690, he was Major General commanding the expedition against Canada. Later on, for some years, he was the Agent of Connecticut at the Court of William III. From 1698 until the time of his death, in 1707, he was Governour of Connecticut. Most of his life in America was spent in Connecticut and, in his latter years, he was much at New London or at the Manor of Fisher's Island. He was noted for his generous hospitality.

After the death of Fitz-John, his younger brother, Wait Still succeeded to the greater part of the landed estate, including the Manor of Fisher's Island. Born in 1642, Wait Still upheld the family tradition for distinguished careers. The greater part of his life he spent in Massachusetts where, for more than thirty years, he was Major-General commanding the Provincial Forces, a Judge of the Superior Court, Judge of Admiralty, and sometime Chief Justice. He died in 1717 and was succeeded as head of the family by his only surviving son, John, usually known as "John Winthrop, F.R.S.," who was born in 1681.

"John F.R.S." graduated from Harvard in 1700. In 1711 he moved from Boston to New London that he might devote himself to the improvement of the family estate in Connecticut and in Fisher's Island. John's habits and tastes were not in accord with this occupation and, in the end he 'became involved in vexatious law suits with his tenants and neighbours. He likewise engaged in ill-advised mining ventures which turned out both expensive and fruitless. Another source of annoyance lay in some decisions by the Courts and Legislature of Connecticut regarding the settlement of his father's estate. Feeling that he had been wronged in this matter, he went to England in 1727 and ultimately got redress for his grievance from the Privy Council. He continued to live in England, however, and became an active member of the Royal Society. He died at Sydenham, near London, in 1747.

The next Lord of the Manor of Fisher's Island was John Still Winthrop, the elder of the two surviving sons of "John F.R.S." The younger son, Basil, died unmarried. John Still Winthrop was born in 1720 and graduated from Yale in 1737. Much of his early life he spent in England. Although he lived in Boston for a time when he was in America, most of his life after his marriage he passed in New London. There he built a great house at the head of Winthrop's Cove, a dwelling described in *Peters's History of Connecticut,* 1787, as "the best house in the Province." John Still Winthrop was a far more capable man of business than his father had been and he succeeded in ridding his patrimony from all the embarrassments under which it had previously suffered. He died in 1776.

In view of the comparatively short tenure by the families of so many of the manors, it is interesting to note that

THE MANOR OF FISHER'S ISLAND

the Manor of Fisher's Island remained in the possession of the direct descendants of Governour Winthrop's family until 1863, at which time the surviving heirs sold it out of the family. Before the Revolution, there were at least three houses on Fisher's Island that were connected with the Winthrop family. The original part of the Manor House is believed to be 200 years old, although it has grown by sundry additions from time to time. There was also another Winthrop house at the eastern end of the Island, believed to have been built by Francis Bayard Winthrop. Both these houses were built of brick with outer facings of wood.

THE MANOR OF PLUM ISLAND
TOWN OF SOUTHOLD

GRANTED 1659: ERECTED A MANOR 1675

THE Manor of Plum Island, adjacent to the Town of Southold, though one of the shortest-lived and least important of the Long Island Manors, served to accentuate the intimate connexion in early times between Suffolk and Connecticut. The land, about 800 acres, was first acquired from the Curchong Indians in 1659 by Samuel Wyllys of Hartford. A confirmation of this purchase was given by Wayandance, Sachem of the Montaukets, the 27th. of April, 1659. The price paid by Wyllys was "a coat, a barrel of biskitt, and a 100 muxes or fish hooks."

Samuel Wyllys was the son of the Honourable George Wyllys, a former Governour of Connecticut. He was born in 1632 at the Manor of Knapton, near Fenny Compton in Warwickshire. In 1638 he came with his father to Hartford. In 1653 he graduated from Harvard and thence onward occupied a conspicuous and honourable place in the public affairs of Connecticut. He was partly instrumental in securing the Connecticut charter, and the famous Charter Oak stood hardby his house in Hartford. In April, 1675, Governour Andros issued a patent of confirmation to Wyllys and created Plum Island a Manor.

Wyllys, it seems, never lived on the island and there was no Manor House. About 1700 the island was sold to

OLD POST HOUSE, SOUTHAMPTON

OLD GAMBREL-ROOFED HOUSE, SOUTHAMPTON

SAYRE HOUSE, DOORWAY, SOUTHAMPTON

SAYRE HOUSE, SOUTHAMPTON

the Beebee family of Plymouth, and from that time ceased the exercise of any manorial privileges and obligations if, indeed, such exercise had ever been more than nominal. Samuel Wyllys died at Hartford in 1709.

SOUTHAMPTON

Although the Village of Southampton was one of the earliest settled places in Suffolk, the visible evidences of this antiquity have been overlaid, to a great extent, by the effects of modern popularity as a social nucleus of the surrounding region. Many of the oldest houses have disappeared, while others have been so altered or so added to that their original quality is not at once evident. With the disappearance or disguise of so many of the ancient dwellings, the highly interesting historic character of the village has been somewhat obscured. Within the limits of space available it was, therefore, necessary to give precedence to the houses of eastern Long Island that are still intact and to those that have an historic connexion of the widest import. When one sees the houses that still represent Southampton's early days, one deeply regrets that the village could not have preserved its pristine appearance unchanged.

THE MAYHEW MANOR OF TISBURY
MARTHA'S VINEYARD
GRANTED 1641: ERECTED A MANOR 1671

THROUGHOUT New England and, as a matter of fact, all the length of the Atlantic seaboard, the historian and the antiquarian are continually coming in contact with curious survivals of British rule, some of them preserved from early Colonial days.

Now and then these traces of the past take the form of social customs, or traditions. Occasionally one finds rents paid in a certain extraordinary manner, but the most notable of all survivals are the old boundaries which remain as, for example, the small triangular parcel of Connecticut that belongs to Massachusetts, likewise the extreme southwestern portion of Connecticut which encroaches on what might be called New York's lawful territory.

Just so, looking over the islands that lie east of Long Island, we find that when the Provincial Assembly of New York, in 1683, created Kings County (now Brooklyn), Queens County, Richmond and Suffolk, that worthy body also incorporated in what they were pleased to call Dukes County the islands of Martha's Vineyard, the Elizabeth Islands, Nantucket and No Man's Land.

New York's claim to jurisdiction over these islands dated from 1663 and is thus accounted for. In 1605 King James I had created the Council for New England and the territory had been distributed to certain of the nobility and gentry who were interested in the colonisation of the New World. "For thirty years this corporate body had been in active operation until, in 1635, it found that the maximum of its powers and usefulness had been reached, and in their wisdom the remaining active members deemed it wise to divide the territory among themselves as best they could, with their limited knowledge of the geography and nomenclature of it, and surrender their Charter to the Crown." The division took place in February, 1634–5, and was confirmed several years later. Two of the active members, Sir Ferdinando Gorges and William Alexander, Earl of Stirling, "drew" islands along the southeast coast of New England as parts of their shares in this distribution, and from this island drawing ensued conflicting claims.

To Sir Ferdinando Gorges, as Lord Proprietor of the Province of Maine, was granted along with other island possessions, the "Isles of Capawock, Nautican &c near unto Cape Codd." Capawock was the Indian name for Martha's Vineyard. To Lord Stirling fell sundry territory near Sir Ferdinando's holdings in Maine and, according to the Council decree, "hereunto is to belong the Island called Mattawack or the Long Island." Sir Ferdinando Gorges was represented in America by an agent, Mr. Richard Vines, who bore the title Steward-General of the Province of Maine. Lord Stirling's agent on this side of the water was James Farrett. Farrett, it appears, interpreted Lord Stirling's grant as including Martha's Vineyard and Nantucket; they were certainly not included by any grant in the domain of Massachusetts.

In the autumn of 1641 Farrett went to Boston to lay

a complaint before Governour Winthrop about the unauthorised entry of settlers from Lynn upon Lord Stirling's land on Long Island. He let it be known, however, that immigration upon Long Island soil, with due acknowledgement of Lord Stirling's proprietary rights, would receive every encouragement.

While in Boston, Farrett fell in with Mr. Thomas Mayhew, a merchant of Watertown, who was just then in a "maelstrom of financial trouble" and open to any suggestion for retrieving his fortunes. Farrett apparently pointed out to Mayhew how desirable it would be for him to acquire Martha's Vineyard and Nantucket and mend his estate by the profits possible from their exploitation.

The upshot of the dealings was, at any rate, that Thomas Mayhew agreed to purchase the islands for a suitable consideration. Mayhew then discovered that these same islands were claimed by Sir Ferdinando Gorges and that his title to them appeared far clearer than Lord Stirling's. This dilemma of disputed title Mayhew ingeniously solved by settling with both James Farrett and Richard Vines—the price agreed upon was not large in either case—and so put his position as owner beyond all future question, regardless of whether Lord Stirling or Sir Ferdinando Gorges was previously the rightful lord of the soil. Nor did Mayhew forget to satisfy the Indian inhabitants and take title from them as well. All this was in 1641.

Mayhew took actual possession of his islands in 1642. The Reverend Experience Mayhew, grandson of the grantee, wrote: "In 1642 he (Thomas Mayhew) sends

THE MAYHEW MANOR OF TISBURY

Mr. Thomas Mayhew Junior his only Son, being then a young scholar, about 21 years of Age, with some other Persons to the Vineyard, where they settled at the East End, and quickly after the Father followed." The settlement seems to have prospered reasonably and increased in numbers.

It is well to bear in mind the unusual position held by Mayhew as master of Martha's Vineyard and Nantucket. In her monograph on the Manor of Tisbury, prepared for the Order of Colonial Lords of Manors in America, Ida Wightman writes: "It is to be remembered that Martha's Vineyard belonged to no chartered province as then established by royal patent excepting its relation as an integral part of the territorial grants to Sir Ferdinando Gorges. For over a score of years Mayhew never, as far as is known, made any acknowledgement of this technical relationship to the Province of Maine, and Martha's Vineyard continued to be what it was in fact— an independent, self-governing entity."

Sir Ferdinando Gorges had died in 1647, England was distracted by the Civil War, and the proprietary interests of Gorges in Maine were usurped for thirteen years by the government of the Massachusetts Bay Colony, so that we can understand in a measure Mayhew's state of undisturbed independence. But this detached status of the islands could not continue indefinitely.

In 1663 James, Duke of York, bought all of Lord Stirling's proprietary interests. Thereupon, in 1664, Charles II granted his brother, the Duke, a patent embracing the territory of New York, Maine, Long Island "and alsoe all those severall Islands called or known by the name of Martin's Vineyard and Nantukes otherwise Nantuckett." Sir Ferdinando's interest in these islands James apparently did not buy, but there is no indication that the Gorges heirs ever tried to revive it so that there was no challenge to the Duke of York's overlordship, and the governours of the Province of New York, therefore, naturally looked upon the islands as within the scope of their lawful jurisdiction.

Governour Francis Lovelace, in 1670, sent for Mayhew to come to Fort James "to consult about those Parts and their settlement," meaning Martha's Vineyard and Nantucket. Mayhew was likewise to shew his title to the islands and "to bring all his Patents, Writings and Papers relating hereunto with him."

It was a year later when Mayhew met Governour Lovelace in New York, and then their conference lasted for six days. When Mayhew, then in his eightieth year, went back home he bore with him the lordship of a newly-created manor, a commission as Governour of Martha's Vineyard "dureing his natural life," and an appointment as Chief Justice of the Courts of Martha's Vineyard and Nantucket.

The Patent of Tisbury Manor to "Mr. Thomas Mayhew & Mr. Matthew Mayhew his Grande Childe" is, in part, as follows:—

"Francis Lovelace Esq: one of the Gentlemen of his Ma'ties Hon'ble Privy Chamb'r and Governour Gen'll under his Royall Highness JAMES Duke of Yorks and Albany &c of all his Territories in America: To all to whom these Presents shall come sendeth Greetings:
Whereas there is a certaine Island within these his Royall

THE MAYHEW MANOR OF TISBURY

Highness his Territoryes in Length over against the Maine
. . . wch said Island was heretofore Granted unto Thomas
Mayhew sen'r & Thomas Mayhew Jun'r his Sonn by James
Forret Agent to William Earle of Sterling in whom the Gov-
ernment then was . . . : NOW for a confirmacon unto the
Said Thomas Mayhew Sen'r & Matthew Mayhew his Grand
Childe the Son & Heyre of Thomas Mayhew Jun'r in their
Possession & enjoymt of the Premises KNOW YE that by
Vertue of the Commission and Authority unto mee given by
his Royall Highness . . . I have Given and Granted & by
these Presents doe hereby Give Ratify Confirme & Graunt
unto the said Thomas Mayhew & Matthew Mayhew his
Grand Childe their Heyres & all the aforementioned Pieces
& Parcells of Land Islands & Premises to bee Erected into
a Mannor & for the future to be called & knowne by the
name of TYSBURY MANNOR Together with all the
Lands. . . . To bee holden according to the Customs of the
Mannor of East Greenwich in the County of Kent. . . .
Yielding Rendring & Paying therefor Yearly & every Yeare
unto his Royall Highness . . . as an Acknowledgment two
Barrells of Good Merchantable Cod-fish to be Delivered at
the Bridge in this City."

This lengthy instrument investing the lord of the manor
with the rights of hunting, hawking, fowling and all
other customary privileges appertaining to manorial
tenure, and stipulating as acknowledgement therefor "two
Barrells of Good Merchantable Cod-Fish to be Delivered at the Bridge" in New York, "Yearly & every
Yeare," if they shall be demanded, is dated the 8th. of
July, 1671.

The history of Tisbury Manor was not marked by any
spectacular episodes. Life went on in a fairly even

tenour, and apparently both lords and tenants led a prosperous and comfortable existence.

In the time of Thomas Mayhew, Senior, very little of the manor land was alienated by sale, and such few portions as were sold off were conveyed with the stipulated payment of some form of quit-rent annually. The custom of demanding quit-rents was scrupulously maintained and insisted upon by Thomas Mayhew's successors for many years. The annual "acknowledgement" to the lord of the manor might be—as it was in the case of one John Haynes—"2 good sheep at the Manor House on November 15th. yearly and every year," or it might be "a good chees," or "one nutmeg," or "six peckes of good wheat," or from "his beloved brother John," for the privilege of occupying certain land, "one mink skin" to be paid yearly "at my mannor house in the mannor of Tisbury." The payment of these "acknowledgements" was kept up until well on in the eighteenth century, not that those who had to pay them were at all enthusiastic about the practice, but they did not wish to jeopardise their land titles. The last vestige of the manorial system of administration was swept away, of course, at the time of the Revolutionary War.

Where the Manor House of Tisbury, mentioned in these land conveyances and stipulations, may have been has not come down in recorded history; no one seems to know anything about it and, in all likelihood, it was not an imposing structure and differed very little, if at all, from other modest-sized dwellings of the period.

The charter granted to the Massachusetts Bay Colony, October 7th. 1691, settled definitely the jurisdiction of that colony over the present territory of Massachusetts "together with the Isles of Capawock and Nantucket near Cape Cod," and this summarily put an end to New York's claim to jurisdiction over Martha's Vineyard which, since that time has been reckoned a part of Massachusetts.

THE MANOR OF SAINT GEORGE
TOWN OF BROOKHAVEN, SUFFOLK

ERECTED OCTOBER 9, 1693

IT RARELY happens that food suggests important historical associations, and yet the Little Neck clams, so justly prized for their flavour and famous far distant from the place of their origin, by their very name call to mind that bit of Long Island shore whereon the great Manor of Saint George had its beginning, and a deal of Colonial history besides.

The Manor of Saint George, in the Town of Brookhaven, in Suffolk, lies at about the centre of Long Island. According to the terms of the letters-patent creating the manor, its lands stretched in a broad strip across the island from the Sound to the ocean. They were included in the geographical boundaries of the Town of Brookhaven, although by the provisions of the charter—as in the case of other manors—the manorial jurisdiction was wholly independent of and distinct from the civil jurisdiction of the town within whose territorial limits it existed.

Colonel William Smith, the first Lord of the Manor of Saint George, was born on the 2nd. of February, 1654, at Weld Hall in the Northamptonshire village of Newton, near Higham Ferrers. Tradition has it that his mother was "a Maid of Honour in attendance upon the Queen." Whether she was a maid of honour to the unfortunate Henrietta Maria before the irksome days of

MANOR HOUSE, MANOR OF SAINT GEORGE, SOUTH FRONT, MASTIC NECK·

NORTH FRONT

DETAIL OF SOUTH PORCH
MANOR HOUSE, MANOR OF SAINT GEORGE
MASTIC NECK

the Commonwealth came to take all the joy out of life, or whether she afterwards became a lady in waiting to the dull and patient Catherine of Braganza, whom the "Merry Monarch" took to wife when he had come back from exile to "enjoy his own again," is not explicitly stated. At any rate, there seems to have been some definite Court connexion that accounts for young William Smith spending his boyhood as a page in the royal household.

As a page, his education was not effected at one of the great public schools with the curriculum commonly prescribed for lads of his station, but was picked up in the chance and rather haphazard manner his Court duties permitted. Such a programme of training, whatever may be said either for or against it, seems to have had the merit of stimulating resourcefulness and initiative and of breeding that stamp of courtier peculiarly fit and willing to accept posts of responsibility and trust under the aegis of royal patronage. Young Smith was undoubtedly a lad of parts and must have commended himself to the favourable regard of the King, under whose eye he had grown up from boyhood, for when he was but twenty years old, in 1674, he was commissioned "Mayor of the Royall Citty of Tanger in Africa" with the military rank of colonel.

When Charles II married Catherine of Braganza, Tangier, the Moroccan capital, came under the English Crown as a portion of her dowry. It was apparently destined to become an important commercial centre and, with this encouraging prospect in view, both the Crown and individual merchants alike invested large sums for the development of the newly-acquired African seaport. To the youthful Colonel William Smith was entrusted the civil administration of the city and, in an official report of the day, he is described as "the greatest Proprietor in the Place."

The Tangier venture, however, did not meet with the glowing success of which its promoters had cherished such high hopes. Within a comparatively few years from its brave beginning the enterprise was abandoned, the little army was recalled, the fortifications were left to fall into ruin, and the Mayor along with all the other officials went back to England. This was in 1683.

Not long after his arrival in Tangier, William Smith had married. In his diary, "The Tangier Book," as it is called, he records his marriage thus:—

"Tang' this twenti-sixth Day of November 1675. This day beeing fryday I William Smith Borne in Newton neare Higham ferris in Northampton was married to Martha Tunstall of Putney in the countie of Surrie by Docct William Turner in the Protestant Church in Tanger."

On his return he remained but a short time in England and, in 1686, set sail for America, reaching New York the 6th. of August in that year. It is said that Colonel Smith, in this same year, brought to New York the first coach used in the Province, an impressive and ponderous affair of the sort then used in England.

The genial Thomas Dongan, then Governour of the Province, had previously been Lieutenant-Governour of Tangier. Him Smith immediately sought out on the strength of former acquaintance and friendship. Kindred tastes and traits drew these men naturally together, and the erstwhile official companionship of Tangier days soon ripened into a warm intimacy.

In looking about for suitable lands whereon to settle, Colonel Smith's attention fell favourably upon central Long Island, more than likely at the Governour's instance. At all events, it was through Dongan's timely intervention that Smith was enabled to make his initial purchases in the Town of Brookhaven, incidentally thereby removing the cause of what bade fair to become vexatious litigation between the neighbouring residents. Just before this the Brookhaven town meeting had ordered that Richard Woodhull and Thomas Helme "should lay out and divide the common land" known as the Indian field, on Little Neck at Setauket Harbour, and apportion it in equable shares to the sundry persons having a joint interest in it.

Owing to the topography of this choice bit of rich land, it was well nigh impossible to satisfy all the claimants and trouble was impending to disturb the peace of the colony. At this juncture Colonel Smith appeared on the scene simultaneously with a diplomatic suggestion, tendered by Governour Dongan, that the tangle could be averted and every difficulty permanently settled if the claimants would all alike sell out their rights to Colonel Smith.

The people accepted the Governour's suggestion, Colonel Smith acquired Little Neck as well as a considerable area of adjacent land, and a town meeting subsequently approved the whole transaction. From this beginning followed successive purchases from the Indians and others until the estate eventually extended clean across the island in the way already indicated.

Though still a very young man, Smith's sterling merits soon marked him as a person of weight in the community, and when Governour Dongan appointed him a member of the Provincial Council, in 1687, the appointment was regarded with general approval. This post of honour he retained for the rest of his life, despite the hostility of a succeeding governour, as we shall see by-and-by. A further honour was awaiting him when, in 1692, he became Chief Justice of the Province.

In due time Colonel Smith filed a petition with the Governour and Council that his estate be erected into a manor, to be known as the Manor of Saint George. Before filing this petition, he seems to have signified his intentions to the town authorities for it is recorded that at a town meeting, on the 28th. of March, 1693,

"Coll. William Smith of Brookhaven did then and there acquaint the Towne, as he did before, that with the Governour's Lycence he had and intended to purchase divers Tracts of land unpurchased of the Indian natives by the Towne, and within ye limits of theire patent and reserved to theire majtis by theire said patent; . . . and did require to know whither the towne layd any claime to the same or not, and whither they were content that hee the said Smith should purchase and peassoblie enjoy the same. Voated and agreed that the above saide Coll. Smith may purchase and peacably injoy as aforesaide."

The Surveyor General of the Province surveyed Colonel Smith's holdings, making his official report thereon the 19th. of September, 1693. On the 9th. of

THE MANOR OF SAINT GEORGE

October immediately following, Governour Fletcher, in the names of Their Majesties, King William and Queen Mary, issued letters-patent erecting the manor and confirming it to their "Loving subject, Coll. William Smith, one of the Members of Council and Chief Justice of said Province." The document continues, in the usual tenour of such instruments, setting forth the customary privileges and obligations:—

that "full power and authority" are given and granted "at all tymes forever hereafter in the sd. lordshipp and mannour one court Leet and Court Baron to hold and keep"; that "the said lordshipp and manor shall be and forever continue free and exempt from the jurisdiction of any town, township or manor"; that unto the "said Coll. William Smith, his heires and assignes," are ratified and confirmed "all and every the forecited necks, tracts and parcells of Land and meadow within the respective limitts and bounds before mencioned and expressed, together with all and every messuages, tenements, buildings, barnes, houses, outhouses, fences, orchards, Guardings, Pastures, meadows, marshes, swamps, pooles, poundes, waters, water-courses, woods, underwoods, trees, timber, quarryes, Rivers, Runs, Rivoletts, Brookes, Lakes, Streames, Creeks, Harbours, beaches, bays, inlands, fferyes, ffishing, ffowling, hunting, hawking, mines, mineralls, (silver and gold only excepted) and all rights, members, Liberties, Privileges, Jurisdictions, Royaltyes, Hereditaments, profits, benefits, advantages and appurtenances whatsoever to the aforesaid severall and respective necks and tracts and parcells of Land and meadow, Bay, Beach and Inlands, with the bay belonging or in any ways appertaining or accepted, reputed, taken, known or occupying as part, parcell or member thereof"; and, finally, after reciting divers other rights and conditions, that the Manor of Saint George was to be holden "in free and common soccage, according to the tennour of our mannour of

East Greenwich in the county of Kent in our Kingdom of England," for the stipulated nominal quit-rent of twenty shillings a year.

Thus began the Manor of Saint George. As soon as he received his patent, Colonel Smith lost no time in publishing it and accordingly caused it to be read before a town meeting on the 27th. of November following its issuance. The trustees assented to the limits and powers set forth and, in consideration of forty-two shillings paid them by Colonel Smith, they did forever release him "from any or all Quitt-rent due from the little Neck and his home Lots." Again, in "publique Towne meeting" convened the 1st. of May, 1694, the patent was rehearsed and it was again voted and agreed that the inhabitants of the Town of Brookhaven consented to the bounds and privileges therein expressed.

The creation of manor courts—court leet and court baron—to which all persons resident within the manorial jurisdiction were answerable, meant that the first, in which all freemen could take part, which more or less resembled a town meeting in its constitution, and over which the Steward of the Manor presided as judge, enacted ordinances, elected constables and other local officers, set up the stocks and pillory, sentenced the offenders who occupied them, and had cognisance of vagrancy, poaching and fraudulent dealing. The second, the court baron, in which all freehold tenants sate, had cognisance of questions pertaining to law and fact, decided disputes between the Lord of the Manor and his tenantry respecting especially such matters as rent or trespass, and conducted actions for debt and the transfer of land.

As to the stocks, pillory and whipping post, the robust-fibred folk of the seventeenth century had a goodly store of rough and ready common-sense and were not troubled by any mawkish sentimentality, prompting them to coddle offenders, nor by doctrinaire qualms about using vigorous bodily punishment when and where needed. They knew that actual corporeal chastisement for certain types of ill-doers was a far better means of correction, and a far more effectual deterrent from further misdemeanours than the milder expedients of fine or imprisonment prescribed by modern advocates of "humane" methods, that are often maudlin besides, based as they generally are on a sense of misplaced compassion. They knew that the certainty and promptitude of a sound thrashing or a turn in the stocks or pillory—which the delinquent didn't like at all because of the physical discomfort—went a long way farther towards amendment and prevention of repeated misdoings than a leisurely term of confinement in a cell—the disgrace of which the culprit probably didn't mind in the least. They had an wholesome, rugged sense of basic justice and well knew that they could instill a lively repentance and the fear of God more quickly and more surely into some transgressors through their skins than through their conscience. If they chastised the evil-doer with one hand, with the other they were ready to help him back again to decent behaviour.

The stocks and whipping-post were common instruments of punishment, and throughout the early court and town records can be found abundant mention of their employment. For example, in 1666, "Arthur Smith, of Setauket, was set in the stocks there to continue till the rising of the court, with a paper pinned on his breast declaring the occasion thereof, viz., that he did not acknowledge the King to be his King, nor the Government to be his Government." In the Town of East-hampton, in 1727, R. Syme held the post of *common whipper* by vote of the town, and his official fee was fixed at three shillings for each person whipped. In the Town of Southampton the principle of "spare the rod and spoil the child" evidently found hearty acceptance; if a lad under sixteen stole any fruit from a neighbour's orchard the law directed his parents to wallop him severely in the presence of a spectator, and if they failed to lay on the rod themselves, the magistrate was to have the job done and fine the parents for neglect of duty. In the same town, a man who spoke disrespectfully of his neighbour might be "severely whipped," while a female scold could be bridled by standing her up in court with a split stick on her tongue. Castigation could be applied even for heterodoxy, for we discover that in May, 1659, one Smith, of the Town of Southold, "for embracing the opinions of the Quakers, is ordered to be whipped and bound in a bond of £50 for his future good behaviour."

On the 17th. of June, 1697, Governour Fletcher issued to Colonel Smith a second patent or confirmation of the earlier instrument creating the manor. All the previously named powers and privileges were reiterated and "if there was any sort or condition of material thing within the boundary lines of the grant, over which the

Lord of the Manor was not expressly given control, it was because the lenses of the surveyor's theodolite were not powerful enough to discern it, the vocabulary of the dictionary ample enough to express it, or the imagination of the attorney sweeping enough to conceive of it."

In 1689 Colonel Smith left New York City and came to live on his landed estates in the Town of Brookhaven. This removal from town to country did not mean any lessening of his public functions. He remained an active participant in all the doings of the Provincial Council, was concerned with all manner of affairs pertaining to the conduct of Government business and, in addition, now took on his full share of local responsibilities. One of them was to accept command of the Suffolk militia.

Not long after Colonel Smith came there to live, the original Manor House at Setauket was the scene of his daughter Martha's marriage to Caleb Heathcote, later to become Lord of the Manor of Scarsdale. But matters of less happy omen than marriages were forcing themselves on William Smith's attention. The time of his going to live on the manor coincided with the troublous period of the Revolution in England, when King James II. was driven from the throne to be succeeded by his daughter Mary and her Dutch husband, William, Prince of Orange.

Of course such an event could scarcely fail to be reflected by some disorder in the Province of New York and the neighbouring Colonies, and that disturbance came in a very grave and unpleasant form, the uprising in Boston and, in New York, the Leisler Rebellion, with all the attendant rowdyism and fanaticism then let loose. Long before the short, troubled reign of James II. reached its abrupt end, suspicions were rife and there was a general feeling of uneasiness throughout the American Colonies. People distrusted the King's intentions. They knew his attitude in religious matters. They fully understood the menace of French Canada to the north, and there was an undercurrent of rumours of impending French and Indian invasion. They were aware of the friendly relations between King James and Louis XIV., and Louis's endeavours to apprehend the Huguenots in his American possessions and carry them back to France for trial and punishment were fresh in their minds. They fancied their own protestant liberties were in jeopardy, and their fears fed the flames of animosity. Furthermore, in the absence of specific facts, they gave free rein to lively imagination and pictured things far worse than they really were. Though order was preserved outwardly, the situation became increasingly tense.

Albeit no overt act of disorder had yet occurred, up to the spring of 1689, Sir Edmund Andros had perceived "a great buzzing among the people" of Boston, ever since tidings in early April that William and Mary had been proclaimed King and Queen of Great Britain, and he had his soldiers ready in case of trouble. At last, on the 18th. of April, the merest trifle started the outbreak that ended in Andros being made a prisoner. This diverting bit of Boston history space forbids us to discuss here. Suffice it to say that the fire in Massachusetts kindled an answering blaze in New York.

THE MANOR OF SAINT GEORGE

Late in April there occurred in the city, to quote the words of the Councillors, a great "uproar through people coming from Boston" who brought "the surprising news that its inhabitants had set up a government for themselves and disabled his Excellency from acting." Subsequently they say "we cannot imagine that any such actions can proceed from any person of quality amongst them, but rather that they were promoted by the rabble."

The altercation with Plowman, the Collector of the Port, and Leisler's refusal to pay him the accustomed duties because he was a Roman Catholic, though invested with a certain dramatic flavour was, after all, only a minor incident in the tale of disorder and violence. Leisler himself has been roundly damned for the part he played, and blamed as the prime mover of the entire uprising; again, he has been exonerated and defended as the victim of circumstances in which he was involuntarily embroiled. The story is long and involved. Leisler's personal guilt or innocence does not affect our immediate narrative. What is quite certain is that the people completely lost their heads, and what *does* have a bearing on our story is the wave of rowdyism and virulent hysterical fanaticism that possessed the rabble at this time and produced the most unpleasant and intemperate aspect of the whole episode.

The baser sort in the city of New York were haunted by a fantastic and unreasoning dread of popery, a phenomenon, curiously enough, not without a modern parallel of periodic occurrence. All the worst inherent defects of a protestant and untutored mentality suddenly became manifest.

"To have risen to eminence or influence under James, to have been loyal to the British Crown, to be considered as belonging to the aristocratic class, to be possessed of land, or of money, put one under popular suspicion of affiliation with Roman Catholicism and as being at heart hostile or indifferent to the new social order which the popular imagination fancied would follow from the enthronement of Protestantism. . . . The well-to-do classes realised that they were the targets of a growing and irrational hatred. The common people were obsessed with the idea that they were the objects of fiendish plots."—*Memorial History of the City of New York.*

The madness spread like wildfire and infected many of the country districts, especially middle and eastern Long Island where the people had always been closer in spirit and temper to New England than to New York. When Sir Edmund Andros sent a messenger to New York, appealing for a special commission to be sent to Boston to demand his release, and requested that Colonel Smith be one of the commission, "so virulent and menacing was the anti-papal excitement" that it was impossible to accede to the call. Under date of the 22nd. of May, 1689, the minutes of the Council record that:—

"Coll Smith shewed and declared his willingness to serve his Excellency Sr Edmond Andros. . . . Butt hee living att Zealtalkett, the middle of Long Island, ware the people already shoocke off this government and taking him to be a papist or a frind off them, fears iff hee should goe to Boston that the people in his town would rise and plunder his house, if not offer violence to his family."

In New York City absurdly grotesque rumours filled the air. "Staten Island was said to be infested with papist conspirators. Governour Dongan was believed to be the instigator of an infernal plot to destroy New York. The Lieutenant-Governour, a loyal Church of England man, was accused of being secretly a papist and scheming the landing of King James on the Jersey coast with a French army to establish the supremacy of the Roman Church in the Province. Thanks to the aberrations of mob mentality, "there arose in the minds of the masses the vision of a judgement day for the rich and a millenium for the poor, when the populace should mount to the top round of the ladder and the aristocracy should be brought down to earth, to guide the plough and to wield the hammer. Such a situation is the historic cue for the demagogue."

Whether we choose to regard Leisler as a particularly vicious demagogue or merely as a well-intentioned but misguided person, thrust by unkind fate into a position about which centred the storms of disorder, there can be no minimising the reality of that prolonged and serious civil disturbance to which Leisler's name has always been attached, nor can we ignore the intemperance and insolence indulged in by the rabble during that topsy-turvy period when they were in the saddle. The duly constituted authorities of the City and Province were set aside and such civic and social leaders as Philipse, Van Cortlandt and Bayard were maltreated and imprisoned. "Dogs," "traitors," "hellish rascals" were the epithets applied to any who presumed to question the validity of Leislerian rule. When some of the city officials had met at Colonel Bayard's house to celebrate the coronation of William and Mary, they "were insolently ordered to the Fort to join with Leisler and his crew in drinking the health of the newly crowned majesties. To avoid giving an excuse for outrage, they complied, but as they passed through the streets the mob gathered about them with riotous threats. Physical violence was inflicted. Some were kicked and pounded with fists. One was hit with a musket and another was struck with a sword. Colonel William Smith was vociferously saluted as a 'devil and a rogue' and was threatened with such serious mishandling that he was compelled to flee for his life."

When Governour Sloughter arrived on the scene with adequate military support and restored order, one of his first official acts was to arrest Leisler, whom he "found in actual rebellion." For the trial a special court was held and Colonel Smith was one of the "distinguished and scholarly men" included in the judicial commission of whom a contemporary writes, "they were gentlemen most capable of discerning the truth and least prejudiced against the prisoners." At the end of the proceedings, conducted by the ablest lawyers in the Province, Leisler was sentenced to death as the ringleader of a treasonable conspiracy.

In 1698 Lord Bellomont became Governour of the Province and promptly reversed every policy and method of procedure that had obtained under his predecessor, Governour Fletcher, so far as it was in his power to do so. Colonel Smith had been on most friendly terms with Governour Fletcher and had given him loyal support in all his governmental programme. Hence he was not *persona grata* to the Earl of Bellomont who straightway ousted him from the office of Chief Justice and would gladly have removed him from his seat in the Council, too, had there not been a serious obstacle in the shape of

Colonel Smith's conspicuous loyalty and the favour with which he was known to be regarded by the throne.

The Earl of Bellomont, partly from personal motives but more especially from considerations of the administrative policy he saw fit to adopt, so shaped his course "as to penalise those who were responsible for Leisler's death and to bring to pass at least some of the theories of social reform which Leisler advocated by imposing all possible checks upon the accumulation of wealth." The new Governour took an extremely antagonistic attitude regarding the great land grants that had been erected into manors. Ignoring altogether the onerous responsibilities assumed by the lords of the manors, and the signal services they were rendering the Province in developing and establishing settlement, he saw only vast tracts bestowed by the Crown without what he considered an adequate return. Accordingly he determined to strike an effective blow at the whole system. He caused a bill to be prepared prohibiting "any one person from becoming proprietor of more than one thousand acres under any circumstances." By this means he hoped to shatter not only the manors—especially the Manor of Saint George—but other considerable holdings as well, such as the endowments of Trinity Church, the estate of Dominie Dellius, and the growing possessions of Caleb Heathcote.

When the Governour pursued such a radical, confiscatory policy toward land holding, besides openly deprecating Leisler's execution and giving countenance to the faction that had sprung up to perpetuate his views, it was inevitable there should be a clash between him and

Colonel Smith who stood staunchly for all the things to which Lord Bellomont was opposed. It was inevitable that Bellomont should try to strip Smith of his powers, so far as he dared. It was inevitable, too, that strenuous opposition to the Governour's measures should arise from all whose lawful interests were threatened. This opposition he disregarded, and stubbornly pressed his determination.

"Rejecting the advice of the Attorney-General that the passage of the proposed measure was well-nigh impossible, and that even if enacted into law it might produce civil war, the bill was laid before the Council. Three were for it and three were against it. Bellomont cast the deciding vote in its favour. Dominie Dellius at once set sail for England to appeal to the King. Trinity Church invoked the aid of the Bishop of London. The Rector of Trinity, the Reverend Mr. Vesey, omitted mention of the Governour and his family in the Sunday prayers and substituted a petition for Dominie Dellius, imploring God to grant him a safe voyage and give him success with the King. The Governour retorted by petitioning the Bishop of London to deprive Mr. Vesey of his benefice. The upheaval was widespread and intense. The Clergy were aroused. The well-to-do classes were up in arms. The merchants openly aligned themselves against the reformatory measures. The London Lords of Trade were so bombarded with angry petitions, remonstrances and memorials that finally, to Bellomont's discomfiture, they laid upon the table his proposal for the destruction of the manors, and the King whispered in his ear a friendly caution to beware of over-encouraging the Leisler faction."—*Memorial History of the City of New York.*

Lord Bellomont died early in 1701 and his successor in the governourship, Lord Cornbury, reinstated Colonel Smith as Chief Justice of the Province. This office, along with some other burdensom dignities, the Lord of Saint George's Manor laid aside about two years before his death, but the presidency of the Council he retained to the end. He died at the Manor of Saint George on the 18th. of February, 1705, and was buried at Setauket in a family burying-ground near the site of the original Manor House. His gravestone bears the inscription:—

"Here lyes intered ye body of ye Hon. Coll. William Smith Chiefe Justice and President of ye Councill of ye Province of New Yorke. Born in England at Higham Ferrars in Northampton Feb. ye 2 165⅘, and died at the mansion of St. George Feb. 18 170⅘ in ye 51st yeare of his age."

His eldest son recorded in "The Tangier Book":—

"Lord day 3 a clocke afternoon   "Man^r of St. Georges Feb^{ry} 18 170⅘. Then Almighty God was pleased (after sixteen days sickness of a Rheumatism &c) to take to himself our hon^d & Deare Father Col^o: William Smith, who ye 21st of said inst, was intered in the Evening where he had directed: & Mr. Geo: Phillips preached his funeral sermon."

In the inventory of Colonel Smith's estate, the value of his wearing apparel is set down at a very considerable amount in comparison with his silver plate, household appointments and other chattels and movable effects. From this it seems quite clear that the first Lord of St. George's Manor was "by no means indifferent to his appearance" and that he took care "to array himself in a fashion properly bespeaking the dignity and responsibility of his rank."

Martha Tunstall Smith, Colonel Smith's wife, was not

only a notable Lady of the Manor, but also a capable business woman whose influence was widely felt in the neighbourhood. In 1700 it is recorded that she owned a whaling station at Smith's Point, with a whaleboat manned by a crew of Indians. The kill averaged about twenty whales a winter; the oil and bone were sent to England. Thus the whaling station was the forerunner of the Manor House on the present site.

The Lady Martha, as she was commonly called in the neighbourhood with a kindly sense of mingled pride and respect on the part of the people, survived Colonel Smith about four years and an half. Great deference was shewn her and, at the close of the Sunday services, it is said that the congregation always remained "respectfully standing as she withdrew from the Church." The general regard for her was well founded, for she was not only gracious and considerate towards all with whom she came in contact, and an able administratrix of the varied and exacting affairs of a broad estate, but she was also a pattern of domesticity and a "past-mistress in the housekeeping craft of the day." The many entries in her handwriting in the "Tangier Book" shew that, besides a thorough knowledge of preparing all manner of good food, witnessed by sundry recipes, she had a comprehensive acquaintance with the lore of simples and the arts of. nursing and healing. With perfect naïvete, mingled in with the records of births, marriages and deaths are recipes "To Make Allmond Pudding in Gutts," "a Quakinge puddinge," "Calves head pye," and directions for preparing "an oyntment for ye Itch," "a shure remedy for ye Janders," a salve for "Blasted face or pysoned by any ill herb or weed," a potion "for ye grippen of ye guttes," a lotion "to wosh ye head to make hare growe," and sundry other concoctions that must have been vastly useful at a time when capable representatives of the medical profession were few and far between on Long Island.

Though she lived mostly in the country, surrounded by simple folk and with comparatively little intercourse with those of her own station in life, she never forgot her earlier days passed amidst all the pomps of courtly elegance. There is a family tradition that she was wont, upon certain occasions, to don her old court dress and walk up and down in her own house that she might always keenly remember all the little graces of behaviour and polite equipage to which she had been accustomed.

Colonel Henry Smith, the eldest son of Colonel William Smith and "Lady Martha," was born at Tangier in January, 1679. Like both of his parents, he was blessed with a goodly share of talents and the ability to use them. He, too, took his part in public affairs and was a Judge of the Suffolk Courts. His first wife was Anna Sheppard, of Charlestown, and the marriage was performed in 1705 by Cotton Mather. Henry died in 1767 at the ripe age of eighty-eight and was succeeded by his eldest son, William Henry, as third Lord of the Manor.

William Henry Smith was born in 1708 and trod the way of his family in the course of public service as Judge of the Court of Common Pleas. He married Margaret Lloyd, of the manorial family of Queen's Village on Lloyd's Neck. He was succeded by his eldest son John as fourth Lord of the Manor.

There is a story that William, the third Lord of the Manor, was talking over sundry family affairs with his neighbour Judge Floyd. Judge Floyd said that he had put down his four daughters in his will for £1000 each. This was a large sum for those days. To Judge Smith's way of thinking, it was much too large; he considered that women had no idea of the value of money. One of the Floyd girls overheard the conversation and repeated it. The result was a perceptible friction between the younger generations of both families. The pique, indeed, did not stop there. When young John Smith, the great-grandson of the first Lord of the Manor, sued for the hand of Betsey Floyd, Mrs. Floyd would not hear of the match and Betsey, dutiful child, refused John. Judge Floyd died not long after, and when his will was read it was found that he had followed Judge Smith's advice and cut down the portions of his daughters. They each got £900 instead of the £1000 they had expected. This naturally aggravated the indignation.

Acting upon his father's suggestion, John gave up Betsey—for the time being—and married Lady Lydia Fanning, daughter of Lord Fanning, who was Governour of Prince Edward's Island. The girl bride came to live at St. George's Manor—Lady Lydia was less than fifteen when she married—but her married life was not of long duration. She died in April, 1777, when her son William was a month old.

John then turned to Betsey Floyd for consolation, but Betsey was inexorable. Thereupon he married Mary Platt, daughter of Judge Platt of the Upper Hudson. Meantime Betsey married Edward Holland Nicoll.

When her wedding took place, Mrs. Floyd sent John Smith word that now she was sure he would never get Betsey. But Mrs. Floyd was wrong. Mrs. John Smith died and Edward Nicoll died. John again offered his heart and hand to Betsey, and Betsey rewarded his perseverance by accepting.

This same much-married John sate in the New York Legislature from 1784 to 1799. He sate in Congress from 1799 to 1804. He then took his seat in the United States Senate in place of DeWitt Clinton on the resignation of the latter. John Smith was also United States Marshall for the district of New York and Major-General of the Militia. He died in 1816.

The Manor House now standing is the third structure upon the same spot and dates from 1810. It is a commodious and comfortable dwelling and is an excellent specimen of the generous architecture of the day. It has a frontage of one hundred feet and there is a broad hallway running through the middle of the house with large rooms on each side. Much of the furniture in the present house is modern, but some of the original family furniture remains, saved from the fire that destroyed the preceding Manor House after the Revolutionary War.

The Manor House has an unparalleled site, standing as it does on a bluff at the eastern end of the Great South Bay. In front of the house, the bay stretches for nearly thirty miles in the direction of Fire Island, while to the south, not more than three miles distant, rolls the open Atlantic. Although the estate is not more than sixty miles from New York City, houses, roads, fields and forest remain almost exactly as they were at the time of the Revolution, and deer are still unmolested in the forest.

The spot where the Tangier Smiths have dwelt for two hundred years has its place in Revolutionary annals. On the plateau to the west of the house may still be traced the remains of a fort built in 1774 to guard the main ship channel to Moriches and the East Bay. It was here, on Christmas Eve, 1777, that by using a clever bit of strategy the Smiths contrived to put three British smacks, which were anchored in the bay off the Manor House, into the hands of the Continentals. They gave a ball at the Manor House to which they invited the British officers and their crews. When the festivities were at their height and all the guests were unsuspecting, the Americans went out to the British boats, overpowered the few men left in charge, and quietly sailed away, leaving the Britons to a rude awakening of surprise when they left the house.

The neighbourhood of Mastic Neck is divided up amongst the holdings of the Smiths, the Floyds and the Woodhulls. They have all been closely related for many generations past and there is an air of intimacy that is not often met with elsewhere. There is something about this secluded bit of Long Island's south shore that is very reminiscent of the long-settled neighbourhoods in Virginia and Maryland.

THE HOUSE OF WILLIAM FLOYD
MASTIC NECK, TOWN OF BROOKHAVEN
C. 1724

ON MASTIC NECK, in the Town of Brookhaven, completely surrounded by old forest growth and reached by a perplexing maze of circuitous woodland roads, is the former home of General William Floyd, one of the signers of the Declaration of Independence.

The progenitor of the Floyd family in America was Richard Floyd who was born about 1620 in Brecknockshire, in Wales, and died at Setauket in 1690. He came to America in 1654, going first to New England. His stay there, however, was not long. Along with Richard Woodhull and a number of other associates, he removed to Long Island where they founded Setauket in 1655.

Richard Floyd was a man of keen intelligence and vigour, and soon evinced his aptitude for leadership. It was not long before he was chosen Judge of Suffolk County and appointed Colonel of the County Militia. These two offices he held during the rest of his life, discharging their duties to the full satisfaction of his fellow colonists.

His eldest son Richard, the second of the name, was born at Setauket in May, 1661, and died there in February, 1737. In May, 1686, this second Richard married Margaret Nicoll, the daughter of Matthias Nicoll who was secretary to the Duke of York's Commissioners who took over New York from the Dutch. Matthias Nicoll was also the first secretary of the Province of New York under English rule. Richard Floyd the second was appointed a Judge of the Court of Common Pleas in 1723. Like his father, he too held a commission as Colonel of the Suffolk County Militia.

A third Richard, the eldest son of the second Richard, was born in 1703 and lived till 1771. In due time, 1752, he also became a Judge of the Court of Common Pleas and succeeded to a commission as Colonel of Militia in Suffolk. The judgeship and the colonelcy really seem to have become hereditary honours in the senior line of the Floyd family. Like his father and grandfather before him, Richard Floyd the third held these offices for the remainder of his life.

He was not only a man of conspicuous integrity and honour but likewise a person of courtly manner, genial disposition and ever kind and generous to those who stood in need of aid. His wife was a daughter of Colonel Samuel Hutchinson of Southold. It was this Judge Floyd of whom the story is told in the account of St. George's Manor. The consequences of his following Judge Smith's advice anent the inheritance portions of his four daughters are there related.

The fourth Richard, eldest son of the third Richard Floyd, was born in 1736. To him, too, came what by now appeared the natural succession of public offices. In 1764 he was appointed a Judge of the Court of Common Pleas; along with the judgeship he held the commission of Colonel of the Suffolk County Militia.

To this Richard Floyd had descended the bulk of the great family estate on Mastic Neck and elsewhere on

Long Island. No one could have been better fitted than he to play the rôle of eldest member and head of a great family, according to the best old English traditions. He was noted for his affable courtesy, his urbane manners and his generous and unfailing hospitality. His house on Mastic Neck was known far and wide for its proverbially open doors. There he entertained Governour Tryon and all the people of consequence in the Province.

Colonel Richard Floyd was a staunch Loyalist and his name was included in the proscription list of the New York Act of Attainder. Exiled from New York with the rest of the Loyalists, he removed to New Brunswick and settled on the St. John's River and lived there till his death in 1791. His wife was Arrabella Jones, daughter of Judge David Jones of Fort Neck House and sister of Judge Thomas Jones. As Judge Thomas Jones had no issue, and was exiled by the Act of Attainder, the Fort Neck estate descended to the eldest son of Colonel Richard Floyd who, upon his succession, assumed the additional patronymic of Jones, according to the provision of the wills, and became David Floyd-Jones.

General William Floyd, the Signer, was the son of Nicoll Floyd and Tabitha Smith, a daughter of the Lord of the nearby Manor of St. George. Nicoll Floyd was the second son of the second Richard Floyd, who married Margaret Nicoll, daughter of Matthias Nicoll. General William Floyd was thus first cousin to Colonel Richard Floyd the Loyalist. This circumstance well exemplifies how different members of the same families were ranged on opposite sides in the Revolutionary struggle. The "Tangier" Smiths, the Nicolls, the Floyds and the Woodhulls have always been the principal land-holders on Mastic Neck, and there has always been the closest intimacy between all the families, as well as the many blood ties and connexions by marriage. One can scarcely imagine, therefore, what painful situations were brought about by conflicting convictions during the hostilities with the Mother Country.

General William Floyd was born on Mastic Neck, in the Town of Brookhaven, on the 17th. of December, 1734. He had the usual education given the sons of well-to-do country families of that period, but this initial education was not continued by a university career. His school training, nevertheless, was well supplemented by keen powers of observation, aided by natural shrewdness and a large store of sound common-sense. His family name and connexions gave him all the advantages of social position and influence he could desire. With these and his own marked personal gifts, he became a man of note far beyond the borders of his own immediate neighbourhood. In the farming and management of his estate, and in business matters generally, he displayed prudence and good judgement. A rigid Presbyterian, he was religiously inclined and lent his support to all the activities of the period for which one of his position and means would naturally feel responsible. It is an interesting fact, often overlooked, that the majority of Presbyterians and Congregationalists were staunch Whigs, while most of the Church of England people were apt to be Loyalists. The Friends, too, were generally Loyalists, or neutrals with Loyalist leanings.

HOUSE OF GENERAL WILLIAM FLOYD, SOUTH FRONT, MASTIC NECK

HOUSE OF GENERAL WILLIAM FLOYD, GARDEN DOOR OF EAST WING
MASTIC NECK

THE HOUSE OF WILLIAM FLOYD

In addition to other varied interests, William Floyd was a close student of all public affairs, and his clear-headedness and sense of justice brought him prominence in the people's cause against the Ministry of the Mother Country. He was an officer of the Suffolk County Militia for a number of years and, in 1775, was Colonel of the First Suffolk Regiment. His military career, though useful, was uneventful with the exception of one occasion when he prevented some British forces from landing on Long Island. At the end of the Revolutionary War he was commissioned a Major General.

General Floyd's temperamental qualifications better fitted him for public business and legislative affairs than for military matters. His contemporaries recognising this fact, kept him from the outbreak of the Revolution onward for many years occupied in the service of his country.

He served a short term in the Provincial Assembly of New York and was then delegated to the First Continental Congress at Philadelphia. So far as the records shew and common tradition can be relied upon, it seems that General Floyd from the very first was in favour of complete independence of the Mother Country. With this political bias, it is easy to understand that he was eager for the Declaration of Independence, of which he was one of the signers.

From 1777 to 1783 he was a State Senator under the first New York constitution, and was *appointed* from the southern district, which was then within the British lines. *Appointment* was necessary; wherever British forces were in control no American elections, naturally, could be held.

During the whole Revolutionary period, the British forces controlled virtually all of Long Island. The property of Loyalists was more or less respected and protected, and save for occasional raids made by whaleboat parties from the Connecticut shore, the King's adherents had little to complain of. The property of the Whigs, on the other hand, suffered severely in many cases.

General Floyd's attitude, of course, was well known to the British authorities. His property was seized and his family fled to Middletown, Connecticut. The British troops, according to all accounts, ravaged the place, used the house as cavalry barracks, and made the whole estate generally uninhabitable. General Floyd, under stress of war conditions and the occupation of his house, was away from Long Island for about six years, so that he scarcely realised what havoc had been wrought in his home until he came back and saw with his own eyes what had taken place.

From 1784 to 1788 General Floyd was again returned as State Senator from this same district, this time, however, being duly elected by the voters who could now register their choice without let or hindrance. From 1787 to 1789 he was chosen a member of the Council of Appointment; in 1792, 1800 and 1804 he was a Presidential Elector.

With the limitations of a country school education, General Floyd was not a brilliant speaker, nor was he anything of a stylist in writing. His thorough knowledge, however, of all the current issues and of all the affairs in hand, his conscientious and zealous attention to duty, and his intensely practical and mature judgement, made him of the greatest value to his Country and State in all legislative and executive deliberations.

Late in life, he withdrew from the old house on Mastic Neck and left the administration of his estate to his children, while he himself undertook the pioneering and carving out of a new home in Oneida County.

The old house, lying on a remote part of Mastic Neck distant from the highway and approachable only by winding woodland roads, presents an ample reward at last to those who overcome the difficulties of search. Facing the south and looking across a broad, open expanse of lawn, sheltered on all sides by dense wooded growth, this venerable eighteenth century dwelling with white weather-boarded walls presents an aspect of mingled serenity and dignity that at once captivates the imagination. One feels instinctively, even without knowing anything of its history, that its walls could tell many a story were they endowed with speech.

The oldest part of the house, so far as the records shew, was built about 1724. Additions were made at an early date, so that the house as we see it now is virtually the same as when General William Floyd lived there, save for several unimportant verandahs tacked on in the nineteenth century.

But even more than the fabric of the house has remained unchanged. The hedges and ditches still mark the original boundaries of the fields, and each field bears its old distinctive name by which it has always been known since the place was first cultivated and the first plot drawn up on parchment, shewing the position of the fields and their extent. In this respect, the estate closely perpetuates all the usages and customs derived from the Mother Country two hundred years ago.

THE HOUSE OF
GENERAL NATHANIEL WOODHULL
MASTIC NECK, TOWN OF BROOKHAVEN

THE old house on Mastic Neck in the Town of Brookhaven, in which General Nathaniel Woodhull lived, has, like some of the other historic homes of Long Island, fallen into a sorry state of decay. The surroundings are overgrown with weeds, and there is all round a general air of disorder and neglect that cannot fail to be depressing. The windows of the house are boarded up, and although the fabric seems still to be sound enough, the general aspect indicates that its days are numbered. It is on the edge of one of the land-booming plot-developments in eastern Long Island, and one cannot help feeling that it will not be very long ere it is demolished before the onslaught of inhabitants who know nothing of its history.

Nathaniel Woodhull was born in Brookhaven Township in 1722, and was a son of Nathaniel Woodhull of Brookhaven, a descendant of Richard Woodhull, who came from Thetford about the middle of the 17th Century and settled first at Jamaica and afterwards at Brookhaven.

Nathaniel, being the son of a large landowner and born to inherit an estate which required careful supervision and adroit administration, was educated with a view to making him a competent administrator and a leader in the agricultural community by which he was surrounded. He was naturally gifted mentally, and his noteworthy abilities soon brought him not only into public notice but into public service as well.

His first military service was in the old French and Indian War, where he served as a Major, in 1753, under General Abercrombie in the campaign against Crown Point and Ticonderoga. He was at the capture of Fort Frontenac, where he gave evidence of distinguished gallantry, and served as a Colonel under Lord Amherst in the campaign against Montreal.

He represented Suffolk County for a time in the Provincial Assembly of New York, and he became President of the Congress of New York, which met at White Plains. He was also President of the New York State Assembly, convened after the Declaration of Independence.

In 1776, in the month of August, General Woodhull, having obtained leave of absence in order to visit his home at Mastic, got word that the British had landed troops and were threatening the position of New York from the Brooklyn side. Thereupon he hastened to Jamaica to join the Queens' County and Suffolk Militia. In this emergency, he was detailed to protect the cattle and crops intended for the supply of American troops, and to drive off from all the farms in the region cattle that might fall into the hands of the British.

His orders were to drive the cattle to the high ridge running through Queens County, with troops guarding them. He was handicapped by too small a force of men at his command, and sent word to headquarters that "he was at the place with less than 100 men and could do

GENERAL NATHANIEL WOODHULL HOUSE, SOUTH FRONT, MASTIC NECK

NICOLL FLOYD HOUSE, EAST FRONT, MASTIC NECK

nothing without reinforcements and would have to retreat unless he had assistance." There were between one and two hundred head of cattle to guard and remove, and the called-for assistance did not come. He was, therefore, obliged on the morning of the 28th to fall back several miles to the east of Jamaica, there to await the reinforcements that had been promised him. Falling back slowly, with a few companions, he came to Carpenter's Tavern, at what is now Hollis, and there took refuge from a thunderstorm. While he and a few who accompanied him were taking shelter at the inn, Sir William Erskine with the 17th Light Dragoons and the 71st Foot came up and surrounded the hostelry, having heard that General Woodhull was there.

Being called upon to surrender, he said that he would do so "if treated like a gentleman." Being assured that he would be so treated, he gave up his sword. It is said that one of his captors bade him say "God save the King," to which he replied, "God save us all and the Continental Army." So far, the accounts of his capture in the main agree.

According to one account, his reply so angered one of the British officers that he struck Woodhull with his broad-sword and would have killed him outright had it not been for the timely interference of Major De Lancey. As it was, General Woodhull sustained serious wounds on the head and on one of his arms, which was badly mangled from the shoulder to the wrist.

According to the other account, which by the way Thomas Jones gives in his history, General Woodhull, taking advantage of the darkness, endeavoured to escape, and while climbing over a fence was wounded by his captors, whose duty it was to prevent his carrying out his obvious intention of getting away. In any event, there is no ground for crediting the slanderous story that Major De Lancey struck and wounded him after he had surrendered. There is not only no good reason for believing the slanderous story about De Lancey, but it is open to doubt whether any officer of the British Army struck a defenceless man unless under some such provocation as attempting to break away after having given himself up.

After he was wounded, tradition has it that he was first taken into the inn and afterwards removed to Jamaica, where he was confined in a church that had been turned into a prison on the spur of the moment. From there, with eighty or more prisoners, he was taken to Gravesend Bay, and imprisoned on a ship that had been used to transport cattle and was in a filthy state. His wounds were infected and their already serious condition much aggravated. His now precarious plight was recognised, and he was then removed to New Utrecht, to the house of Nicasius de Sille. Although his arm was amputated, mortification had already set in and he died at the house of de Sille on September 30, 1776, at the age of 54 years.

His wife, who had been summoned, arrived before he died, accompanied by a waggon-load of food, which General Woodhull directed her to have distributed amongst the hungry soldiers of the Continental Army. This she did, and after his death she bore his body back on a waggon to Mastic, where he was buried in the family burial-ground.

THE MANOR OF QUEEN'S VILLAGE
LLOYD'S NECK, QUEENS
ERECTED 1685

THE Manor of Queen's Village lies on Lloyd's Neck, a point of land that projects into the waters of Long Island Sound between Cold Spring Harbour and Huntington Harbour. This tract, of about three thousand acres, was first bought from the Indians, in 1654, by Samuel Mayo, Daniel Whitehead and Peter Wright, three of the earliest settlers at Oyster Bay. The price they paid was three shirts, three coats, two cuttoes, three hatchets, three hoes, two fathoms of wampum, six knives, two pairs of stockings and two pairs of shoes.

From the three original owners the land passed through sundry sales, parcellings and transfers until, at length, in 1679, it all came into the possession of James Lloyd of Boston. Since that time the neck, once known as Caumsett by the Indians, has been called Lloyd's Neck.

James Lloyd was the third son of "John Lloyd of Bristol, Gentleman." In 1670 he left England and came to Boston where he engaged in commerce. He married Griselda, the daughter of Nathaniel Sylvester, of Shelter Island. By his marriage he acquired a considerable portion of the land that was afterwards incorporated in the manor. And thereby hangs a bit of romance. The land that Grisell Sylvester owned at "Caumsett" she had inherited from her betrothed, Latimer Sampson. When Latimer Sampson was setting out on a voyage to England, by way of Barbadoes, he willed his holdings on "Caumsett" to Griselda in event of his death. Whether he was prompted by some premonition, it is impossible to say. At any rate, he perished at sea in 1668, and Griselda came into possession of the land.

In 1685, by letters-patent issued under Governour Dongan, the estate was erected a manor, with confirmation of the usual privileges and responsibilities assumed by the grantee. Curiously enough, the instrument conveys the right of Court Leet but not the right of Court Baron. The quit-rent was "four bushels of good winter wheat, or the value thereof" to be paid on Lady Day, the 25th of March, in each and every year, if demanded.

James Lloyd, the first Lord of the Manor, never lived continuously on the Neck called after him. In fact, no Manor House was built there till 1711. James Lloyd died in 1698 at the age of forty-seven, devising the manor by will to his three children, Henry, Joseph and Grisell. Henry, the eldest, born in 1685 and reared as a merchant in Boston, bought out the interests of his brother and sister and became sole owner of the estate as well as second Lord of the Manor.

Coming to Lloyd's Neck to live in 1711, although keeping up his connexion with Boston and with Stamford, he made the manor his chief place of residence till his death in 1763. In 1708 he had married Rebecca Nelson, the daughter of Captain John Nelson, of Boston. By this marriage he had seven children, four sons and three daughters. As Lord of the Manor, he jealously guarded and maintained his rights, and the people of the neighbouring town of Huntington found that they could

MANOR HOUSE OF QUEEN'S VILLAGE, LLOYD'S NECK

not poach on the manor lands with impunity nor carry off wood and thatch at will and without just payment.

But if the Lord of the Manor was a stickler for his rights, the people of Huntington were no less aggressively punctilious about what they considered their prerogatives. Indicative of the fact that the villagers of Huntington stood on their dignity, an amusing incident occurred in 1717. Most of the Huntington people were rigid Presbyterians and viewed with some suspicion the Lord of the Manor, who was a staunch adherent of the Church of England.

On August 6th., 1717, at a town meeting it was

"ordered and agreed by the Major part of the Trustees of the town that Henry Lloyd of Queen's Village shall have Liberty to build a pew in the Meeting house at his own Cost and Charge for the use of his family and his heirs, provided that he shall not use the priviledge for the introduction of any minister to officiate in sd. meeting house of any different perswasion than is or has been usuall in this place here to fore, but in case he does the sd. pew shall accrew to the use of the town as much as if this priviledge had not been granted."

As a matter of fact, the Presbyterian trustees of the town really need not have troubled themselves about the "priviledge" they so circumspectly granted. There was no church of that "different perswasion"—meaning, of course, the Church of England—in Huntington till 1750. The family from the Manor House, therefore, generally crossed the Sound in a sail-boat to attend service at St. John's, Stamford, where a pew had been set apart for their use in recognition of Mr. Lloyd's benefactions to the parish.

Upon the death of Henry Lloyd, the second Lord of the Manor, his daughters received their share of his estate in money, while the manor lands went to the four sons, Henry, James, John and Joseph, in unequal portions. Henry, the eldest received a third. It was about this time that the second and present Manor House was built. Henry was a merchant in Boston. His letters shew that as early as 1764 he was most anxious to wind up his affairs in Boston and come to live most of his time at the manor. This ambition, however, he seems never to have realised. His commercial interests took so long to settle that he was still in Boston when the Revolution broke out.

He remained loyal and eventually went to England where he spent the closing years of his life in London. As an old man he was of striking presence with white hair and a ruddy face almost devoid of wrinkles. The story is told that, in 1794, when he was eighty-six years old, he and his wife, along with another elderly couple, appeared in a box at the Drury Lane Theatre and sate throughout the play. The King, who happened to be there also, looked intently at the party in the box for a long time and then sent an attendant to enquire who "those venerable persons" might be. Henry Lloyd was named in both the Massachusetts Act of Banishment and the New York Act of Attainder.

Dr. James Lloyd, the brother of Henry, was inclined to the Loyalist side but seems to have rendered medical services to both the British and American armies. John and Joseph reconciled their convictions to the Whig point of view and remained in Connecticut during the war, apparently in favour with the American authorities.

Henry Lloyd's share of the Manor of Queen's Village was confiscated because of his adherence to the Mother Country. At the conclusion of the war it was sold by the State of New York, but was bought in by his nephew, John Lloyd junior, who had previously acquired much of the other part of the manor. In March, 1790, the owners applied to the State Legislature for a renewal of the ancient manor privileges enjoyed before the war, but their application was refused. The Lloyd family, however, continued in possession and occupancy of the Neck for many years afterward.

During the war the British troops took possession of Queen's Manor and despoiled the place of much of its fine growth of timber, felling the trees and cutting them up for firewood, not only for their own immediate use but for commercial purposes as well. It is said that between fifty and a hundred thousand cords of wood were sold off the place at this time. Besides cutting wood at the Manor, the troops also built a fort there under the direction of that Benjamin Thompson who afterwards became famous as Count Rumford. Thompson occupied the Manor House as his headquarters, and there he entertained William Henry, Duke of Clarence, who was afterwards to become King William IV.

Thompson, a Massachusetts boy by birth, was a Loyalist from the outset and, in 1781, raised the King's American Dragoons by his own exertions. Possessed of extraordinary talents and great versatility of genius, he was not a person to remain in the background when anything was forward, and there were abundant opportunities of using his gifts. By 1783 he held the rank of Colonel in the British Army and commanded the regiment he himself had raised. Early in 1783, this regiment, then encamped about three miles to the east of Flushing, the Duke of Clarence honoured by presenting it with a stand of colours.

When he was only nineteen, Thompson married a lady fourteen years older than himself. Her home was in the town of Rumford (since renamed Concord) in New Hampshire. Hence was derived the title by which Thompson was subsequently known when the Elector of Bavaria had made him a Count of the Holy Roman Empire. Before that, however, he had become Sir Benjamin Thompson, being knighted in recognition of his distinguished services. In military and naval matters he left no mean record, as a philanthropist and public administrator he was a man of mark, but it is chiefly for his conspicuous attainments in chemical science that his name is remembered. In allusion to his remarkable versatility Gibbon, the historian, referred to him as "Mr. Secretary-Colonel-Admiral-Philosopher Thompson." He died in France in 1814.

The neighbouring town of Huntington being preponderantly Presbyterian was also preponderantly Whig in its political sentiments at the outbreak of the Revolutionary War. When tidings came of the Declaration of Independence, a local chronicler tells us,

"The British flag was hauled down . . . and a Liberty Pole was raised. An effigy of King George was fabricated out of some coarse material. Its face was blackened, and its head adorned with a wooden crown, stuck full of Roosters' feathers. It was then rolled up in a British flag lined with gunpowder, hauled up on a gibbet, exploded and burnt to ashes amid jeers and groans."

After the Battle of Long Island, however, when the British troops occupied Huntington and Lloyd's Neck, the Huntington folk found it expedient to be less demonstrative in their bearing. They chafed at the restraint they were obliged to manifest, and they kept a meticulously accurate account of every item of food, wood or any other sort of supplies used by the King's officers and men. Their bottled-up feelings are fairly represented by the agreeably amazed old woman who hailed what to her appeared to be a portent. A British dragoon, seeing a temptingly fat goose by the roadside, baited a fish hook with a kernel of corn. The goose swallowed the bait, the dragoon drew the fishing line taut and rode off, and the goose perforce followed flapping and squawking. At this juncture, the goody of the house "appearing in the doorway, threw up both hands in astonishment, and being unable to see the string, or to comprehend the exact situation, exclaimed:—'Well, I never! If our old goose isn't fighting the British!'"

Lying on the north shore, immediately across from Connecticut, Queen's Village Manor and Huntington saw much of the excitement caused by the whaleboat expeditions. When General Silliman was captured by a whaleboat party of Connecticut refugees, who had fled to Long Island, he was landed at Lloyd's Neck before proceeding to New York. It is of interest, too, to know that Nathan Hale was captured on East Neck, not far from Queen's Manor.

THE MANOR OF EATON
EATON'S NECK, TOWN OF HUNTINGTON
GRANTED 1646: ERECTED A MANOR 1686

IN 1646, Governour Theophilus Eaton, of the New Haven Colony, bought Eaton's Neck, as it came to be called, from its Indian owners. By a succession of transfers it passed to one, George Baldwin, who had a confirmation of his title from Governour Richard Nicoll, in 1666. Baldwin subsequently sold Eaton's Neck to Richard Bryan and his son Alexander, "both of Milford, merchants."

At the petition of the Bryans, Governour Sir Thomas Dongan, on the 23rd. of August, 1686, "gave, granted, released and confirmed" the land to their possession and, by the same instrument, "erected, made and constituted" the estate a Manor, to be called the Manor of Eaton. All the usual manorial rights were conferred, including the right to hold Court Leet and Court Baron. For quitrent, the Lords of the Manor were to pay every year, on the 20th. of May, "four bushells of good winter wheat," if demanded.

Apparently the Bryans never fully exercised their manorial prerogatives and their tenure of the Manor was of comparatively short duration. In 1710 they sold it to John Sloss, of Fairfield. John Sloss Hobart lived there until after the Revolution. In 1792 it passed to the Gardiner family.

SAGTIKOS MANOR
APPLETREE NECK, BAY SHORE, WEST ISLIP
HOUSE BUILT 1692: MANORIAL PATENT, 1697

ON THE north side of the Merrick Road, between Babylon and Bay Shore, in the Town of Islip, stands Sagtikos Manor House, built in 1692 or 1693 by Stephanus Van Cortlandt. The original building is quite intact and carefully preserved both without and within. It is quite easy to pass it, however, without becoming immediately aware of its presence and character for at both the west and east ends extensive modern additions catch the eye and, at first, draw attention away from the older structure that forms a connecting link between them.

The house is of heavy timber construction covered with weather-boarding and painted white. Wide-throated chimneys, staunchly built of red brick, rise above the shingled roof and the massive kitchen chimney occurs as a projection outside the west wall of the main body of the house. The old kitchen is within the one storey wing at the west. All the fireplaces are of a width and depth to correspond with the generous size of the chimneys; the fireplace in the original kitchen is more than eight feet wide and quite capable of taking the enormous back-logs of ancient repute that had to be dragged in by horses. There is still all the appropriate accompaniment of cranes, hooks, Dutch oven and all the now mysterious appurtenances that seventeenth and early eighteenth century housewives knew how to use with such masterly

128

SAGTIKOS MANOR HOUSE, SOUTH FRONT, LOOKING TOWARDS SEA, ISLIP

SAGTIKOS MANOR HOUSE, THE ORIGINAL KITCHEN
NOW A MORNING ROOM, ISLIP

results. This kitchen now does duty as an extra sitting-room and a means of communication with the more recent part of the house at the west.

On the 26th. of September, 1692, Stephanus Van Cortlandt received the Governour's licence to purchase lands hereabouts from the Indians. Negotiations with the Indians had apparently been going forward toward this end for some time previously as the actual purchase was made only a few days later than the date of the licence, to wit the 1st. of October, 1692. The survey of the patent was made three months later, in January 1692—be it remembered that the year then began with Lady Day, the 25th of March, so that January came *after* October—and apparently the house was built immediately thereafter, both tradition and probability being fully borne out by the structural evidence of late seventeenth century methods of joinery and by all the details of interior woodwork. The panelling of the doors, the design of the stair balustrade, and the manner of the panelled dadoes afford especially convincing testimony in this respect. These virile details, thoroughly characteristic of the age, present valuable material for architectural study. At the tops of the upper panels of the door from the entry into the "Van Cortlandt Parlour" are two round holes, glazed with clear glass, the purpose of which seems to have been to let enough firelight shine out into the entry at night, when the door was shut, to avoid the necessity of a candle.

The original patent for "Saghtekoos Manour, or Appletree Neck Wicke" at Islip, granted by King William III, and issued in his name by "His Excellency Collonell Benjamin Fletcher, Captain General, Governour in

Chief of the Province of New Yorke, and Vice Admirall of the same," is dated the 2nd. of June, 1697. It recites that "Whereas our Loving Subject Collonell Stevanus Cortlander hath . . . . . prayed our grant and confirmation of a certane Neck of land Lying and being situate, on our Island of Nassau, on the South Side of Huntington, in our County of Suffolk, Commonly called and known by the Indian Name Saghtekoos and by Christians called Appletree Neck," the said Stephanus Van Cortlandt is to have all the usual rights and privileges of "ffishing, ffowling, Hunting and Hawkeing," and all the other customary prerogatives appertaining to a lord of a manor.

This document, which is still intact with the great seal appended, further rehearses that the estate is

"TO BEE HOLDEN of us, Our Heirs and Successors, in ffree and Common Soccage as of Our Mannor of East Greenwich, in Our County of Kent, within Our Realm of England, yielding, Rendering and paying therefor yearly, and every year, forever, unto Our Heirs, and Successors, at Our city of New Yorke, on the feast day of the Annunciation of our Blessed Virgin Mary, the yearly rent of One Shilling Currant money of our Said province in Lieu and Stead of all other rents, services, dues, dutys and demands whatsoever."

Although the patent distinctly calls the estate a "manor," and it has always been reckoned as a manor, it is worth noting that neither judicial jurisdiction nor the advowson and patronage of churches are granted the lord of the manor according to the usual custom in such grants. The explanation for such an omission in this case seems to lie in the exceptionally small size of the manor; within such circumscribed limits there could have been no occa-

SAGTIKOS MANOR HOUSE, FIREPLACE IN VAN CORTLANDT PARLOUR, ISLIP

SAGTIKOS MANOR HOUSE, CORNER CUPBOARD IN EAST PARLOUR, ISLIP

sion for conferring rights of legal jurisdiction or rights of ecclesiastical patronage. The *shape* of the manor land, too, yields some clue to the omission just mentioned. The manorial domain of 1200 acres extends backward from the sea in a narrow strip eight miles long but only a few hundred feet wide. As shewn in a survey, it closely resembles a golf club in shape, the narrow strip running back towards the centre of the island being the handle.

In exactly what year Sagtikos Manor ceased to be a Van Cortlandt possession is not quite certain. In any event, the records shew that by the year 1712 it was in the hands of one Timothy Carll. Quite naturally the great Van Cortlandt Manor on the banks of the Hudson, in Westchester County, claimed chief place in the interests and affections of the family, while Sagtikos, little and remote, was an altogether subsidiary factor in their affairs. It was farther away from the city than Croton, and it could not well be reached by *periagua*. To get there one had either to drive or go on horseback, and although the manor was in a place by no means newly-settled, the prospect of a monotonous journey across Salisbury Plain, if not actually irksome, had certainly not the attraction of a thirty-mile sail up the Hudson. We are too apt to forget to-day how dependent the early colonists were upon water communication and how much they preferred it.

The next change in the lordship came in 1758 when Jonathan Thompson purchased Sagtikos Manor for his son Isaac. The price of purchase was £1200, New York money. According to family tradition, Jonathan Thompson rode over on a grey horse from his home on the north side of the island to Sagtikos and carried the money in his saddle-bags.

The new Lord of the Manor, Isaac Thompson, is always known in local history as Judge Thompson. He was a magistrate for more than forty years, a Judge of the Court of Common Pleas, and represented the County of Suffolk in the New York Assembly in 1795. It was during his lifetime that all the stirring events of the Revolutionary period took place and Sagtikos Manor was not without its share in the alarums of war. Judge Thompson took an active part in organising the Long Island Militia and was chairman of the Islip committee.

On one occasion, in 1777, a troop of more than three hundred British light horse bivouacked for the night around the Manor House and, as was their usual wont, made free use of Judge Thompson's property. The various officers commanding the British troops frequently stayed at Sagtikos Manor House in their tours of the Island. Sir Henry Clinton was among these recurrent military visitors and the room in which he slept is still known as Sir Henry Clinton's room and sundry mementoes of his visit are preserved there.

Once some straggling British sailors assaulted the house at night. Judge Thompson was a man of distinguished and courtly manners and his company was much esteemed by the officers who stayed at his house, but his mild and gentle bearing was apparently not appreciated by the nocturnal sailor assailants. They shot at him while he was going upstairs but, fortunately, missed their aim and the bullet embedded itself in one of the steps where the hole it made may still be seen. Another of their polite attentions was to drag him across the highway in front of the house by a rope around his neck. The drunken Jack Tars were about to hang him when he was saved by one of their number saying that, as he was a magistrate under the King, they could not hang him, so he was released. This same raiding party took with them some of the furniture out of the Manor House and carried it on board of a frigate at New York. Judge Thompson finally succeeded in having it restored to him, but only after much trouble and delay.

The Manor House is now occupied by Daniel Thompson Gardiner, Esquire, and his sister, who inherited it from their uncle, Francis Diodati Thompson. Everything is punctiliously maintained in an admirable state of preservation and many historical relics are to be found there, including the bedstead which General Washington really *did* sleep in when he visited the house after the Revolutionary War on his progress through Long Island.

We may be sure that His Excellency, on the occasion of this visit, was entertained with all due ceremony and the stately hospitality which the Lord of Sagtikos Manor was wont to dispense. By way of sharp contrast to his treatment at Sagtikos, Washington must have chuckled over an incident that took place at Patchogue during this same progress. The story goes that a certain lad by the name of Hart, along with his playmates, was baking sweet potatoes at a roadside bonfire when the President and his cavalcade halted nearby. Encouraged by the General's pleasant voice and kindly manners, Hart thrust his way up to the side of His Excellency's horse and offered him one of the baked sweet potatoes hot from the ashes. Washington accepted the present with a broad smile, gave the lad a bright shilling as a keepsake, and munched the potato with evident relish.

THE OLD BRICK HOUSE: TRYON HALL
FORT NECK, QUEENS
1696–1837 :: 1770

AFTER the King's Grace was defeated at the Battle of the Boyne, in 1690, many of the Jacobite military officers sought service in French privateers operating under letters of marque. One of the officers who became so engaged was Major Thomas Jones of Straubane, County Tyrone. The family, it seems, was English of Welsh descent but had been some time settled in Ireland.

Born about 1665, Thomas Jones was less than thirty years old when we find him at Jamaica in 1692, at the time of Port Royal's destruction by earthquake. Later in the same year, he gave up his sea life and, for a time, took up his abode at Warwick, Rhode Island. There he met and married Freelove Townsend, the daughter of Thomas Townsend, a prominent member of the Society of Friends.

During their residence in America, notwithstanding the persecutions and disabilities suffered by the Quakers, the Townsends had become possessed of very substantial land holdings, a good deal of their land being on Long Island. In 1695 Thomas Townsend deeded to Thomas Jones "my son-in-law and Freelove, his wife, my daughter" a large tract of land that had formerly been held by the Massapequa Indians at Fort Neck on the south shore of Long Island.

Tradition has it that Thomas Townsend had previously

135

offered this land to his son John, but John had refused it, saying, "Does my father want me to go out of the world?" The tract in question had been bought, in 1679, by Thomas Townsend and eleven other patentees from the Sachems Tackapousa and "Will Chippy." Some time prior to 1695 Thomas Townsend had bought the interests of the other eleven patentees, so that he was sole owner and, therefore, able to turn over the whole estate unconditionally to his son-in-law and daughter. The only encumbrance was a claim, preferred in 1696, by the son of old Will Chippy that he should receive "on each 1st. of December one good new cloth coat, in each and every year" throughout his natural life. So simple and modest a quit-rent could scarcely be looked upon as a burden. It could really have been reckoned a *charity*.

In 1696 Major Thomas Jones and his wife moved to Fort Neck and there, at the head of the creek, built the small but substantial brick house shewn in the illustration. It was always known as "the Old Brick House" and, for the time of its building, was a pretentious abode. At various times subsequent to his settling on Fort Neck, Major Jones acquired sundry adjacent parcels of land from the Indians and other owners, and through inheritance by his wife, until he was master of about six thousand acres.

When Lord Cornbury was Governour of New York he commissioned Thomas Jones Captain of the Queens County Militia. This was in October, 1702. Two years later he was appointed High Sheriff of Queens, while in 1706 he became Major of the Queens County Regiment. In September, 1710, Governour Hunter appointed him

THE OLD BRICK HOUSE, FORT NECK.   ERECTED 1696
From the copy of Mount's original sketch by Sarah Hall Floyd-Jones

FORT NECK HOUSE, FORMERLY TRYON HALL, FORT NECK
From an old print

FORT NECK HOUSE, FORMERLY TRYON HALL, FORT NECK, PRESENT VIEW

THE OLD BRICK HOUSE: TRYON HALL

Ranger General of the Island of Nassau with all "rights, or franchises, of estrays, of hunting Royal fish, treasure trove, mines, deodands, forfeitures, and the like," appertaining to the office. Incidentally, tenure of this office gave Major Jones "virtually a monopoly of the whale and other fisheries from both the north and south shores of Long Island."

The house that Thomas Jones built in 1696 was a thoroughly convincing little structure. It had brick walls, gabled roof of steep pitch, chimneys rising from each gable end, and a lower portion at the back covered by a lean-to roof, all which characteristics are clearly discernible in the sketch which is all that remains of it. This early home of the family was unfortunately demolished in 1837, but not before it had become the subject of sundry bits of romance and legend. One of the weird stories attached to the "Old Brick House" is that after the death of Thomas Jones, the *emigrè,* strange noises were heard from time to time, and that one of the small circular windows flanking the chimney at the top of the gable could never be kept closed. Sashes and even boards were forcibly shot out of the aperture when anyone essayed to shut it. When they tried to stop it more effectually with bricks and mortar, the same invisible agent sent them violently flying outwards directly the bricklayer had finished his work.

Of course the negroes on the estate, and ignorant supeistitious folk in the neighbourhood, set their tongues wagging busily and, no doubt, amplified the yarn with all manner of gratuitous additions. Even after the demolition of the old building, in 1837, its ruins oppressed the

137

blacks with eerie fears that lent speed to their feet whenever they had to pass the spot after nightfall.

Major Thomas Jones died in December, 1713, and was buried on the banks of the creek not far from the house. The inscription on his grave stone, which he had composed himself, reads:—

"Here Lyes Interd The Body of Major Thomas Jones
Who Came From Straubane, In The Kingdom of Ireland,
Settled Here and Died December 1713
From Distant Lands to This Wild Waste He Came,
This Seat He Choose, And Here He Fixed His Name.
Long May His Sons This Peace Full Spot Injoy,
And No Ill Fate his Offspring Here Annoy."

No doubt the absurd yarns and extraordinary legends, circulated about Major Jones after his death, can be attributed to the fertile imaginations of the negroes and the superstitions of the plainer sort of white people in a credulous age. It was known that Major Jones had sailed a privateer for two years under letters of marque. It was likewise known that afterwards, as Ranger General, he had enjoyed rights granted by the Crown which carried various perquisites. With this foundation of fact, the babbling tongues of the irresponsible soon managed to turn him into a pirate. Common rumour had it that much treasure of gold and silver had been buried with him and more than once the Major's bones were disturbed by the fishermen of the Bay digging for plunder. So strongly did this rumour persist that even an hundred and thirty-five years later the grave was violated and one of the culprits with a clam shell scratched on the grave stone

THE OLD BRICK HOUSE: TRYON HALL

"Beneath these stones
Repose the bones
Of Pirate Jones.
This briny well
Contains the shell,
The rest's in hell."

Even down to the middle of the nineteenth century there were not a few who gave credence to the absurd tales of piracy and buried treasure.

When Major Thomas Jones died in 1713, his son David, born in 1699, was fourteen years old. Although he did not come into full control of his patrimony till 1737, he married, in 1722, Anna Willett, the grand daughter of Thomas Willett who was the first Mayor of New York City under British rule. He was a Judge of the Supreme Court of the Province of New York and was also a member of the General Assembly of the Province till 1758. For thirteen years he was Speaker of the Assembly and in various other capacities likewise was closely identified with public life. His second wife was Margaret, widow of John Tredwell.

Under his wise management, the estate left him by his father increased materially in value and, in 1770, at some little distance from the "Old Brick House," he built a splendid country seat which he called Tryon Hall, in honour of Governour Tryon. Later on the name of this house was changed to Fort Neck House, coinciding with the name of the estate. This was the summer home of the family; the winter or city house was at Fort Pitt, where Pitt Street now is.

Tryon Hall or Fort Neck House faced the Great South

Bay and had a frontage of ninety feet. The great entrance hall was thirty-six feet long by twenty-three feet wide, and all the appointments were according to the best manner of the day. In every way it was one of the finest houses of the period. Over the door leading to the staircase hung a great pair of antlers from a buck taken in the Mohawk Valley, a present from Sir William Johnson to the master of the house.

David Jones died in October, 1775, at the age of seventy-six. By the terms of his will, which created a carefully guarded entail, he left his estate to his son Thomas, with remainder to his daughter Arrabella, in case Thomas failed to have issue. Both Thomas and Arrabella were children by the first wife. Arrabella had married Richard Floyd, of Mastic, and had children. David Jones, foreseeing the possibility of Thomas dying without issue, inserted a clause in his will providing, under such circumstances, that the Fort Neck estate should descend "to and for the use of my Grandson, David Richard Floyd, Oldest Son of my Daughter Arrabella," and thence, according to the usage of primogeniture, in perpetuity to the successive eldest heirs male, "they and Each of them using and taking the Sirname of Jones, in addition to their other names."

Thomas Jones, born in 1731, also became a Judge of the Supreme Court of the Province and, during his father's lifetime, was always known as "the Young Judge." In December, 1762, he married Anne, the daughter of Lieutenant-Governour James Delancey. Upon the death of his father, in 1775, Thomas Jones succeeded to the estate at Fort Neck.

THE OLD BRICK HOUSE: TRYON HALL

When the Revolutionary War broke out, Thomas Jones remained firm in his allegiance to the Crown and, because of his loyalty, a dramatic bit of history attached itself to Fort Neck House. Early in May, 1779, General Silliman of the Continental Army had been seized by some of the active Connecticut Loyalists who had previously taken refuge in Long Island. Under the leadership of Captain Bonnell, they had crossed the Sound in whale-boats, taken the General at his home, Holland Hill, near Fairfield, and carried him first to New York and thence to Oyster Bay where he was held a prisoner. General Silliman's own account of his capture is given in a letter, of May 12th., to his father-in-law, the Reverend Joseph Fish of Stonington. He writes:—

"Before this reaches you, you will have received the news of my captivity, I doubt not. I was surprised in bed at my own house about 1 o'clock in the morning of the Sabbath, the 2nd. inst. by a party of refugees from Connecticut (except two that were foreigners) commanded by one Bonnell, who used to live in my neighbourhood. This party went from the Island for this purpose. Billy is with me. We both receive kind and complaisant treatment."

Mrs. Silliman's account of the incident, written in 1801, gives all the intimate details—the General looking out of the window in the moonlight at the assailants before his door, his attempt to shoot and the failure of his gun to give more than a flash of powder in the pan, the breaking in of a window and the entrance of armed men, the permission for the General to dress and bid his wife adieu, provided he made haste, the forbearance of the captors, upon the General's remonstrance, to take more than a very little plunder; and the hurried departure of the party to the shore before an alarm could be given.

The American Army at this time held no British prisoner of equal rank with General Silliman whom they might offer in exchange. It was clearly necessary to secure such a prisoner and, after mature consideration, the Honourable Thomas Jones, of Fort Neck, seemed the most available person, notwithstanding the fact that he had previously been taken and released on parole and was, therefore, presumably safe from molestation.

On the night of November 4th., 1779, a party of twenty-five American volunteers, under Captain David Hawley, crossed Long Island Sound in whaleboats from Bridgeport to Stonybrook, hid their boats and set out for Fort Neck on the opposite side of the island. According to Mrs. Silliman's account, Captain Hawley had not intended to permit any looting of Fort Neck House but was obliged to yield to the insistent demands of his men. Before starting on what they recognised as a risky undertaking, they pointedly enquired, "What are *we* to get?" and would probably not have gone without some prospect of plunder.

They travelled by night and by day lay concealed in the woods. On Saturday evening, the 6th. of November, about nine o'clock they reached Fort Neck House. Inside there was music and dancing, and when the kidnappers knocked at the door they were apparently not heard. Thereupon Captain Hawley broke through the door and led his men into the hall where they found Judge Jones and one of his guests. Securing both the Judge and the young man with him,. the raiders then began to pillage. What followed is best told in the Judge's own words, quoted from his "History of New York during the Revolution":—

". . . on the 6th. of November following, the crews of three whaleboats, commissioned as privateers by the Governour of Connecticut to cruise against the enemies of the United States, the subjects of Great Britain, and to seize their property, either upon the seas, or upon any lands or territories under the jurisdiction of Great Britain, broke into Mr. Jones's house, (while he was peaceably living at home, as he thought, in perfect security, in consequence of his parole aforesaid,) and plundered it of property to the amount of several hundreds of pounds. They even robbed Mrs. Jones of her wearing apparel, and took that of two young ladies in the house, (the clothes upon their backs only excepted) and, after plundering the house, insulting the family, and regaling themselves with good old Madeira, they ordered Mr. Jones to proceed with them. He pleaded his parole. It had no effect. The answer was 'the Governour wanted him, and go he must, but he might depend upon beeing soon exchanged.' They compelled him to march two nights, through woods, swamps, and morasses, and over hedges, ditches, and fences, sixty miles on foot, and sleep two days in the woods, without fire, victuals, or drink, (a little mouldy cheese and an hard biscuit with a little water, given him by the party, excepted.)"

Reaching the north shore, the party found their boats where they had hid them and made off with their prisoners and booty to the Connecticut shore with all possible haste. Captain Hawley landed all his men at Fairfield, excepting six who had loitered behind and been captured by the pursuers. Mrs. Silliman's account there takes up the narrative. She writes:—

"News came to me in the morning that Captain Hawley had arrived with Judge Jones. Although I was glad the event had taken place, yet my heart was full of sympathy for him and his family, whom I knew well how to pity as I had so recently myself gone through the same trial. Wishing to make his captivity as easy as possible, I sent my son to invite him to our house to breakfast and he came under a guard."

Her story then goes on to tell of Judge Jones's coming. In talking over their experiences, Judge Jones asked, "Did they plunder when they took your husband?" "I said, 'Not much.'" Said Judge Jones, "They have plundered my house—I don't believe they have left my wife a second sheet."

Warm-hearted Mrs. Silliman did all she could to make Judge Jones comfortable during the two or three days he remained at her house until he was taken to Middletown. Mrs. Jones wrote Mrs. Silliman a grateful letter thanking her for consideration and kindness and, along with the letter, sent a pound of choice green tea. It is pleasant to relate that, from the disagreeable incident of captures and the ensuing kindliness mutually displayed, there sprang up a family friendship that was afterwards continued by the descendants on both sides.

At the end of the following April, 1780, an exchange was effected by which General Silliman and Judge Jones were returned to their respective homes. The boat that went down the Sound, with Judge Jones on board, to meet the boat bringing General Silliman, carried a fine, fat turkey sent by Mrs. Silliman "for the General's comfort on his voyage home." When the boats met, they hasted to dress the turkey "that the Judge might dine with him [General Silliman] before he went on, which he did." Thus ended this episode with roast turkey and, it may be presumed, better feelings on both sides than at the beginning. Judge Jones and General Silliman had been at Yale together and knew each other well.

Judge Jones was one of those proscribed by name in the Act of Attainder passed by the New York Assembly in October, 1779. That act, which charged fifty-six men and three women of the most prominent families in the Province with "adherence to the Enemies of this State," provided "that each and every one of them who shall at any time hereafter be found in any part of this state, shall be and are hereby adjudged and declared guilty of felony, and shall suffer death as in case of felony, without benefit of clergy." This savage enactment, back of which can be traced personal bitterness, old grudges and greed, was unparallelled amongst any civilised people either before or since.

Judge Jones, whose health was much impaired, in 1781 sailed for England with his wife, his niece, Miss Elizabeth Floyd, and two servants, intending to take the waters at Bath. There he got much better and was looking forward to a return to his home at Fort Neck, but the Act of Attainder becoming operative on the conclusion of peace made him an exile. He was obliged, therefore, to remain in England. He finally removed to Hoddesdon, in Hertfordshire, and there he died, July 25th., 1792. He and his wife are buried in the south aisle of Broxbourne Parish Church.

It was a sore grief to Judge Jones that he could never

come back to America. "To his native land his eyes always turned with affection, and his heart ever beat true. He died, as he'had lived, an American and a son of New York." His exile, occasioned by the infamous New York Act of Attainder, was a public loss. Corresponding with his relatives and friends in America was one of his greatest pleasures, during his remaining years, and the letters that have been preserved on both sides vividly picture the political and social affairs in each country.

When Judge Jones had become officially dead by reason of the Act of Attainder, his nephew, David Richard Floyd, the only son of Richard Floyd and the Judge's sister Arrabella, succeeded to the Fort Neck estate with his mother's assent and, by act of legislature, added the surname Jones to his own patronymic. Fort Neck, since that time, has remained the home of the Floyd-Jones family.

Judge Jones's letters to his nephew David, the new master of Fort Neck, shew not only his unfailing affection for his relatives and his old home, but also his just and kindly estimate of those to whom he had been politically opposed. In one letter he writes,

"Consult your Father-in-law in everything. He was a friend of your Grandfather's, he was a friend to all our family, he was a friend of mine, and tho' he and I differed in politicks during the late war, I know him to be an honest man."

This same father-in-law was Henry Onderdonk, at one time the most influential Whig in Queens County, char-

THE OLD BRICK HOUSE: TRYON HALL

acterised by Judge Jones in his *History* as "an arrant rebel." In another letter, he counsels his nephew,

"My love to you, my dear David. Behave with caution and prudence, and let me beg of you by your conduct never to disgrace the families of your two Grandfathers. Always remember one was first in Queens, the other in Suffolk."

It often happens, in the case of an old house, that the personality of some one of its former occupants attaches itself to the place with peculiar vividness. In this way the gracious personality of the Honourable Thomas Jones seems to pervade not only the house but the whole neighbourhood of Fort Neck.

RAYNHAM HALL
OYSTER BAY

1740

RAYNHAM HALL, at Oyster Bay, was built about 1740 and was thoroughly representative of the better sort of Long Island wooden houses of the middle and eastern parts. In all its characteristics it was thoroughly English, with somewhat of a New England flavour since the affiliations of the Oyster Bay people, and especially the Townsends, were with Connecticut and not with the Dutch of the western end of the island. Dutch influence is not to be found in the fabric of Raynham Hall.

Unfortunately, numerous alterations of the Victorian era have done much to obscure the fine eighteenth century qualities of the building, but these changes that were deemed improvements in their day have not done irreparable damage and intelligent restoration could easily bring the structure back to its pristine state. Happily, the nineteenth century carpenters could not efface history as readily as they could disguise architectural merit.

The Townsend family in America are sprung from the Townsends of Norfolk, whose family seat is Raynham Hall. Hence the name of Raynham Hall at Oyster Bay in allusion to the home in the Mother Country. About 1100, Sir Ludovic de Townshende, a Norman knight, came to England and "married Elizabeth de Hauteville, sole heiress of the manor of Raynham; daughter of Sir Thomas de Hauteville, of the famous family of de Haute-

Photograph by *Country Life*

RAYNHAM HALL, SOUTH FRONT, OYSTER BAY

Photograph by *Country Life*

RAYNHAM HALL, THE HALLWAY, OYSTER BAY

ville or Havile, which family at this time appears to have been a most important one. They were of Norman extraction, and, settling in the County of Norfolk, became possessed of a considerable property, said to have been granted them by William the Conqueror, a portion of which by this marriage came to the Townsend family." In 1630, three Townsend brothers, John, Henry and Richard, came to America and landed in Massachusetts. From John was descended Samuel Townsend who built Raynham Hall at Oyster Bay for himself in 1740.

Samuel Townsend, the first owner and occupant of Raynham Hall, was fourth in descent from John Townsend the immigrant and was born in 1717. He married Sarah, daughter of William Stoddard, of Oyster Bay, but formerly of Rhode Island. A part of the Townsend family, some time prior to Samuel's birth, had joined the Society of Friends, for Samuel was a birthright member of meeting. His wife, though born and baptised in the Church of England, became a Friend and went to meeting with her husband. A relative, Dr. P. Townsend, in his Note Book, has left a pen picture of Samuel describing him as

"a fine old gentleman, of regular features, straight nose, a large blue eye and high forehead." He often wore "a snuff-coloured or grey suit, with silver knee and shoe buckles, a white stock of cambric lawn gathered in five plaits, fastened behind with a paste buckle, shewing no collar, narrow ruffles at the shirt bosom, gold-headed cane and cocked hat. A certain Solomon Seaman, uncle to Samuel, used to say he 'hated to see Sam and Sarah Townsend come into meeting, they looked so tall and proud.' "

Samuel Townsend may have been a strict Friend, but he could not have been a very *plain* Friend or he would not have dressed in the manner described by his relative. Plain or not, however, he was active in the affairs of meeting and when visiting Quaker preachers came to Oyster Bay they always stopped at Raynham Hall.

Samuel was a merchant in the British and West India trade, and prospered so that he was blessed with substantial means. Before the Revolution he had been a Justice of the Peace for about thirty years. He likewise played a conspicuous part in the political life of the Province, and when the Revolutionary troubles were brewing his sentiments led him to espouse the Whig side although he was a Quaker. He was a member of the First Provincial Congress and, in 1776, was appointed one of a committee of thirteen to frame a constitution for the State of New York. During the war, as a consistent Friend, he could not enter actively into the affairs of the period but, upon the conclusion of peace, he became a State Senator and a member of the first Council of Appointment under the Constitution, in 1789, and continued in public life until his death in November, 1790.

Samuel's known Whig sympathies subjected him to more or less inconvenience and annoyance under the British occupation of Long Island during the Revolution. Nevertheless, he and his family managed to maintain pleasant relations with the officers of the British Army several of whom were quartered in his house. Samuel's children were Solomon, Samuel, William, David, Audrey, Sarah and Phoebe. To his daughters Audrey and Sarah must be attributed, in great measure, the consideration shewn him; both of them made a deep impression on the hearts of their unbidden military guests and visible evidences of their attachment to the Townsend girls are still in existence.

For a considerable period Lieutenant-Colonel Simcoe and some of the other officers of the Queen's Rangers were quartered at Raynham Hall and the house naturally became the scene of a good deal of military gaiety and entertaining. Simcoe was especially smitten with Sarah Townsend's charms. He was in his twenty-sixth year and still warmly impressionable and accordingly demonstrative. For St. Valentine's Day, 1779, he composed an elaborate effusion in verse addressed to the young lady who had captured his affections. It begins,

> "Fairest maid, where all are fair,
> Beauty's pride and Nature's care;
> To you my heart I must resign;
> O choose me for your Valentine!"

and, after many lines of impassioned appeal, it ends,

> " 'Fond Youth,' the God of Love replies,
> 'Your answer take from Sarah's eyes.' "

What answer Sally Townsend returned to this ardent declaration we know not. It is said that she did not altogether discourage Colonel Simcoe in his hopes. What we do know is that she never married and was reputed to have been a changed girl when her lover finally departed, later in life to become the Lieutenant Governour of Upper Canada. Years afterward Sarah Townsend's nieces discovered this historical valentine carefully and tenderly laid away. Then it became easy to surmise the details of this old romance and how Sally's heart was torn between love for her suitor and loyalty to her brother, who was closely identified with the American cause.

Major André stayed at Raynham Hall not long before his visit to Arnold at West Point and his subsequent capture at Tarrytown. This handsome and accomplished young officer was likewise a great admirer of Sally Townsend. He loved to be constantly using his pencil and on one occasion, without her knowing it, he sketched Sally and surreptitiously slipped the sketch under her plate for her to discover later. The sketch shews her as a beautiful girl in a riding habit. This picture was a treasured possession at Raynham Hall until comparatively recent years, when it was stolen by a visitor to whom it had been shewn. The Simcoe valentine, too, after generations of careful preservation, disappeared and is believed to have met the same fate as André's sketch of Sally.

The still visible evidences of the admiration inspired by Audrey and Sally Townsend in the breasts of the British officers are inscriptions cut with a diamond on the panes of a small window above a doorway. The first reads, "The Adorable Miss Sarah"; under "Sarah" appears "Sally Townsend." Two lines are drawn through this and signed "J. McGill." Just why the words "Sally Townsend" were erased nobody knows; it was possibly because J. McGill, a lieutenant under Colonel Simcoe, repented the familiarity of "Sally" and later inserted "Sarah." A second pane has, "Miss A. T. The Most Acompl young lady in Oyster Bay." A third pane has "Sally Coles." A. T. stood for Audrey Townsend. "Sally Coles" was probably a cousin of the Townsend

Photograph by *Country Life*

RAYNHAM HALL, DINING-ROOM, OYSTER BAY

Photograph by *Country Life*

RAYNHAM HALL, THE ORIGINAL STAIR, OYSTER BAY

girls, for the Coles family, who lived in the neighbour-hood, were related to the Townsends.

The legends of Raynham Hall shew André as a practical joker. In the old china-cupboard, in what was then the dining room but is now the library, he hid the dough-nuts and cakes that Sarah had made for a tea party, and not until Sarah was in a state of frantic excitement and perplexity did the mischief-loving André reveal their hiding-place and let the guests have what had been made for them.

Solomon Townsend, the eldest son of Samuel, and brother to Audrey and Sarah, was launched by his father on the career of an India merchant. In 1766, when he was in his twentieth year, Samuel Townsend put son Solomon in command of the ship *Glasgow,* belonging to Walter Buchanan. Captain Solomon prospered at his seafaring until the outbreak of hostilities between the Colonies and the Mother Country. Then the *Glasgow* was left in London and Captain Townsend went to Paris. There he got from Benjamin Franklin the following cer-tificate just before sailing for America:—

"Passy, near Paris, June 18th., 1778

I certify, to all whom it may concern, that Captain Solomon Townsend, mariner, hath this day appeared volun-tarily before me and taken the oath of allegiance to the United States of America, according to the Resolution of Congress, thereby acknowledging himself a subject of the United States.

B. Franklin."

This paper is still in the possession of the family.

Landing in Boston, Captain Solomon Townsend, who

had just plainly declared his attitude by his oath of allegiance to the United States, could not go to his father's house in Oyster Bay where the British officers were then quartered. He crossed the country to the other side of the Hudson and went to the house of his relative, Peter Townsend, at Chester, in Orange County, New York. At Chester he engaged in the iron business. When he wished to see his family, he met them by appointment on Shelter Island.

Solomon Townsend was associated with Peter Townsend just after the chain had been forged that was stretched across the Hudson from West Point to Constitution Island. This chain was 500 yards in length and was made of the "best sterling iron," three and an half inches square, with links 45 inches long and 14 inches wide. It cost about $400,000. Lossing's *Field Book of the Revolution* says of the making of the chain,

"Colonel Timothy Pickering, Attorney-General of the Army, accompanied by Captain Mackin, arrived at the home of Peter Townsend, late on a Saturday night in March, 1778, to engage him to make the chain. Peter Townsend readily agreed to construct it, and in a violent snow-storm, amid the darkness of the night, the party set out for the Sterling Iron Works. At daylight on Sunday morning two forges were in operation. New England teamsters carried the links, as fast as they were finished, to West Point and in the space of six weeks the whole chain was completed. It weighed one hundred and eighty tons" and on the first of May "it was stretched across the river and secured."

In the library at Raynham Hall is a photograph of the "Articles of Agreement between Noble, Townsend & Co., proprietors of the Sterling Iron Works, in the State of

New York, of the one part, and Hugh Hughes, Deputy Quartermaster General to the Army of the United States, of the other part."

Dealing with the stern metal did not prevent the growth of tender sentiment in the heart of Solomon Townsend for his counsin Anne, the daughter of Peter Townsend. Solomon and Anne were married, and Peter gave his daughter the old family clock which she brought to Raynham Hall as a bride. There the clock still remains, and tradition says that Washington more than once consulted it when he visited the Townsend home in Chester regarding the construction of the chain.

Solomon Townsend bought land adjoining his father-in-law's property and established extensive iron works. After the War he carried on a large iron business in New York City and likewise had a bar-iron foundry on the Peconic River in Suffolk County. He sate for a number of years in the State Legislature, of which he was a member at the time of his death in March, 1811. Captain Solomon was the second owner of Raynham Hall.

Solomon, the son of Captain Solomon, was a merchant in New York engaged in the importation of coffees and of teas and spices from China. This Solomon "the Merchant" was the third owner of Raynham Hall.

Near the house are two great boxwood trees that were more than a century old when the British officers sate in their shade and had tea. Close by these box trees lie two links of the West Point chain made by Peter Townsend in 1778. Raynham Hall is still in the possession of the family and contains many relics and heirlooms full of historic associations.

CARPENTERS TAVERN
JAMAICA
1710

CARPENTERS TAVERN, in what is now Hollis, was the scene of General Woodhull's capture by the British army and the spot where he received the wounds from which he subsequently died. This historical incident is the chief one associated with the old tavern and one which will always live in the public memory.

The oldest part of Carpenters Tavern was built about 1710, and from thence onward was a popular place of call for the stage coaches and also a favourite place of entertainment for the gentry of Long Island, both those who were travelling in their private coaches and those who lived more or less in the neighbourhood and utilised the large rooms of the inn for social gatherings.

In the days before the Revolution, balls were frequently given in the ballroom of the inn, and after the beginning of the Revolutionary War, when the British army was in occupation of Long Island, its reputation as a place of entertainment was fully sustained, for the officers dined there very frequently and likewise perpetuated the balls that had taken place in the days preceding the outbreak of the war.

We are told that Sir Henry Clinton danced the minuet there on more than one occasion, and there are many mementoes of the presence in the inn of the younger officers and the fair maids of the neighbourhood, who came

CARPENTER'S TAVERN, HOLLIS, JAMAICA

to attend the military dances, in the shape of names scratched with diamonds on the small panes of the windows, names cut by the young gallants of their fair friends' linked with their own names.

The inn contains many interesting domestic relics in the nature of chairs, fire irons and other domestic fitments that had been part of its furnishings for the last hundred years or more. There are also some amusing traditions whose lighter vein relieves the sombre memory of General Woodhull's capture and death. One of these stories tells how the children hid under the trundle beds when they heard that the British soldiers were coming. At the same time, the servants buried their coins in glass bottles, and one old black slave was so terrified at the rumours he had heard that he sought safety by climbing up the big chimney.

There could scarcely be a more suitable object of efforts for preservation than this old tavern; such buildings might suitably be made into historical museums.

KING PARK
JAMAICA

THE former home of the Honourable Rufus King, at Jamaica, stands in what is now King Park and is the only one of the homes of Long Island's famous men that has become public property, with the exception of the John Howard Payne, or "Home, Sweet Home," house, which the village of Easthampton has recently acquired. The house stands on the main local thoroughfare, Fulton Street or Jamaica Avenue, and is carefully preserved in an ample park composed of what were once the immediate grounds of the building.

Built about 1750, this ample gambrel-roofed building, whose exterior walls are covered with white weatherboarding, presents a pleasant blending of comely Georgian features with the local Colonial manner in which, as in this case, both English and Dutch fashions were combined.

The house is of ample size and for many years of its early existence it was used as an hostelry and kept by a widow. Late in the eighteenth century it passed through sundry vicissitudes of ownership until Mr. Alsop, who held a heavy mortgage upon the place and controlled it, through his close relationship by marriage with Rufus King, induced the latter to buy it. On coming into possession, Mr. King made some improvements but undertook no radical changes of any sort. This was in 1805.

KING PARK, JAMAICA, SOUTH FRONT

KING PARK, JAMAICA, NORTH EAST VIEW

Richard King, the son of John King of the County of Kent, was the first of his line born in America. John King settled in Boston about 1700 and some time not long after this date Richard King was born, but of his early life very little is known. That he was liberally educated and a man of parts is proved by his public record and the positions of trust he held and discharged with distinction. We find him settled at Watertown in 1740, associated with one of the principal merchants of Boston engaged in the timber business. In the spring of 1745 Governour Shirley appointed him Commissary of Subsistence, with the rank of Captain, for the expedition against Cape Breton. He sailed with the expedition to Louisbourg and was present at the capture of that fortress. Returning to Massachusetts, he sold his properties at Watertown and went to live permanently at Scarborough in Maine. He died there in 1775.

Rufus King, the son of Richard King, was born in Scarborough in 1755. His mother was Isabella Bragdon. After going to school at the Byfield Academy, he entered Harvard and graduated with distinction in 1777. He then studied law at Newburyport in the office of Theophilus Parsons, who was afterwards Chief Justice of Massachusetts. Attached to the expedition of General Sullivan to Rhode Island in 1778, he was thenceforward actively in public service until almost the end of his life.

In 1783 he became a member of the General Court of Massachusetts, where his worth and ability almost immediately won recognition, and in 1784, by almost unanimous vote of the Legislature, he was sent as a delegate to the old Congress sitting at Trenton. This post he continued to hold in 1785 and 1786. In 1785 he moved that "there shall be neither slavery nor involuntary servitude in any of the States described in the resolution of Congress in April, 1784, otherwise than in punishment of crime, whereof the party shall have been personally guilty, and this regulation shall be an article of compact, and remain a fundamental principle of the Constitution between the original States and each of the States named in the said resolve."

Although this resolution against slavery was not acted upon at the time, the principle was ultimately adopted, almost word for word, in the ordinance of 1787 for the government of the Northwestern Territory, a provision prepared by Mr. King and introduced into Congress by his colleague Nathan Dane while Mr. King was in Philadelphia as a member of the Constitutional Convention from Massachusetts.

At the Constitutional Convention he was one of the members entrusted with the task of making a final draught of the instrument, and when the question of its adoption was submitted to the several States, Mr. King's familiarity with all its provisions, his lucid explanation of them, and his eloquent setting forth of its claims and advantages contributed greatly to its ratification by Massachusetts.

In 1786 Rufus King married Mary Alsop, the daughter of John Alsop, Esquire, of New York. This event wrought a complete change in his life. Not long after his marriage, he moved to New York City and lived at the house of his wife's father at the corner of Maiden Lane and William Street, mingling much in the brilliant society that adorned the first Republican Court. Washington's diary of this period makes frequent mention of the distinguished young couple who were constant visitors at the President's house. Mary Alsop was a lady of remarkable personal beauty, gracious and engaging manners, unusual talent and mental attainments, and well calculated to adorn by her presence any society into which she might be thrown. She possessed all those qualities that would appeal strongly to President Washington, who was extremely susceptible to feminine charms, and we can well understand the numerous allusions to the Kings in his diary.

In New York Rufus King's marked ability won immediate recognition no less than in his native Massachusetts. In 1789 he was returned to the State Legislature and there "received the unexampled welcome of an immediate election, with General Schuyler, to the Senate of the United States." In 1794, when the Jay Treaty with Great Britain was up for ratification, King was an ardent advocate of its adoption. When he and his firm friend Alexander Hamilton were prevented from explaining its provisions to the people in public meeting in New York, they united in publishing the Camillus Papers. King wrote those pertaining to mercantile affairs and maritime law.

While serving his second term in the United States Senate, President Washington, in 1796, appointed him Minister Plenipotentiary to England. This post of honour and responsibility he continued to hold during the administration of President Adams and for two years during that of Thomas Jefferson, in other words till 1804.

During his tenure of office at the Court of Saint James he secured numerous important modifications in the commercial relations between the two countries. His intelligent, courteous and firm presentation of any matter under discussion won the confidence and esteem of the British Government and, at the same time, both claimed and obtained for his own country the respect paid to it as one of the important world powers.

In 1804 he returned to New York, believing and hoping that his public career was now at an end and that he might be able to enjoy some of the satisfactions of private life. In 1805 he bought the house and farm at Jamaica and settled down to the life of a country gentleman, hunting, fishing, reading, cultivating his estate, and making himself generally helpful in the community. He was an enthusiastic agriculturist, delighted in constantly improving his property, and stocked his farm with a fine herd of Devonshire cattle which he imported from England. Likewise, he was a keen gardener and lover of trees, and many of the trees now flourishing in King Park were set out by Mr. King himself soon after he came into possession of the place. One of the most striking of these trees, that have now reached great size, is a magnificent oak that has grown from an acorn Rufus King planted with his own hands. The pine and fir trees, sent to Mr. King from Portsmouth, New Hampshire, are believed to be the first of their kind in this part of Long Island.

In 1813 Mr. King's retirement was broken by his election for a third time to the United States Senate, and from that date until almost the time of his death he was continually in public service. In 1816 he was nominated for the Governourship of New York but was defeated. He was also the candidate of his party for the Presidency in opposition to James Monroe. He was elected a fourth time to the United States Senate in 1820. Though fully minded to retire to private life again a few years after this, John Quincy Adams persuaded him in 1825 to accept the post of Minister to Great Britain a second time. After a year's service, however, failing health compelled him to resign and he came back to America, spending the last year of his life partly in New York City, partly at Jamaica. He died on the 29th. of April, 1827, and was buried in the churchyard of Grace Church, Jamaica.

After Rufus King's death, his son, the Honourable John Alsop King, sometime Governour of New York, lived at King Park. The place remained in the possession of the family till the death of Miss Cornelia King in 1896. It was then bought by Jamaica and became public property. Amongst other things, the house now contains a collection of Long Island historical relics.

THE BOWNE HOUSE
FLUSHING
1661

IN THE town of Flushing there stands on Bowne Avenue, several hundred feet from Broadway, a venerable house filled with associations that reach out far beyond the personal history of its erstwhile occupants. It is the Bowne house, and besides being once the home of one of the staunchest and most determined pioneers of religious liberty in America, it was one of the first meeting-places of the Quakers and kept its semi-public capacity for this purpose for forty years or more after it was reared by John Bowne in 1661.

John Bowne, the son of Thomas Bowne of Matlock in Derbyshire, was born in 1627 and, in 1649, with his father and sister, migrated to Massachusetts. In 1650 he returned to England but arrived again in America in 1651. He landed at Boston in May, and in June "he visited Flushing in company with Edward Farrington, who is supposed to have married his sister Dorothy." Not long afterwards the whole Bowne family established themselves in Flushing. John Bowne was a substantial merchant, well educated and possessed of considerable means according to the reckoning of his time. In 1656 he married Hannah Feake who was nearly related to the Winthrop family of New England and seems to have been a person of much natural charm as well as force of character.

BOWNE HOUSE, FLUSHING

THE BOWNE HOUSE

With the entrance of the woman on the scene begins the train of events that gave John Bowne and his house a conspicuous place in Colonial history. In the very same year of her marriage Hannah Bowne became well acquainted with several of the Flushing Friends. At that time they were holding their meetings in the woods to escape, as far as possible, the annoyances and persecutions under which they laboured at the hands of both the English and Dutch colonists. Subsequently Hannah Bowne herself became a member of the Society. Experimentally-minded woman, like Eve with the apple, then leads the man to make a venture. Hannah having professed membership amongst the Friends, "her husband from curiosity attended a meeting, and was deeply impressed with the beauty and simplicity of their worship. He invited them to meet at his house, and soon after he joined in membership with them." This was just after he had finished his new dwelling.

This was too much for the equanimity of his English and Dutch neighbours of Calvinistic persuasion. It was bad enough to have any of the despised and hated Quakers amongst them as village pests, but to see these "harmless but frequently irritating people," under their very noses, openly holding meetings in one of the best and largest houses in the place was more than they could stomach. Hence we find it recorded: "Complaints made 24th. August, 1662, by the magistrates of Flushing that many of the inhabitants are followers of the Quakers, who hold their meetings at the house of John Bowne."

The persecutions and disabilities suffered by the early Friends have already appeared in the Introductory chap-

ter. The persecution of one individual, and what came of
it all, we now see unfolded. The puritanical English settlers who had migrated from New England to the Dutch
end of Long Island, opposed as they were to every brand
of religious liberty except liberty to be religiously uncomfortable in their own particular manner along with liberty to impose their own notions willy-nilly on everybody
else, were open-eyed if not open-minded. At their aggressive instance the Dutch West India Company, in
1662, ordered that "besides the Reformed religion, no
conventicles should be holden in the houses, barns, ships,
woods or fields, under the penalty of fifty guilders for the
first offence, double for the second, and arbitrary correction for every other." The old order issued long before
by the Directors of the Company for "the maintenance of
the Reformed religion in conformity with the decrees of
the Synod of Dordrecht," and the ban on public toleration
of any other sect, had never been very rigorously or
harshly interpreted. The new order, however, exactly
suited the waspish, meddlesome genius of self-righteous
bigots, and in less than a fortnight after the Flushing
magistrates had lodged their complaint with the Director
General, John Bowne was arrested on the charge of "har-
bouring Quakers and permitting them to hold their meeting at his house." He was summarily haled to New York
and cast into the gaol at Fort Amsterdam to await trial.

Under date of September 14th., 1662, the minutes of
the Council shew the following entry:—

"Whereas John Bowne, now a prisoner residing at Vliss-
ingen, on Long Island, has dared, in contempt of our orders
and placards, those of the Director General and Council in

New Netherland, not only to provide with lodgings some of that heretical and abominable sect named Quakers, and even permitted that they kept their forbidden meetings in his house, at which he not only, but his whole family has been present, by which the aforesaid abominable sect, who villify both the magistrates and the preachers of God's holy word, and who endeavour to undermine both the state and religion, are not only encouraged in their errours, but other persons are seduced and lured from the right path, all which are transactions of the most dangerous consequences, from which nothing else is to be expected, as calamities, heresies and schisms, directly contrary to the orders of the Director General and Council in New Netherland; which, therefore, deserves to be punished for an example to others; so is it, that the Director General and Council in New Netherland, having heard the conclusion of the matter, and the confession of the prisoner, doing justice, in the name of their High Mightinesses the States General of the United Netherlands, and the Lords Directors of the privileged West India Company, department of Amsterdam, condemn the aforesaid John Bowne in an amende of £25 Flanders, and to pay the costs and mises of justice, with the express warning to abstain himself, in future, of all such conventicals and meetings, on the penalty that, for the second time, he shall pay double amende, and, for the third time, to be banished out of the Province of New Netherland.

Done and condemned, at a meeting of the Director General and Council in Fort Amsterdam, in New Netherland, September 14th., 1662."

Bowne resolutely declined to pay the fine and was unflinchingly steadfast in adherence to his principles and the dictates of his conscience. In the eyes of his accusers, he was merely incurably obstinate and contumacious. As they held his fate in their hands, for the time being, he stayed in prison in solitary confinement, with a diet of bread and water. Although he still remained inflexible, he was subsequently held in the State House, his rigorous treatment was somewhat relaxed, and he was occasionally allowed to see his wife and some of his friends. However, since he persisted "in great contempt of the authority of the Director General and Council," and still "declined very obstinately to pay the amende," the Council minutes of the 14th. of December record that the authorities are "resolved to transport from this Province the aforesaid John Bowne, if he continues obstinate and pervicatious, in the first ship ready to sail, for an example to others."

Threats of banishment utterly failed to shake Bowne's determination, and the Council minutes of the 8th. of January state that:

"Whereas, John Bowne obstinately declines to submit to the judgement of the Director General and Council, so is it, in conformity to the resolution of the 14th. of December last, commanded to depart from here in the ship *Fox,* now ready to sail, while it is once more left to his choice either to obey and submit to the judgement, in paying the amende imposed upon him, or otherwise at sight of this, to depart in the aforesaid ship."

A few days later John Bowne embarked in the *Fox* for Holland. The stubborn Derbyshire Quaker was too tough a nut to be cracked by the stubborn Peter Stuyvesant and his Council.

Delayed by adverse winds, the *Fox* put into Ireland. There, upon his personal engagement to appear in Holland in due season, Bowne was allowed to land and continue his way through England. The Amsterdam Chamber of the West India Company, when they had examined him, "finding him a discreet man and steadfast in his religion, set him at liberty." Before going back to his family in Flushing, he paid visits in England and then returned by way of Barbadoes. Meanwhile, the Amsterdam Chamber had sent a rebuke to Stuyvesant that was virtually a vindication of Bowne and tacitly a sanction of his course. The letter, dated at Amsterdam the 16th. of April, 1663, said:—

"We, finally, did see from your last letter, that you had exiled and transported hither a certain Quaker named John Bowne, and, although it is our cordial desire that similar and other sectarians might not be found there, yet, as the contrary seems to be the case, we doubt exceedingly if rigorous proceedings against them ought not to be discontinued, except you intend to check and destroy your population, which however, in the youth of your existence, ought rather to be encouraged by all possible means.

Wherefore it is our opinion that some connivance would be useful that the consciences of men, at least, ought ever to remain free and unshackled. Let everyone be unmolested as long as he is modest, as long as his conduct in a political sense is unimpeachable, as long as he does not disturb others or oppose the government. This maxim of moderation has always been the guide of the magistrates of this city, and the consequence has been that from every land people have flocked to this asylum. Tread thus in our steps, and we doubt not you will be blessed."

Roman Catholic Maryland, years before, had guaranteed religious liberty to all within her borders, and the guaranties were no empty shadows. The promises were punctiliously kept. This letter from the Amsterdam Chamber, however, was the first official proclamation of religious liberty in the Protestant north. As might be expected, it broke the back of Quaker persecution at the Dutch end of Long Island.

When Bowne at last reached his home, he found the Province had passed under the sway of the British Crown. Assured of freedom from interference, he and his fellow Friends went on holding meetings in his house and, in 1672—only ten years later—sentiment had so changed that George Fox, when he visited Flushing on his American journey, was not only an unmolested guest beneath Bowne's roof but also preached there until his hearers so increased in numbers that the house would no longer hold them and he was obliged to move out of doors under shelter of the wide-spreading branches of two ancient oaks, afterwards known as the "Fox Oaks."

John Bowne died at Flushing in 1695, "the 20th. day of Tenth month." According to the records of the Flushing Meeting, "He did freely expose himself, his house, and estate to the service of truth, and had a constant meeting at his house near about forty years. He was thrice married. His second wife was Hannah Bickerstaff, and his third was Mary Cock. He also suffered much for the truth's sake."

Although the old house was always wrapped in the atmosphere of Quakerism, it was not without its gentler side of romance in contrast to the stern determination and passive resistance of its first master. On one occasion, when John Bowne and his wife Hannah Feake were both in England on a religious visit to Friends, Cupid stole into the house and caused a flutter in one heart, however subdued and decorous the outward manifestation may have been. Young Benjamin Field tendered his heart and hand to Hannah, daughter of John and Hannah Bowne. Presumably his heart was somewhat a-flutter, too. And this is how daughter Hannah, holding Cupid at arm's length, with characteristic Quaker deliberation, demurely and prudently announced in a letter to her parents the tender attachment:—

"And, dear Father and mother, I may also acquaint you, that one Benjamin Field, the youngest son of our Friend Susanna Field, has tendered his love to me, the question he has indeed proposed is concerning marriage, the which as yet I have not at present rejected, nor given much way to, nor let out my affections too much toward him until I have well considered the thing, and have your friends' advice and consent concerning it."

Daughter Hannah did eventually marry "one Benjamin Field."

There was still another and later romance, of which we are told the *"dramatis personae* were Daniel Bowne, *his* daughter Hannah, and Walter Franklin, a wealthy merchant of New York City. Ere the Revolutionary War had disrupted the country, Franklin one day set forth in his travelling carriage to journey on Long Island. Arrived in Flushing, he was passing the Bowne house when he espied thirty fine cows in the barnyard at milking time, with the milkmaids at their evening task. Of the fairest he asked whose was the farm. "My father's, Daniel Bowne," came the prompt reply, and then she hospitably added, "Wilt thee not alight and take tea?"

Franklin was a bachelor and past the first bloom of youth, but not too old to be highly susceptible to feminine beauty. He gladly accepted the invitation and went into the house. The master knew him well by name and received him cordially. They fell to talking and Franklin, according to the account of a grand-niece, "conversed with the farmer on his fine cows, etc., but not a word about the fair milkmaid. Presently the door opened, and she came in to make tea for the 'city friend,' when her father said: 'Hannah, this is friend Walter Franklin, from New York.' She blushed deeply, finding he made no allusion to having seen her before. The blush heightened her loveliness. She had smoothed her hair, and a fine lawn kerchief covered her neck and bosom." It was clearly a case of love at first sight. Franklin made three more trips to Flushing and then asked for Hannah's hand. His suit prospered, and not long afterwards she rode back with him to New York to preside over one of the stateliest mansions in the city—the house at Cherry Street and Franklin Square later occupied by Washington in his first Presidency. One of the daughters of Walter Franklin and Hannah Bowne became the wife of DeWitt Clinton.

THE PRINCE HOUSE
FLUSHING

ONE of the most engaging objects that meets the eye of the visitor to Flushing as he approaches that ancient town across the drawbridge is the Prince House nearly at the end of Bridge Street. It is a seemly structure of the mid-eighteenth century, simple indeed, yet withal having some pretensions to architectural amenity, as the illustration shews.

William Prince, the founder of the nurseries, was a lineal descendant of Thomas Prince who was Governour of the Plymouth Colony in Massachusetts for a period of eighteen years. After his death the property remained in the possession of his family and the business was continued on an extensive scale by his descendants until well past the middle of the nineteenth century, when the boundaries of the establishment were greatly diminished by the opening of streets and the conversion of large tracts into building lots.

The neighbourhood of Flushing has always been kindly to the growing of fruits and flowers and in that respect recalls its namesake town in Holland. The Huguenots, many of whom settled in the neighbourhood of Flushing, were skilled horticulturists and cultivated their acres in a manner unknown in other parts of the colony. The tradition they established has always persisted, and Flushing since early in the eighteenth century has been a centre of arboriculture and horticulture.

MANORS AND HOMES OF LONG ISLAND

In witness to Long Island's natural kindliness of soil and climate to the growing of fruit, Denton, in his early description of the country, says, "Mulberries, Posimons, Grapes, Huckleberries and Strawberries, of which last is such an abundance in June that the Fields and Woods are dyed red; which the country people perceiving instantly arm themselves with bottles of Wine, Cream and Sugar and instead of a Coat of Male everyone takes a Female upon his horse behind him and, rushing violently into the fields, never leave till they have disrobed them of their red colour and turned them into their old habit."

The Lady Apple and the Belle Pear trees today bear witness to the Huguenots who brought them thither. Many other choice fruits also first came into this country through the Huguenots. In the first half of the eighteenth century William Prince started the Prince Nurseries, which were known as the Linnean Botanical Gardens. There were two entrances to them, one in front of Mr. Prince's house and the other in the south side on Bridge Street.

At the time of the Revolution the nursery suffered badly. Three thousand cherry trees were cut down and sold for hoop-poles. When the British troops entered Flushing ready consideration was shewn the gardens, for General Lord Howe stationed troops at both gates to protect the property from injury. This protection was continued as long as there was any occasion to guard against carelessness or malice.

During the Revolutionary period, while the British troops held control of Long Island, William Henry, Duke of Clarence, afterwards King William IV, was

PRINCE HOUSE, FLUSHING

regaled at an ox-roast and a feast in the grounds. After the war General Washington was entertained at the house and his visit is recorded by an entry in his diary, saying, "I set off from New York about 9 o'clock in my barge to visit Mr. Prince's fruit gardens and shrubberies at Flushing." Considering Washington's keen interest in horticulture, the visit was doubtless a genuine pleasure to him.

Lombardy poplars were also grown at the Linnaen Botanical Gardens in great numbers and from there were spread all over the country. An advertisement that appeared in December 1798 says: "For Sale. Ten thousand Lombardy Poplars from ten to seventeen feet in height, by William Prince, Long Island."

From 1819 to 1835 the Princes formed and continued an experimental vineyard embracing four hundred varieties of foreign vineyard grapes. These they secured from the government nursery of the Luxembourg at Paris. They collected from every part of our own country as well every possible native variety.

Another branch of arboriculture in which the Princes engaged was the raising of mulberry trees. The William Prince of that day raised these trees especially with a view to fostering silk culture. As a matter of fact, he himself experimented in silk culture, feeding the worms on the branches brought from his own fields. His cocoonery produced large quantities of cocoons and he contrived a filature that was highly successful. It is said that Prince lived in a manner his name might indicate and it is interesting to note that he had woven of his own silk a number of gloves and stockings that were manufactured for him in Philadelphia.

By the autumn of 1827 the collection of different varieties of mulberry trees was complete so that it was possible to acquaint the public with the merits of each. About this time a resolution of Congress directed the Secretary of the Treasury to prepare a manual of information on the culture of mulberry trees, a list of those varieties best adapted to the different parts of the United States, and instructions relative to the manufacture of silk.

The mulberry trees which the Princes grew were propagated from cuttings they imported from Marseilles. The original plant came from Tarascon, near Marseilles, and cost five francs.

The nursery was continued in the best of condition and with extended territory until 1860.

THE HOUSE OF DE WITT CLINTON
MASPETH

THE former summer home of Governour DeWitt Clinton, at Maspeth or Newtown, in what is now a part of Brooklyn, is but a ghost of its erstwhile self. Indeed, in the state to which it has descended, it can now be regarded as little else than a derelict and an eyesore. It was once a dwelling of gracious and distinguished aspect and, in the heyday of its existence, it was doubtless one of the finest as well as one of the largest houses at the western end of Long Island. Now it is but an half-dismantled tenement with some of its members lopped off, a pathetic wreck about ready to fall down.

An old sketch, made some fifty years ago or more, shews it a comely gambrel-roofed structure with a two-storey verandah in front and a lower pitch-roofed wing at one side—see cover-design of this volume. It was covered with white weather-boarding and had a shingled roof whose contour closely coincided with the customary lines of Dutch roof design prevalent in the neighbourhood. Although simple in treatment and altogether devoid of any effort at conscious ornament, the whole exterior is instinct with quiet, homely dignity and an air of domestic comfort and contentment.

Judge Joseph Sackett, a Judge of the Court of Common Pleas, built the house and lived in it till his death at an advanced age about twenty years before the outbreak of the Revolutionary War. Eventually the Sackett family sold the property to Walter Franklin, the wealthy New York merchant who had married the pretty Quakeress, Hannah Bowne, of Flushing. Walter Franklin lived there till his death in 1780. The next occupant was Colonel Corsa, an officer who had won renown for his notable chivalry displayed at Fort Frontenac during the Old French War.

DeWitt Clinton married Maria Franklin, the daughter of Walter and Hannah Franklin, who was also a niece of Colonel Corsa. The romance of Walter Franklin's courtship of Hannah Bowne is told in the story of the Bowne house at Flushing. No doubt the daughter of this marriage inherited a love of this immediate vicinity and this feeling, after she became the wife of Clinton, as likely as not had some effect on the decision to live here.

Clinton is said to have rented the place and occupied it for several years; then he bought it, making it not only his summer home but living there for long periods at other times as well. It is generally understood that it was in this house that he planned the scheme for the Erie Canal and carried the project through to realisation. This successful undertaking brought him tremendous popularity and was doubtless instrumental, in great measure, for putting him in the Governour's chair, despite the opposition of the powerful interests that militated against him.

There is a story more or less current in connexion with this house that Clinton secluded himself here in deep dejection after his defeat as a candidate for the Presidency, hoping in the quiet of its retirement to escape to some extent the attacks of his political enemies. The story further has it that one cold winter's night a group of prominent and influential friends came to him here and succeeded in reawakening in his breast a desire to enter again into public life.

Whether this story be altogether true or not, it is quite certain that it was while living here, prior to becoming Governour, that DeWitt Clinton formulated some of his most significant projects.

After the death of his first wife, Maria Franklin, Clinton married Catharine Livingston Jones, the daughter of Dr. Thomas Jones, of Philadelphia, and grand daughter of Philip Livingston. This second marriage took place the 21st of April, 1819. At the time of her marriage, the second Mrs. Clinton is said to have been a spinster of great pride and haughtiness and her manner of superiority increased perceptibly upon becoming Mrs. DeWitt Clinton. She gave the name to the barge "Lady Clinton" that formed one of the Governour's fleet when he made his progress through the whole length of the Erie Canal upon its completion.

DeWitt Clinton died in February, 1828. This gave "Kittie Jones," as she was always called before her marriage, a chance to pose with new lustre. She was exceedingly eccentric and is said to have been inordinately proud at being the widow of the former Governour. In her later days, one of her peculiarities was to "vamp" the coachmen and footmen of her friends and acquaintance and impress them into her own service. She would come out from a reception or rout, pop into one of the best looking equipages she could see, and then order the coachman or footman to drive her home. If the retainer addressed objected to obeying her command without orders from his master, "Lady Clinton" would draw herself up in her most dowagerial manner and say in her stammering speech, "I am Mrs. DeWitt Clinton, drive on!" This was generally sufficient to gain her point.

Another of her peculiarities, it is said, was that she would never allow any fire in her house in winter time except in the kitchen. Julia Clinton, her youngest step-daughter, died suddenly from the effects of a cold generally believed to have resulted from being compelled by her step-mother to go out on foot in stormy weather to take a music lesson. The widow Kittie seems to have been a veritable czarina within her circle so that the lot of her step-children could scarcely have been compared to a bed of roses. When one of her step-daughters married David S. Jones at the command of Widow Kittie, as it was generally reported, the young lady must have obeyed with glad alacrity and a sigh of immense relief at escaping from the sway of the tyrannical dowager.

During the Revolutionary War, before DeWitt Clinton owned it, the house was occupied by General Warren of the Royal Army. It was from here, too, that General Lord Howe directed the embarkation of the British army in boats on Newtown Creek, whence they crossed over the East River to land at Kip's Bay and take possession of the City of New York after the Battle of Long Island and the retirement of Washington and the American army.

Not far from the house there was a landing on Newtown Creek which figured for many years as a busy depôt whither were brought for shipment large quantities of the district's famous product, the delicious Newtown Pippins.

MOORE HOUSE
ELMHURST, (NEWTOWN)
BUILT 1661

ONE of the oldest, if not indeed the oldest, house in that part of Brooklyn known as Newtown is the dwelling built in 1661 on land granted to the Reverend John Moore. The illustration shews a small middle porch on the general frontage of the house, and it is this part of the building that dates from the 17th Century. The larger and more conspicuous section of the house is of more recent date.

In 1652 a company of Englishmen, being dissatisfied with the conditions existing in New England, and desiring more liberty of action as well as liberty of conscience, left New England and came to Long Island. Having approached the Governour, Peter Stuyvesant, they sought his permission to start a town for themselves, and the Governour granted their request. Accordingly, the town of Newtown was laid out.

The Reverend John Moore, who had accompanied the party in their migration from New England, had been extremely active in the purchase of Newtown from the Indians, and, in recognition of his services, the town awarded his children eighty acres of land. On part of this land, in 1661, Captain Samuel Moore, a son of the clergyman, built the house which remained in possession of the family long after that date, although the descent has sometimes been in the female line.

THE MOORE HOUSE, ELMHURST (NEWTOWN)

COE HOUSE, MILL CREEK, NEWTOWN

MOORE HOUSE

It was in this house that Lord Howe had his headquarters for a time during the Revolutionary War. When the Duke of Clarence, afterwards King William IV, of England, visited America just before the termination of the Revolutionary War, he was a guest under this roof.

The neighbourhood of Newtown and Flushing seems always to have been associated with the growing of plants and the establishment of nurseries for the cultivation of trees and shrubs. Many fine types of fruit trees, as well as plants of a different nature, are attributable to efforts of nurserymen in this vicinity. The Newtown Pippin, a very famous type of apple, was first grown here.

Another admirable example of the early domestic architecture of western Long Island is furnished by the Coe house, of which an illustration is given.

THE LEFFERTS HOUSE

FLATBUSH, BROOKLYN

THE Lefferts homestead, which has now been removed for safe preservation to Prospect Park in Brooklyn, formerly stood at 563, Flatbush Avenue, in that part of Brooklyn embracing the ancient borough of Flatbush.

The original Lefferts house, which was built at some time in the latter part of the seventeenth century on land granted to Lefferts Pietersen Van Hagewout in 1660, was partly burned in 1776, but as the destruction was arrested, it was not a difficult matter to restore the structure to substantially its original state soon after the fire.

Judging from the analogy of other Dutch houses in the neighbourhood and the fact that the Dutch were exceedingly conservative and held tenaciously to all forms to which they had been long accustomed, we shall probably not be far wrong in concluding that the restorations and repairs closely followed the pattern of what had existed before the fire.

The occasion of the burning was this. The British troops landed at Bath in August, 1776, and were approaching Flatbush. To prevent the supplies of grain from falling into their hands, the American soldiers were ordered to fire the crops. A party of American riflemen accordingly set fire to the wheat stacked in the fields and barns of Flatbush and it was at this time that the Lefferts

LEFFERTS HOUSE, PROSPECT PARK, BROOKLYN

BOERUM HOUSE, KENT AVE., BROOKLYN
From an old sketch

house was set on fire, whether by accident or intent it is now impossible to say.

The owner, at the date of the conflagration, was John Lefferts, great grandson of the first settler, Judge of the Court of Sessions and Common Pleas, and a delegate to the Provincial Congress. Later, his son Peter was both Judge of the Court of Sessions and Common Pleas and a State senator. It was of him that John Baxter wrote in his *Diary,* in 1790, "There's Senator Lefferts across the street in his homespun suit that made the statesmen at Albany jealous when he was there. His wife spun every thread of it."

The house is of thoroughly Dutch type, as that type is often seen in Long Island and North Jersey, the outside walls covered with wide siding. The shingled roof over the main part of the house is of gambrel form with short top slopes and the lower slopes flared out bell-wise at the eaves and projecting far enough forward from the walls to form a verandah. Its aspect is eloquent of substantial domestic comfort and one can readily associate with this old building the homely charm of thrifty Mrs. Lefferts spinning the thread from a well-stocked store from which her husband's clothes were made.

John or Jan Lefferts, who owned and lived in the house at the time of the fire in August, 1776, died in October, 1776. He was born in 1719 and was the son of Pieter Lefferts. Pieter Lefferts, born in 1680, lived till 1774 and was County Treasurer from 1737 to 1772. In 1767 he had conveyed the Flatbush homestead to his son Jan or John for £1400, a very substantial value for that period.

Pieter Lefferts was the son of Lefferts Pietersen van Hagewout, the eldest son of the immigrant and progenitor of the family in America. Lefferts Pietersen van Hagewout the elder came from Holland to America, in 1660, on the ship *De Bonte Koe* (The Spotted Cow) accompanied by his wife and four children, of whom the eldest, Leffert Pietersen, was then fifteen years old.

In some records Lefferts Pietersen van Hagewout is spoken of as Pieter Janse, and in others as Peter Haugewout. Pieter Janse or Lefferts Pietersen is recorded to have bought an house and lot in Flatbush from Cornelis Janse Bougert in 1661. In this statement there is nothing incompatible with the statement that in 1661 he also acquired land in Flatbush, the deed for which was signed by Governour Peter Stuyvesant. This property descended through his son Leffert Pietersen to Pieter Lefferts, the father of John, and remained continuously in the possession of the family until the house became an historical museum in the keeping of the Borough of Brooklyn.

The men of the Lefferts family were very generally of powerful physique and long life. John Lefferts is said to have been over six feet in height and powerfully built. He was a kindly soul of gentle disposition but, nevertheless, was not disposed to countenance trifling in either man or beast. Now the Lefferts family had a donkey which, like many of his kind, was not always responsive to gentle suasion. One day the beast absolutely declined to go from one field into an adjoining pasture. Mr. Lefferts wasted no time in fruitless coaxing but picked up the obdurate Dutch donkey by the nape of his neck and his tail and moved him to the desired spot, very much to the animal's surprise.

Pieter Lefferts, the son of Lefferts Pietersen, married Ida Suydam and one of their sons, Jacobus Lefferts, married Catrina Vanderveer and was the father of Abigail, who figured in a Revolutionary love romance. This romance, by the way, was connected with another Lefferts house, afterward known as the Zabriskie house, and since demolished.

Jacob, the brother of John of the homestead, and father of Abigail, seems to have been a Loyalist. Now it so happened that Bateman Lloyd, a young American officer who had been taken prisoner by the British, was held in custody in Flatbush from February, 1776 to April, 1781. He was probably quartered in the gaol, but was billeted for his meals at the house of Jacob Lefferts. Lloyd was allowed considerable freedom on parole and had liberty to go pretty much where he pleased within certain limits. Having met Abigail at her father's house, Captain Lloyd no doubt improved the opportunity of his semi-freedom and often joined Abigail in her walks.

The romance progressed apace and much of the courting was done at the house of Abigail's uncle, Jacobus Vandeventer who had no Loyalist scruples and was willing to aid and abet the affair as he was much attached to Lloyd. The upshot of it all was that one afternoon Abigail, Bateman Lloyd and a clergyman conveniently chanced to meet at Jacobus Vandeventer's house. With such a fortunate coincidence, it was quite natural that a wedding should take place.

As Abigail had left home that afternoon ostensibly to go to her uncle's, there was no uneasiness when she did not return that night. The next morning Jacobus Vandeventer went to the house of Jacobus Lefferts. "Is Abby at your house?" asked Abigail's father. "Yes, and her husband, too," replied Vandeventer. There was immediately a storm, as well as much surprise, but eventually Jacobus Vandeventer succeeded in pouring oil on the troubled waters and peace was restored. The family being reconciled and the paternal blessing given, Jacobus Lefferts and his son-in-law became firm friends. In 1802 Jacobus Lefferts conveyed the property to Bateman Lloyd. It is a pity that an house so representative of Long Island Dutch architecture as the Jacobus Lefferts or Zabriskie house should have been demolished.

The Lefferts family owned Steinbokkery Pond, a sheet of water that once covered nearly two acres near Bedford Avenue. When the country thereabouts was all open land, the superstitious attached extravagant stories to this innocent-looking pool. The Indians had indulged in the fancy that the pond was the home of fire dragons which flew from one pond to another. Joris Van Nyse, a credulous and imaginative Dutchman, not to be outdone by the aborigines, declared that it was a breeding-place for sea-serpents and the haunt of ghosts. Furthermore, to prove his assertions by his own experience, he averred that one night he had seen four or five huge sea-serpents, with lambent flames playing over their raised heads, gliding out of the pond and following the creek seaward. The country folk stood greatly in awe of these fearsome apparitions of flame-crested serpents. Mr. Lefferts and his neighbours could see only phosphorescent lights rising from the swamps.

The Boerum house, of which an illustration appears, has now vanished.

THE HOUSE OF JAN DITMARS
FLATLANDS
BEFORE 1700

THE house of the Ditmars family, in Flatlands, now a part of Brooklyn, was built some time prior to the year 1700, although the exact date is not certainly known. It is shingled on the outside, in the typical Long Island manner, with long shingles exposing a foot or more of their length to the weather. The gambrel roof is of the characteristic Dutch contour, with long lower slopes and a bell-flared kick-up at the eaves. In this case, the flared eaves, instead of projecting a long distance and being supported on posts to form a verandah, project only a short distance in the manner of a penthouse. A great many of the houses of this general type have only the ground storey and an attic above it, but the Ditmars house is of such depth that it is easy to have an upper floor and, again above that, an attic within the upper slope of the gambrel. Architecturally, it is about as representative of the Dutch or western Long Island manner as any example that could be found and may be fittingly employed as a subject for contrast with the distinctly English or eastern Long Island manner.

Johannes Ditmars, who occupied the house at the time of the Revolutionary War, was an ardent adherent of the American cause, although his guardian, a near neighbour and an old friend of the family, was equally pronounced in his loyalty to the Crown. Young Ditmars had inherited a substantial fortune and was reputed one of the wealthiest residents of Kings County. Notwithstanding the attitude of his Loyalist guardian, Ditmars advanced large sums to the American cause, a fact that was generally known.

When Lord Howe was preparing to land his troops on Long Island, General Washington issued orders directing the farmers of Kings and Queens Counties to stack their grain and hay in the fields so that they could set fire to it without endangering their barns and houses, if the British forces approached.

With this order, Johannes Ditmars's guardian, being a staunch Loyalist, refused to comply. When it was known that the British forces had landed and were advancing, the Whig farmers ran hither and thither in great excitement "dropping their silver into wells, concealing their valuables, driving off their livestock, and last, but not least, setting fire to their fodder and grain." Johannes Ditmars had obeyed Washington's orders and fired the stacks in his own fields, but when it was seen that his guardian had ignored the instructions—which, under the circumstances, it was quite natural and proper that he should—the American soldiery hastened to fire the barn belonging to his Tory neighbour and friend.

Thereupon Ditmars rushed into the building, stamped out the fire, mounted a pile of hay and shouted to the excited Colonials, "If you burn this barn, you burn me along with it!" This quick action saved the day. The American soldiers, conscious of the services young Ditmars had rendered their cause, thought better of their first intention and marched away. So intent was Johannes on his service to his neighbour and former guardian that he gave little heed to the flaming stacks of grain in his own fields.

Another story connected with the old house tells of a night attack by a roving band of British soldiers. They believed that there was valuable treasure in the house and had heard that several bags of gold were concealed somewhere in a cupboard. They broke in, seized Johannes Ditmars and his mother and pinned them down beneath a feather bed while several of the party began to search for the gold.

Two faithful black slaves who were sleeping upstairs in the attic heard the commotion below and dashed down to the rescue. The soldiers were trying to force Ditmars or his mother to unlock the cupboard where they imagined the gold was hidden, and when they were unsuccessful in this, they attempted to break down the door.

The slaves seized old blunderbusses or such discarded weapons as slaves were allowed to carry, hastened down the back stairs making as much noise as possible in order to create the impression that more were coming, and laid about them so lustily that they soon had the assailants wounded and under control. In fact, they overpowered them and made them prisoners. Two of the culprits escaped, however, with a goodly collection of bruises and cuts, but the third they lodged safely the next morning in the Flatbush gaol. The gaol keepers seem to have been somewhat lax in the discharge of their duty for the prisoner was soon allowed to escape.

Old Cominey and Cuff, the faithful slaves, were just in time to save their master and mistress from being smothered to death. Naturally their action won them undying gratitude. They were always regarded with affection and lived all their lives in the Ditmars family, being taken good care of when they were too old to work any longer.

This assault on the Ditmars house took place about a month before the evacuation of the country by the British troops.

Johannes or Jan Ditmars of our story was the eldest son of Johannes Ditmarsen of Flatbush, grandson of Jan Van Ditmarsen, and great grandson of Jan Jansen. The mother of Johannes Ditmars was Fennetje Voorhees. In December, 1781, he married Margrietje Rapalje.

Note: The Ditmars house has gone the way of most historical or architectural treasures that chance to be in growing and "improving" neighbourhoods. It has disappeared.

THE BERGEN HOUSE
BERGEN BEACH, FLATLANDS

THE Bergen house at Bergen Beach, in the Town of Flatlands, is a seventeenth century dwelling of characteristic Dutch appearance. A peculiarity of Long Island, Hudson Valley and North Jersey Dutch Colonial domestic architecture is that the settlers made use of whatever building materials came readiest to hand, whether they had been accustomed to these in the land of their birth or not. This is the reason why we find such a diversity of materials in different places—stone, stucco, brick and wood. Sometimes a number of materials will be combined in one structure and in such a manner that the ready resourcefulness and adaptability of the builders is at once apparent.

In this part of the Dutch colony, where stone and brick were not plentiful, it was the usual custom to build of wood, shingling the outside with broad shingles which it was comparatively easy to obtain. Notwithstanding the variety of materials made use of, the contour remained typically Dutch; the Hudson Valley and North Jersey stone farm-houses, the brick houses of Long Island, and the much more usual shingled houses all followed much the same type of general design and plan. Ordinarily these farm-houses were of one storey with a long sloping roof within which there was a capacious attic for the storage of household goods and farm products. The roofs usually had a pronounced bellwise flare at the eaves; in some cases the eaves projected in the manner of a broad

BERGEN HOUSE, BERGEN ISLAND, FLATLANDS

penthouse, sheltering the lower walls and shading the tops of the windows, at other times the eaves projected still farther and were supported at their outer edge by posts so as to form a verandah.

The Bergen house is of the former type. The main body of the house is not only long but also of great depth. Fortunately the original roof lines have never been disturbed so that the contour is not broken up by the later addition of restless dormers which destroy the customary aspect of calm repose. The one unusual feature of the exterior in this case seems to be the possession of lower wings at each end. While it was not at all uncommon to have one low wing, the presence of two was of much rarer occurrence. It is not at all unlikely that both these wings were added at some time subsequent to the building of the main body of the structure, nor is it improbable that they were built on separate occasions.

This old house at Bergen Beach is historically remarkable only as the outcome of what seems to have been the first instance of real estate booms and land development on Long Island. All the land hereabouts had been patented to Captain John Underhill in 1646. Underhill sold it in 1652, to Thomas Spicer, and, in 1665, Spicer sold it to Elbert Elbertse, the ancestor of the Stoothoffs, who had emigrated in 1637, at the age of seventeen, from Nieukerken, in North Brabant. Stoothoff had previously, 1662, bought adjacent lands and buildings from the executors of Wolfert Barretson Van Couwenhoven. From certain indications, it seems possible that the main part of the house was built as early as 1639, though it is much more likely of somewhat later date. By a devious course of descent, agreements, transfers, and suits to recover rights, the property came into the possession of the Bergen family.

A Bergen house that has much greater glamour of romance and historic association, is the dwelling of Garrett Bergen which, unfortunately has been demolished.

During the Revolutionary War, the British were in full possession of this other house for a long period and Lord Howe lived there for a considerable time. The British officers occupied quarters there quite long enough to make themselves very much at home, and one particular in which they proceeded to make themselves comfortable was to hang three paintings on the wall of the hallway. The subjects of these paintings were the Duke of Clarence, afterwards King William IV, the portrait of a lady of the Court, and a battle scene.

After peace was finally declared and the British forces left America, the Bergen family once more took up the quiet course of life in their old home. But the paintings were allowed to remain; no one, in fact, would take them down. There they hung, exactly as the British officers had left them, until the house was demolished about 1899.

The strange part of the story is this. Lord Howe, it seems, had always been deeply interested in these pictures and, according to generally accepted tradition, his ghost used to come back and visit them. It was said that every year, on the exact anniversary of the Battle of Long Island, and exactly at midnight, strange sounds were heard that seemed to issue from behind the three pictures. Then heavy footfalls could be heard coming slowly down the stairs, accompanied by the clanking of swords and the clatter of spurs.

These heavy, firm footsteps seemed always to pause for a while directly in front of the paintings, and then passed on to the door at the back of the hall. Next there would be a loud rattling of chains and thrusting back of bolts, and then the sound of the steps would seem to pass out of doors.

This ghostly visit was looked for as an annual occurrence and never failed to take place. Once, when there were guests overnight in the house on the eve of the battle anniversary, no mention was made of the ghost story. In fact, the anniversary date had been completely forgotten for the time being. At midnight, when everybody was in bed, the guests heard the tramping along the hall and, opening their bedroom door, cried out "Who's there?" but got no reply. Their calls, however, brought the members of the family to the scene. Everybody, it seems, had heard the same sounds. Then it was remembered that it was the anniversary date of the Battle of Long Island and that Lord Howe had been making his yearly visit to the paintings. All was thus accounted for and quiet once more reigned.

A romance of pre-Revolutionary date attached to this house was that Sally Bergen, a daughter of the family, fell in love with Captain John Grant, of the Forty-second Highland Regiment and became his wife. This wedding took place the 30th of August, 1759. According to tradition, Sally Bergen was celebrated for her beauty. In 1762 the Colonial Government issued a warrant to Captain Grant for £957 bounty and enlisting money for

·eighty-seven volunteers from Kings and Queens Counties. At this time, it seems, he commanded a company in the Second New York Regiment. In 1764, he marched his company from New York to Fort Herkimer on the Mohawk. Being a Loyalist during the Revolutionary War, at its conclusion Colonel Grant was given a tract of 3000 acres, near Windsor, in Nova Scotia, whither he removed, accompanied by the "fair and faithful Sally," and all of his family, save his eldest son, Michael Bergen Grant.

The Bergen house was several times struck by cannon balls during the Battle of Long Island and these balls were long preserved as mementoes of the struggle that took place so nearby.

THE HOUSE OF NICASIUS DE SILLE
NEW UTRECHT
1658–1850

NICASIUS DE SILLE was a very important personage in the Colony of New Amsterdam. He is always turning up at one place or another in the early annals, and always in a position of dignity and trust.

He was born in Holland about 1600, and in early life received a thorough legal training. In 1633 the Dutch West India Company commissioned him the first councillor in their provincial government of New Amsterdam, and on the 24th. of July of that same year he landed on the scene of his future public services and activities. His record shews that his contemporaries esteemed him both an experienced lawyer and a statesman.

Apparently he was a man of consequence and very substantial means before he left Holland. He brought with him to this country, so we are told, more silver plate than anyone else ever had before him; in this possession he took a pardonable pride and not a little satisfaction in letting it be seen and admired. He also built himself a large house on the corner of what is now Broad Street and Exchange Place, and there he was accustomed to dispense generous hospitality in the same elegant manner to which he had been used at the Hague.

Although de Sille naturally maintained his close connexion with the city of New Amsterdam on account of his official duties—he was Schout Fiscal or Attorney-

General under the rule of Peter Stuyvesant—and kept his house there, he was also closely identified with the town of New Utrecht from the very outset.

In 1657 it was felt necessary that the settlers on the western end of Long Island should form town organisations, both for the sake of protection and also for convenience of administration, and orders were issued to that effect. Almost immediately after the publication of this order, steps were taken for the establishment of one of the towns subsequently incorporated in Brooklyn. On the 16th. of February, according to the record, "as fourteen Frenchmen, with a Dutchman, named Peter Janse Wit, their interpreter, have arrived here; and, as they do not understand the Dutch language, they have been with the Director-General and requested him to cause a town plot to be laid out at a proper place; whereupon his honour fixed upon the 19th. instant, to visit the place and fix upon a site." Three days afterwards, on "February 19th., the Director-General, with the Fiscal, Nicasius de Sille and his Honour Secretary Van Ruyven, with the sworn surveyor, Jaques Corteleau, came to Mispat (Mespeth) and have fixed upon a place between Mispat kil (Newtown Creek) and Norman' kil, (Bushwick Creek) to establish a village; and have laid out, by survey, twenty-two house lots, on which dwelling houses are to be built." This was the beginning of New Utrecht.

Nicasius de Sille built the first stone house in New Utrecht and covered its roof with red tiles imported from Holland. Here he lived for many years when he was not resident in the city. When he built a palisade about his house and the trim garden surrounding it, his neigh-

NICASIUS DE SILLE HOUSE, NEW UTRECHT, BROOKLYN

bours at first thought he was timid and they whispered it amongst themselves that the Honourable Fiscal feared an attack from the Indians. As a matter of fact, Nicasius was not thinking about Indians at all but was merely taking protective measures against the incursions of depredating herds of swine that roamed the neighbourhood and were particularly apt at rooting up and devouring the contents of gardens. It was only a little while after Nicasius de Sille had put up his palisade barrier—which would never have stopped hostile Indians—that Surveyor Cortelyou complained bitterly about the trespassing pigs of Anthony Jansen Sale. We are told that this same Anthony Jansen Sale was a "Moor and a rover," which probably means that he was a migratory negro. At any rate, he had no respect for either Dutch tradition or Dutch habits of cleanliness, and he had spent several years in dickering with the Indians, which was quite contrary to all provincial regulations. From the Indians, for some trifling consideration such as one of his kind might supply, he had purchased land, part of which was a salt meadow, and there he kept his hogs, or rather gave them an abiding place whence they might readily wander at their own sweet will and prey upon the lands and crops of neighbours.

But Nicasius de Sille had other troubles than wandering pigs to contend with in his village of New Utrecht. His nineteen proprietor neighbours were disposed to be more or less contentious and likewise litigious. They were constantly squabbling about land, plantations, houses and rights of one sort or another to which they laid claim. Sometimes they actually came to blows, their swine and cattle got destroyed, their fences were broken down and, worse still, the peace was further disturbed by lusty thieves who practised by day as well as by night. To cap the climax of all these vexations, on one occasion that militant New Englander John Scott, commanding a band of an hundred Puritan guerillas, dashed into New Utrecht brandishing swords and blaring trumpets. They badly scared the villagers and roundly abused the peace-loving Fiscal in a tongue he didn't understand. It was only after hard work and some tactful diplomacy that de Sille succeeded in getting rid of Scott and his fist-shaking, sword-brandishing band of Puritans.

Notwithstanding the fact that de Sille's life in New Utrecht was not exactly a dream of unalloyed pastoral bliss, he faithfully kept the town records of New Utrecht and, being both a scholar and something of a poet, he naïvely relieved the dull monotony of official entries by interspersing amongst them poems of his own, more or less germane to the subjects of record.

His death took place some time prior to 1674, for local records indicate that on the 29th. of March, in that year, the house was sold to Rutgert Joosten Van Brunt, by order of Nicholas Bayard, who was executor for Nicasius de Sille and trustee for his wife.

It was in this old stone, red-tiled house, built by Nicasius de Sille, that General Nathaniel Woodhull died after the Battle of Long Island. Lodged for the night, Church at Jamaica, the next morning he was taken down along with other prisoners of war, in the Presbyterian Jamaica Bay to New York Bay in an hay-boat and taken on shore at New Utrecht almost in a dying condition. He

THE HOUSE OF NICASIUS DE SILLE

was first placed in the church at New Utrecht, but shortly before the arrival of his wife he was removed to the de Sille house and stayed there till he died.

It is most unfortunate that the house was demolished in 1850 without any apparent reason for this act of vandalism. Those who tore it down had no respect for either historic association or architecture. The illustration is reproduced from an old sketch which, happily, conveys some idea of the architectural interest attaching to the structure. In May, 1916, the General Nathaniel Woodhull Chapter, Daughters of the American Revolution, dedicated a tablet marking the site of the de Sille house on what is now 84th. Street, New Utrecht, thus atoning as far as they could for the ruthless idiocy and negligence of a previous generation.

THE CORTELYOU HOUSE
NEW UTRECHT

SIX coats, six kettles, six axes, six chisels, six small looking-glasses, twelve knives, and twelve combs were the price of all the land from Gowanus to Coney Island, including what is now New Utrecht. This price the Dutch West India Company paid the Indians in compensation for the tract just described. This transfer took place in 1645. From the Dutch West India Company Cornelius Van Werckhoven received the first patent for the land now occupied by Fort Hamilton; this was his initial step towards the foundation of what he purposed ultimately to build into a patroonship. He had as tutor for his children Jacques Cortelyou, whom we shall meet again and again in the early history of New Netherland and New York.

After attempting to plant a settlement on the land he had patented, Van Werckhoven returned to Holland to further his arrangements for bringing out the stipulated quota of colonists and the requisite supplies to establish them on their farms. Jacques Cortelyou he left as his agent. Not long after his return to Holland, Van Werckhoven died. His death ended the project of a patroonship on the newly patented land at Gowanus and sundry complications arose in the settlement of his estate. In the final outcome, Cortelyou seems to have wound up Van Werckhoven's affairs in New Netherland faithfully and to the satisfaction of all concerned, after which he became possessed of considerable holdings in the neighbourhood of the present Fort Hamilton.

In 1657 Cortelyou, who combined surveying with his other accomplishments, sought permission and was directed to lay out the town of New Utrecht, which apparently he named in honour of Van Werckhoven's birthplace.

Jacques Cortelyou was a person of parts, and evidently made a most favourable impression upon Jasper Dankers and Peter Sluyter, the Labadists, who spoke of him in highly commendatory terms in their "Journal of a Voyage to New Amsterdam in 1679-1680." They say of him:—

"Jacques is a man advanced in years. He was born in Utrecht, but of French descent, as you could readily discover from his actions, looks and language. He had studied philosophy in his youth and spoke Latin and good French. He was a mathematician and sworn land surveyor. He had also formerly learned several sciences and had some knowledge of medicine. . . . We went looking around the country and toward evening came to the village of New Utrecht, so named by him. This village was burned down some time ago with everything about it, including the house of this man, which was almost an hour distant from it. . . . It was now almost rebuilt, and many good stone houses were erected, of which Jacques' was one, where we returned by another road to spend the night. After supper, we went to sleep in the barn, upon some straw spread with sheep skins, in the midst of the continual grunting of hogs, squealing of pigs, barking of dogs, crowing of cocks, cackling of hens, and especially, a goodly quantity of fleas and vermin. . . . and all this with an open barn door, through which a fresh northwest wind was blowing. Though we could not sleep, we could not complain, as we had the same quarters and kind of bed as their son usually had, who had now on our arrival crept in the straw behind us."

The Labadists' allusion to a "good stone house," built after the fire in the village of New Utrecht, apparently did not refer to the house shewn in the illustration. The establishment, where Dankers and Sluyter had sleeping quarters of such questionable comfort allotted them in the barn, was replaced by a more commodious dwelling at a date subsequent to their visit. There is occasional mention of a stone house built in *1693* but, so far as can be ascertained, the house of the illustration was built and occupied about 1700 by Pieter Cortelyou—son of Jacques the immigrant. This abode which Pieter Cortelyou reared is said to have been constructed in part with stone from the 1693 house. Lacking any infallibly *definite* data on the subject, what seems more likely is that the house of the illustration was built by Pieter Cortelyou somewhere about 1693 and that part of the stone used in its construction came from the earlier stone house of Jacques Cortelyou mentioned by the Labadists in their account. The building of an house in those days was an even more serious undertaking than it is now and it is scarcely probable that a dwelling of 1693 would be replaced by another of 1700! That would have been a piece of extravagance unpardonable in the eyes of thrifty Dutch and Huguenot settlers. What is more likely still is that there were *successive* additions and that some portion of the structure shewn in the illustration represented the stone house of Jacques Cortelyou spoken of by Dankers and Sluyter. In any event, this building was generally known as the "Simon Cortelyou house" from the name of the owner and occupant during the Revolutionary era. Pieter, who gave it its final form, was succeeded by his son Jacques, and Jacques, in turn, was succeeded by his son Simon.

Up to the time of the Revolution, the history of the house and its occupants appears to have been generally prosperous and uneventful. With the breaking out of hostilities, however, and all the consequent opportunities for romances, matters changed and from that date onward sundry interesting happenings were connected with the fabric.

It is said that when Lord Howe's army was about to land on Long Island there were three houses standing within the present reservation of Fort Hamilton. One of them was the Simon Cortelyou House, which was on the south side of the tract, the second the Bennet house, and the third was the stone dwelling of Denyse Denyse. According to tradition, when the British ships of war were at anchor in the bay, Nancy Cortelyou, who was strongly Loyalist in her sympathies, impulsively rushed out on the high ground near her home and, using a red petticoat as a flag, waved it as a signal when it was a favourable time for the Royal troops to disembark. Another version of the story has it that Nancy waved her petticoat as a gesture of welcome and encouragement after the soldiers had actually begun their landing. In any event, Nancy and her red petticoat seem to be established facts of history. Nancy was a full grown woman at this time and not a young maiden, as the story is sometimes told.

The British soldiers, more than 15,000 in number, swarmed on the Bath shore on the twenty-second of August, 1776, upon land which belonged to Captain Abraham Van Brunt and Isaac Cortelyou, the latter a descendant of the original Jacques Cortelyou and a brother of Simon. The Americans had taken up a post on an high protected position near the Cortelyou house before the British forces landed and from this point of vantage picked off a great many of Lord Howe's men as they were making their way across the beach. This effort of resistance doubtless had something to do with Nancy Cortelyou's petticoat waving; the close presence of this picket post doubtless obliged her to exercise considerable caution. It was not long, however, before a troop of Hessians silenced the little opposing post, and then Lord Howe and his staff made the Cortelyou house their headquarters, remaining there for about a month.

Jane Cortelyou, a daughter of Simon, is said to have fallen in love with one of the young officers of the invading force. The lad in a very straightforward way sought her father's permission to marry Jane. Simon Cortelyou flew into a temper and the suitor was promptly told to leave the premises, while Jane was shut up and denied all communication with the outside world.

But love will always find a way. Jane and her lover waited, and their waiting was rewarded by a favourable turn of chance. One clear moonlight night, a horseman reined up beneath the window of the imprisoned girl. There was a hurried consultation in low whispers, and then Jane, throwing a scarf over her head, quietly climbed out of her window. The eloping couple made off to the bay and stepped into a boat none too soon.

Close at their heels rushed frantic members of the Cortelyou family. The story continues with vivid details of gun barrels flashing in the moonlight, wild excitement, the pursuers reaching the shore only in time to hear the plash of receding oars, the roar of a gun breaking the silence of the night, a cry, then stillness, and a little slipper found the next day on the sand of the shore.

The story goes on to tell how, some time afterward, Jane and her husband came back to seek forgiveness and reconciliation. But their quest was in vain; the Cortelyou family received the elopers with adamantine obduracy and gave them nothing but harsh and bitter words. In despair at the prospect, the groom shot himself on the beach over which he had carried his bride on the night of their flight, and Jane went mad from grief.

The romance as told by one of the Cortelyous, who has filled the rôle of family historian, is somewhat different. According to this presumably more trustworthy version, Jane did not elope. She was secretly married to a young Hessian officer named Conrad. It was a case of love at first sight. Conrad, according to all accounts, was a fine fellow of unblemished character and of excellent record in his army services. Jane's choice, however, did not meet with favour in her father's sight and he shewed his displeasure in no uncertain manner. Jane was summarily locked up and denied sight or sound of her lover and husband. In vain did Conrad shew the marriage certificate, in vain did he plead, and in vain did Jane add her tears and prayers and pleadings. Simon Cortelyou was immovable and kept Jane in custody under lock and key.

At last, after a final bitter interview, which failed of any mitigating result, Conrad, leaving his curses for Simon Cortelyou, strode from the house to the bluff overlooking the Narrows and shot himself. Jane's reason became deranged and she ultimately died of a broken heart. When her child was born it was named Hannah Conrad.

All through the Revolutionary War possession of the Cortelyou house was hotly contested by both British and Americans, and the quarter round about was more or less debatable ground. The Cortelyou family were loyal in their allegiance to the Crown, and the story goes that men sent by Lord Stirling on a guerilla expedition captured Simon and Jacques Cortelyou—"Two famous Tories in the enemy's lines, and specie and property to the amount of $2,000." The prisoners were put on parole in New Brunswick, and, according to an account of the time, were to be "exchanged for two citizens of Jersey in captivity with the enemy."

Lord Stirling's agent in making the capture just alluded to was that same Captain William Marriner who captured Major Moncrieffe. He took Simon Cortelyou of New Utrecht to New Brunswick "as revenge for his conduct to the American prisoners," so he said and, incidentally, he kept Cortelyou's silver tankard and several other articles of value—the kind of conduct one would expect from other actions exhibited by the said Marriner.

The Cortelyou family historian says his forebears were Neutrals, not Loyalists, but, in the face of sundry incidents vouched for by history, the hostile attitude towards

CORTELYOU HOUSE, FORT HAMILTON, BROOKLYN

VAN BRUNT HOUSE, NEW UTRECHT, BROOKLYN

them on the part of ardent supporters of the American cause, and the evidence of New York State documents, it is difficult not to conclude that Simon Cortelyou and his brothers were like many others in the Province of New York, loyal to the Crown from honest conviction and not merely from expediency or time-serving motives.

VAN BRUNT HOUSE
NEW UTRECHT
CIRCA 1658

A T THE corner of Eighty-fourth Street and Bay Parkway, in that part of Brooklyn known as New Utrecht, stands the Van Brunt house, now only a pathetic wreck of what it once was, tenanted by foreigners and rapidly falling to pieces, although the walls and timbers are still stout and need only reasonable care to make them last indefinitely. The illustration is from a photograph made a number of years ago and does not tell the tale of ruin and neglect to which this relic of Dutch Long Island has been needlessly subjected.

The house was built about 1658 and is thoroughly representative of the type of dwelling the prosperous Dutch farmer of that neighbourhood provided for himself. The walls of the lower storey are most substantially built of stone covered with roughcast stucco and whitewashed. Immediately above the windows of the ground floor, in a very unusual manner, begins the wooden construction— weather-boarding on the long sides, and shingles on the gable ends. The shingled roof, along the road front, flares out bell-wise at the eaves; at the back the roof slope is longer and ends in a wide-projecting penthouse. It is scarcely necessary to add that the dormers and the porch protecting the house-door are much later and inappropriate additions. Many of the floor boards in the rooms are well over a foot wide, and the great cavernous fireplaces are surrounded by robust seventeenth century mouldings of highly engaging character.

There seems to be some question as to whether the house was one of three built by Jacob Hillakers, a carpenter, just after New Utrecht was first surveyed by Jacques Cortelyou, in 1657, or whether it was reared by the emigrant ancestor of the Van Brunts with his own hands. At any rate, whoever may have been the actual builder, there is no doubt that it was one of the first dwellings finished in New Utrecht and that it was the home of the Van Brunts from the outset.

The first Van Brunt, Rutger Joesten by name, came from Holland to America in 1653. He was a farmer and, before the end of his life, became possessed of a very substantial landed estate which descended to his issue, of whom there were four sons—Nicholas, Cornelis, Rutgert and Joost. Nicholas, who died before his father, had taken to wife Helena Cortelyou, daughter of Jacques Cortelyou of the Narrows, and so had forged one of the early links in that bewildering meshwork of interrelationships that bound almost the whole of the western or Dutch end of Long Island into one gigantic family connexion, destined to be alike the paradise and the despair of genealogists.

Rutger Joesten Van Brunt died at some time prior to 1713, but not before he had become a personage of no little consideration and weight in the community and had fulfilled various commissions of public trust. Indeed, as early as 1660, when the Attorney-General—to give him a modern title—Nicasius de Sille, officially visited New Utrecht, Van Brunt was one of those entrusted with the important task of entertaining him with bountiful food and drink and creating a good impression—a commission we may be sure he discharged with credit. Rutger Joesten likewise did the honours for "Peter the Testy" who came in person to New Utrecht with de Sille, admonishing the people to build suitable dwellings, enclose the village with a strong palisade, and keep in each family a man servant able to bear arms. The orange flag of the Dutch was then unfurled over the house for the first time in New Utrecht. At a later date Rutgert Van Brunt, who had married Elizabeth Van Voorhees, was Colonel of Militia and High Sheriff of Kings County.

At the time of the Revolutionary War, New Utrecht lay directly in the path of the British Army as they disembarked before the Battle of Long Island. Indeed, scarcely more than a stone's throw away, 15,000 soldiers and forty pieces of ordnance were landed from the British transports on the 22nd. of August, 1776.

The Van Brunts were active Whigs and Adrian Van Brunt, the master of the house, was Captain of the Home Guard and had joined the American forces. Mistress Van Brunt, who was Engletie Rapalje before her marriage, had stayed in the house with the children and slaves and was managing the place during her husband's absence. Very naturally she was not glad to see the British forces landing. She was a resourceful body, however, quick to make up her mind and act, and as her slaves gathered about her in consternation, she bade one of them harness a cart. As soon as it was ready, she bundled her children into it, and such of the servants as she could, and off they drove at a round pace along the King's Highway towards New Lotts, hens, pigs, cows, horses and all their other possessions disregarded in the haste of flight.

They were none too soon in making their departure. They were but a little distance away when the red coats of the British soldiery could be seen nearing the home they had just left.

They had gone only a short distance when Altje, the small daughter of the family, missed her pink sunbonnet, a bit of headgear to which she was deeply attached. She thereupon set up such a terrible hubbub about the forgotten treasure that Mistress Van Brunt decided to go back and rescue it if possible. By this time the British soldiers, who had practically come in at the back door as the Van Brunts went out at the front, were in full possession of the place and all it contained.

Having made up her mind to come back and face the music, Mistress Van Brunt was not the person to be mealy-mouthed in her demeanour. As she drove up and saw the troopers lounging about the door, she demanded of them, "What are you doing here?"

"We live here," they replied, "this is our house."

"Indeed it is not your house," flashed Mistress Van Brunt. "This is *my* house and I have brought my family home. If you must have a part of it, you must, but you'll have to make room for my family and for me."

She had scarcely alighted when one of the officers appeared. She tartly asked him, "Where are my cows?"

"Your cows, madam? You have no cows," he said. "They are our cows, and they have been turned out into a common pasture."

"Your cows, indeed!" snapped Mistress Van Brunt. "How do you think this baby is to be fed? Tell me that! I need a cow, and I need it right away."

History records that Mistress Van Brunt got the cow, and got it immediately. Incidentally, she picked out the best in the herd and, it is said, she likewise succeeded in salvaging some of her poultry. She seems to have been signally successful in bullying the soldiers and apparently overrode with ease all opposition in getting whatever she wanted. Her sharp tongue probably did not contribute to the comfort of the troopers' stay under her roof.

One of the Van Brunt daughters, Maria, afterwards married Robert Chesley, a British soldier, and later went to live in St. Mary's County, Maryland. In 1785, two years after peace was declared, Adrian Van Brunt and Altje went to Maryland to visit them. While there, Adrian was taken ill and died, being then about fifty. Altje, of pink sun-bonnet fame, eventually married Engelbert Lott of Flatbush and came back with him to dwell in New Utrecht where, surrounded by her children and grandchildren, she lived till 1861.

Washington is said to have stopped at the Van Brunt house on his progress through Long Island during his first presidency, but this statement can be taken with the same quantum of salt usually required by similar assertions.

THE OLD STONE HOUSE
GOWANUS
1699

THE old stone house at Gowanus, commonly called the "Cortelyou" house, was almost completely destroyed some years since, and quite needlessly, by the heedless march of what was supposed at the time to be civic improvement. The venerable structure was left in an hollow and almost buried by the grading of newly opened streets, and what was not buried was allowed to fall utterly to ruin. It is gratifying to note that there is now a strong movement on foot to rescue it from total destruction and restore it to its pristine condition. The illustrations are taken from old sketches made before the course of modern progress had robbed it of its original charm.

It was a stone structure with the upper parts of the gable ends built of brick. The brickwork was used with highly decorative and interesting effect. The parapets were laid with skewed brick stepped, and the face of the wall exhibited a chequer pattern made with black headers; the parapets ended at the line of the eaves with kneelers. At each gable end, the date of erection, 1699, was marked by wrought iron figures at the termination of the tie irons. In every way the aspect of the house was as typically Dutch as though it had been transplanted bodily from Holland, and by comparing it with old pictures of the port of New Amsterdam its close resemblance to the earliest houses of the infant metropolis can be seen at a glance. Even though the house had no history attached to it, its restoration would be invaluable as a document in the architectural history of America.

But there is history attached to the walls of this old building. It was in the very thick of the Battle of Long Island and it is more than likely that some of the chief actors in that memorable event passed beneath its windows or stepped across its threshold.

The house was built by Nicholas Vechte, who doubtless took great satisfaction in its close resemblance to the dwellings of his native Holland. It was the only stone house in Gowanus at the time of its erection and old Nicholas Vechte, or the masons he employed, built better than they knew. The walls were several feet thick and stood unscathed the shock of the battle that later raged round them. When the walls were partially destroyed within recent years to make way for the projected street, gatling guns had to be used to force the stones apart.

It is not impossible that Nicholas Vechte had in mind some notion of defence when he built his dwelling so stoutly. Gowanus Bay was a convenient place for privateers or pirates—oftentimes there was not much difference between them—and Nicholas may have felt the need of protection against unwelcome visits from these gentry of the high seas. There were plenty of them about to suggest the possibility of their attentions in lonely spots such as Gowanus then was. Indeed, in the very year when Nicholas reared his thick walls, Captain Kidd sailed to Easthampton, made his visit to Gardiner's Island and buried some of his treasure there.

Vechte, a substantial farmer like most of his neigh-

bours, was an eccentric body of independent notions and firm determination to put his whimsical fancies into practice. The house stood on a little rise a few feet above the salt meadow and about an hundred yards distant from the navigable waters of the creek. Impelled by his Dutch love of canals, dykes, and waterways of any description, he dug a canal from the creek to his kitchen door. Thus, in perfect ease and comfort, he could load his boat with cheeses, butter and other farm produce and paddle off through his own private waterway to the creek and thence to the city market in New York. The only difficulty was that the ebb tide often left his boat stranded in his own little canal. This annoying condition he remedied in 1709 by contracting with Abram and Nicholas Brower, who owned Denton's Pond nearby, to supply him with water when he needed it. Then he dug a channel from his canal to a water gate at the edge of the pond so that he could readily flood his canal at will. Thereafter, with perfect equanimity, he would seat himself in his produce-laden boat, high and dry on the mud and, by hoisting his paddle, signal to his negro slave to open the sluice. Then off he would float on the rising water and laugh at his neighbours who had to await the next flood tide to float their stranded boats, while he beat them by hours to waiting customers.

Besides his contract for occasional water-supply from Denton's Pond, Nicholas also contracted for the right to plant oysters, and so became one of the earliest systematic purveyors of bivalves to the New York market, though to what extent he carried this industry it would be difficult to say.

Although the name of the Cortelyou family is generally associated with the Old Stone House, it did not come into their possession until a comparatively late date. In 1779 the descendant of the original Nicholas Vechte of canal-digging fame willed the place to Nicholas Couwenhoven, a Loyalist. On March 10th, 1790, Couwenhoven conveyed the premises to Jacques Cortelyou of the Narrows, a grandson of the first Jacques Cortelyou who surveyed and founded New Utrecht, that enterprising capable and active Huguenot whose name seems to have been associated with almost every event of any consequence that took place in the colony. While the Loyalist Couwenhoven sold the property in 1790 to Jacques Cortelyou, Isaac Cortelyou, the brother of Jacques, had been the tenant during the greater part of the Revolutionary period and remained as occupant after Jacques took title. The house was never occupied by a Jacques Cortelyou till 1840. The three Cortelyou brothers—Jacques, Simon and Isaac—were all Loyalists as well as Couwenhoven and, according to New York State records, were under indictment as Tories.

On the 27th. of August, 1776, the soldiers of the Maryland line under Lord Stirling fought and died round about the Stone House. A bronze tablet, pourtraying the scene of the battle where scores of Maryland's sons fell, has been placed nearby at what is now the corner of Fifth Avenue and Third Street. The inscription on it reads: "The site of the Old Cortelyou House on the Battlefield of Long Island. Here on the 27th. of August, 1776, two hundred and fifty out of four hundred brave Maryland soldiers under the command of Lord Stirling were killed in combat with the British under Lord Cornwallis."

On the day preceding the battle General Washington had viewed the works of defence nearest the British lines. It is quite probable that on his tour of inspection he came to the Cortelyou house and from there overlooked the slopes of Gowanus, anxiously scanning every point and pondering seriously over the situation. It is said that he was "very anxious" on the night before the battle and that he had a premonition of a joint attack by land and sea. After tossing restlessly for a long time, he finally fell asleep consoling himself with the thought that "the same Providence that rules to-day will rule to-morrow."

Lord Stirling set out from the Cortelyou house at three in the morning of the 27th. on his way to face the British troops. He advanced past Greenwood (Lookout) Hill to meet the enemy who had made a landing several days before at Gravesend and what is now Fort Hamilton. Meanwhile the British were directing their lines towards the Stone House and detachments of the opposing armies met at early dawn near the border of Greenwood. Washington and all the people of the neighbourhood had been roused long before by the rattle of musketry, and the Commander-in-Chief was in his saddle before daybreak hurrying towards the Brooklyn lines. There he saw the slaughter of Stirling's men under the attack of Cornwallis. It was, as John Fiske called it, the first real battle of the Revolution. In comparison with it every engagement that had taken place previously was but a skirmish. It began with the engagement between Grant and Stirling at Greenwood, and ended with the fight with Cornwallis at the Cortelyou house.

A very storm of fire from cannon, muskets and rifles kept up from hour to hour between the forces of Grant and Stirling, the latter valiantly holding his own till word came that Sullivan had been wounded and taken prisoner by the Hessians and that the British troops were advancing behind him. At this time the Cortelyou house was held by Cornwallis and his men. Taking a long chance of saving himself and his troops, Stirling decided to attack Cornwallis. Time after time the Americans stormed about the house, and though guns had been planted both inside the house and round it, success was beginning to crown their efforts and Cornwallis was preparing to fall back when strong British re-enforcements arrived.

Stirling then realised that escape was hopeless and that every avenue of withdrawal had been closed. With six companies of the Maryland rifle regiment, he turned once more on Cornwallis, facing the hail of British, bullets till two hundred and fifty-six of his men had fallen. Then he turned and fled across the hills, refusing to surrender to a British General and yielding himself to the Hessian General, De Heister.

The canal dug by Nicholas Vechte proved a fatal barrier to fugitives trying to escape from the battlefield on that memorable August day. The hedges growing along the canal's brink completely screened its width, to the delusion and distress of those who tried to leap across. Not a few of them fell short and were left on the treacherous bog to fall back into the channel. After the Maryland battery at the Old Stone House had been repulsed, many of the routed men were either shot or drowned in the trap formed by the hedged canal.

In the retrospect over her fallen sons, there was added pathos in the message sent by the Maryland Council of Safety to the New York delegates in Congress on the 16th. instant preceding: "We shall have with you in a few days four thousand men, which is all that we can arm and equip, and the people of New York, for whom we have great affection, can have no more than our all."

THE VOORHEES HOUSE
NECK ROAD, GRAVESEND

A N OLD, weather-beaten milestone, standing in front
of the Voorhees house on Neck Road, in Gravesend,
bears the legend "8¾ miles to Brockland Ferry." And
thereto attaches a pretty bit of romance and a story of
love at first sight.

In the days when New York was a Royal Province, the
authorities set out this milestone and many more like it
beside the Long Island roads. Tradition has it that one
sweltering summer's day a young British officer rode out
to Gravesend to superintend the placing of this stone.
Hot and thirsty, he asked for a drink of water at the
farmhouse. This a beautiful daughter of the Voorhees
family graciously gave him and, incidentally, captured
his heart in return. The upshot of it all was a marriage
and the fair Gravesend maid crossed the water to far-off
England as the bride of the officer. It is said that in a
certain noble house in England there hangs to this day
a picture of this same old Gravesend milestone in front
of the home whence the young nobleman, for such he
was, got his radiant bride.

The house is believed to have been built very early in
the eighteenth century by John Coerte Voorhees, son of
the first of his name to settle in Gravesend. Its walls are
covered with siding, and the bell-flare of its roof at the
eaves projects as a penthouse or long hood just above the
tops of the ground storey windows. Were it a little wider

it would probably have been used as the roof of a verandah, but it is much more agreeable as it is without posts.

The early history of the house seems to have been uneventful, but at the time of the Revolution it came into more general notice as the home of Stephen Voorhees who joined the American army. The order issued by General Washington when Lord Howe's troops first landed on Long Island was indirectly the cause of bringing the house a peculiar sort of fame.

Washington knew he could not stand off the British troops and prevent their landing on Long Island, but he was determined they should not derive any more advantage from their occupation of the country than he could possibly help. He directed all supplies to be destroyed, all the grain to be burned in the fields, and all the cattle that could not safely be driven off by the American soldiers to be killed. As a result of this order, much of the country was laid waste before the invading army set foot in it and we are told that on a lonely road outside of Gravesend heaps of cattle bones lay bleaching where they had been hastily slaughtered and left.

Despite the general instructions to kill all cattle, Mrs. Voorhees was permitted to keep one cow to give milk for her baby. This precious cow, for safety's sake, was concealed in the house. Soon afterwards a marauding Hessian, on the lookout for beef, discovered the cow's presence and was just about to drive it off when Stephen Voorhees appeared on the scene. He had got separated from his regiment after the battle of Long Island and had then hurried home to see how his wife fared. He naturally opposed the cow-stealing Hessian, they fell to blows and the Hessian was killed.

Foreseeing that the Hessian's companions in arms would, in all likelihood, institute a search for him and find out what had happened, Voorhees and his wife, so says local tradition, buried the slain man in the cellar. Under cover of night, Voorhees then hurried away to rejoin the American army. Whether the Hessian, thus summarily disposed of, ever walks of nights or utters ghostly groans, history does not inform us.

Another old Brooklyn house of thoroughly characteristic Lond Island Dutch aspect is the Derick Remsen house, of which an illustration is given. It is little short of a calamity that most of these old Brooklyn Dutch houses have either completely vanished or are rapidly disappearing.

DERICK REMSEN HOUSE, NEW LOTS, BROOKLYN

THE VAN PELT HOUSE
NEW UTRECHT, BROOKLYN

THE Van Pelt house, which still stands in that portion of modern Brooklyn known as New Utrecht, is commonly called the Van Pelt Manor House although there was never a duly and legally constituted Van Pelt Manor and this appellation has no defence whatever on any historic grounds. In 1675, 1678 and 1680 considerable tracts of land were acquired by Teunis or Tonis Jansen Lanen Van Pelt, the *emigré,* and added to what he already had previously. These additional holdings in New Utrecht, mentioned in Governour Dongan's Patent of 1686, may have created the impression that the Van Pelts, who were always a prominent family in the neighbourhood, were paving the way for the erection of their possessions to the legal and administrative status of a manor, but if they cherished any such intention it was never consummated.

Teunis or Tonis Jansen Lanen Van Pelt, the first of his family in New Amsterdam, came from Luyck in the Netherlands. He was often called "Tonis the Fisher." His son, Aert Tunise Van Pelt, born in New Amsterdam in 1663, was a magistrate of New Utrecht in 1694, Lieutenant of Militia in 1705, and Captain of Militia in 1715. In 1694 he bought a farm from Hendrick Mathysen Smack, but just what part of the Van Pelt possessions this purchase represented it is now difficult to say.

Peter Van Pelt, the son of Aert Tunise Van Pelt, was

227

Captain of the New Utrecht Militia in 1750. He it was who occupied the house during the Revolutionary period. Although he was well advanced in years at the time—he died in September, 1781—he was actively represented on the American side by his sons Rem and Aert. He was the "Old Man Van Pelt" alluded to by Captain William Marriner in his post-Revolutionary narrative to General Johnson of the capture of Major Moncrieffe.

According to Marriner's account, he and Lieutenant John Schenck, with twenty-eight militiamen, started from Middletown Point, New Jersey, on the night of June 13, 1778. Landing from their two long boats on New Utrecht beach, they called on a number of their friends, "Old Man Van Pelt" being one of the first visited. Marriner had been quartered at the Van Pelt house when a prisoner of the British and knew which rooms each of the family occupied. Knocking softly at Mr. Van Pelt's window, he roused the old gentleman and told him the nature of their mission. Mr. Van Pelt gave Marriner and his companions some advice, wished them luck and sent them on their way to his son Rem's house. Thence they made their final arrangements and started off with the intention of capturing Mayor Matthews of New York, who was then on Long Island, Miles Sherbrook, Major Moncrieffe and Theophylact Bache. Matthews and Sherbrook were away from their quarters and so escaped capture, but the raiding party succeeded in securing Moncrieffe and Bache and, in addition, Captain Forrest. The three of them were taken from their beds, marched to the beach, and carried prisoners to New Jersey.

VAN PELT HOUSE, NEW UTRECHT, BROOKLYN

BUSHWICK TOWN HALL AND CHURCH, BUSHWICK, BROOKLYN
From an old sketch

THE VAN PELT HOUSE

On account of this midnight raid, the British authorities arrested Rem and Aert Van Pelt and also Colonel Van Brunt, of Gravesend, and his brother under suspicion of complicity in the plot. Colonel Van Brunt, it is said, bribed their gaoler into allowing them an interview by night. The four suspects then agreed upon a story that they would one and all tell at their hearing without variation. Fortunately for them, they were found not guilty and discharged.

The house was built in 1664 and has been continuously owned and occupied by members of the Van Pelt family. It is a typical Dutch structure, the lower storey solidly constructed with thick stone walls, while the upper storey, outwardly visible and distinct from the roof only at the gable ends, is weather-boarded with wide siding. The expansive shingled roof comes down with beetling, bell-flared eaves to the top of the ground storey and its lower projection beyond the walls forms the covering of a verandah. Unfortunately, the mid-Victorian "improvers" fell to work on the exterior and substituted fretwork and jig-saw verandah supports in lieu of the old posts, but inside the early character of the dwelling is retained, the rooms are low-ceiled, and the old Dutch storied blue tiles are still to be seen about the capacious fireplace. Washington is said to have visited the house and General Howe is believed to have spent much time under its roof. Upon one of the small-paned windows are scratched the names of prisoners confined there at Howe's order.

In front of the house runs what was once the King's Highway, and along this ancient thoroughfare in Colonial times passed all the travel between Long Island and

Philadelphia. An old milestone dating from the reign of George II—one of the few remaining milestones in King's County—is still at the corner near the house. In 1790, when Washington as President made his progress through Long Island, he passed over this road and was greeted by the village people of New Utrecht, then a community separate from the nearby Brooklyn which was afterwards to absorb it.

When news came that the President was soon to pass by, there was a stir of excitement amongst the eagerly expectant townspeople. The children at the little school hardby the Van Pelt house were hurried home to be tidied up and then sent back to stand in line, in their "best bibs and tuckers," to welcome the Great Man. A little Peter Van Pelt of that day, it is said, stood at the end of the line and was the last lad to whom the General spoke.

Local history records that Washington, patriarchally laying his hand on Peter's head, said solemnly, "Be a good boy, my son, and you will be a good man." This sounds like a Parson Weems yarn, made out of the same kind of material as the cherry-tree and hatchet fable. If the story be true, it only goes to illustrate very aptly one phase of Washington's martyrdom in facing the appalling ordeal of dispensing vacuous platitudes to unknown school-children. Little Peter eventually grew to be a parson and, in due time preached a panegyric when Washington was gathered to his fathers.

Not far from the Van Pelt house is the Dutch Reformed Church of New Utrecht, and in front of the church stands the New Utrecht Liberty Pole, surmounted by an eagle and a weather-vane spelling "liberty." This pole, of which the New Utrecht folk are mightily proud, marks the spot where the American flag was first hoisted in New Utrecht, in 1783, upon the evacuation of the British troops. The present pole is the fourth that has occupied the spot, but the wooden eagle is the original bird, although in the course of years he has grown an iron bill and legs and has had his wings strengthened with iron bands. This fourth liberty pole was the gift of Mr. and Mrs. Townsend Cortelyou Van Pelt.

Whether the President arrived at New Utrecht on horseback or in his coach it is impossible to say. He was quite accustomed to making journeys partly in the saddle, partly driving, his saddle horse being led, while he was in his coach, and ready whenever he wished to change. The coach used on the Long Island progress must have made a profound impression on those who saw it. Drawn by four grey horses, with outriders, it was a very magnifical affair. Suspended from leather straps attached to great curving springs, it was one of the most luxurious equipages in the country and was quite comparable to the best on the other side of the water. The body and running gear were cream colour with gilt ornament and on the panels of the doors were blasoned in full heraldic colours Washington's arms with the proper accompaniment of mantlings and crest. On the four other panels were allegorical pictures emblematic of the seasons, exquisitely painted on copper by Cipriani. The windows at the sides, in front and at the back had green Venetian blinds. The rest of the upper part of the body was finished with black leather, and the inside was lined with "bright black leather"—did the chronicler of this gorgeousness mean *patent* leather?—the same material appearing as trim for the hammer-cloth. Washington was always meticulous to have everything about him *elegant* and *in the fashion,* and this splendid coach must have been exactly to his liking. It is sad to have to record the final fate of this stately vehicle. It was ultimately "broken up and the fragments made into walking sticks, picture frames and snuff-boxes, which were the stock in trade of charity fairs and realised more in this way than its original cost."

BENSONHURST

NEW UTRECHT, BROOKLYN

BENSONHURST is to be found in New Utrecht near Gravesend Bay and stands between the modern streets known as Benson Avenue and Bay Twenty-Fourth Street.

Although it has sustained several episodes of alteration, the house is clearly of the old Dutch pattern, solidly built of stone with a shingled roof coming down to the top of the ground storey. At the threshold lies an old millstone, originally brought from Holland, which, outworn after years of service grinding corn, was finally set as a door-step to this ancient house by the sea, famous for its hospitality.

Nicholas Couwenhoven built this dwelling for himself early in the eighteenth century. When his granddaughter Maria married Egbert Benson, it passed into the possession of the Benson family, and generation after generation of Bensons lived in it until a comparatively recent date. At an early period the family took an active part in public affairs and served the State with credit. "Fighting Anthony" Benson bore arms on the American side in the Revolutionary War, and, after being taken prisoner, was confined in the prison-hulk *Jersey,* anchored in Wallabout Bay, until he died of starvation and disease. Egbert T. Benson was born in 1746 and died in 1833. He graduated from Kings College in 1765 and was noted for his great legal learning and his brilliance as a pleader.

At the outbreak of the Revolutionary War, he was a member of the Committee of Safety. In 1777 he became the first Attorney-General of the State of New York, and was elected to the first legislature.

In 1783, at the coming of peace, he was one of the three commissioners who directed the embarkation of the Loyalists for Nova Scotia. In 1788 he was active in securing the adoption of the Constitution by the New York Legislature. From 1794 to 1802 he was a Judge of the Supreme Court of New York.

General Washington is said to have been a frequent visitor at Bensonhurst. Whether his visits were frequent or rare, at any rate a dinner service is still preserved and treasured from which the first President ate when he dined there. Washington, as we know, was fond of lingering at the table and tradition says that in the springtime after these leisurely meals at Bensonhurst he was wont to walk with his host down to the beach where the shad were caught, for which New Utrecht was then famed, to watch the fishermen hauling in their nets.

A later visitor who often stayed at Bensonhurst was Henry Clay. He was a close friend of the then master of the house and the story goes that the two of them had many a pipe and bottle of applejack together. Until a few years ago—and possibly still—there was carefully guarded by the Benson descendants a bottle of this very applejack that had come all the way from Henry Clay's plantation.

Martha Lamb at one time occupied Bensonhurst and it was there that she wrote a great part of her *History of New York*.

BENSONHURST—NICHOLAS COUWENHOVEN HOUSE
NEW UTRECHT, BROOKLYN

HOUSE SAID TO HAVE BEEN THAT OF LADY DEBORAH MOODY
NECK ROAD, GRAVESEND, BROOKLYN

THE HOUSE OF LADY DEBORAH MOODY
GRAVESEND
1643

IN 1643, accompanied by a small party of English colonists, Lady Deborah Moody descended upon the Colony of New Amsterdam and settled herself at Gravesend. The house which is said to have been her habitation was probably built at that time, as Lady Deborah was not a person to delay when once she had made up her mind to anything. Half hidden by a dense growth of hedges, shrubbery and cherry trees, this house is still standing—though in none too good condition—on Neck Road in Gravesend, midway between Gravesend Avenue and Van Sicklen Street. In the cemetery opposite, so it is said, Lady Deborah is buried, but her grave has never been identified. Whether Lady Deborah built and occupied the house, as many contend, or whether she did not, as others maintain, it is certainly of very early date, is distinctly of architectural interest, and, since it has always been associated with her name and fame, it serves as an engaging memorial of an extraordinary and forceful personage who left a deeply-graven mark on the record of the days of small beginnings.

Whether Lady Deborah was somewhat of a contumacious virago or whether she was rather a capable, far-sighted pioneer with brains to think for herself, clear judgement and determination to put her convictions into effect, seems never to have been fully agreed. There is something to be said on both sides. At any rate, there can be no question about the reality and striking force of her personality. Withal, this seventeenth century forerunner of the modern feminist is a refreshing character to contemplate and her rôle in the Colonial drama is unique.

Lady Deborah Moody was the widow of Sir Henry Moody of Garesden, Wiltshire, one of the baronets created by King James I in 1622. Her maiden name was Dunch and she came of an old Berkshire family whose members had been conspicuous for their championship of liberty of conscience and their opposition to Royal exactions. Lady Deborah's father, Walter Dunch, had been a member of Parliament in the reign of Queen Elizabeth, and her uncle, Edward Dunch, was a member of Parliament in the reigns of both James I and Charles I. Her cousin, Sir William Dunch, was uncle by marriage to Oliver Cromwell, and this Sir William's son was a vigorous champion of popular rights in the Parliaments of Charles I and continued to sit at Saint Stephen's after the beheading of the King. Considering of what sort were her antecedents and relatives, it is not difficult to understand how Lady Deborah was naturally prone to self-expression in no uncertain manner.

If Sir Henry Moody had any restraining influence upon the actions or opinions of his spouse, that influence came to an end at his death which occurred somewhere about 1632. Lady Moody was left with two children, a son, Sir Henry Moody the younger who accompanied his mother to America, and a daughter, of whom nothing is recorded. The first indication of anything that might be construed as bumptious independence on Lady Moody's part crops up in England about five years before she crossed the Atlantic to hew out her niche in the history of the Colonies. Apparently she had come up from the country to stay in London for an indefinite period and had contravened the statute that no person should reside beyond a limited time away from their own homes. Accordingly we find the Court of Star Chamber, on the 21st. of April (probably 1635), taking cognisance of Lady Moody's actions and ordering that "Dame Deborah Moodie and the others should return to their hereditaments in forty days in the good example necessary to the poorer class."

Now, whether "Dame Deborah" had been unduly active in some agitation of religious dissent and had thus brought down upon her head the displeasure of the Court of Star Chamber, we do not know. We can only surmise. Neither do we know whether she did peaceably as she was bid and went home to the country. In any event, it seems likely that she had a sense of galling repression and determined to go where she believed she would have greater freedom of action and be away from controlling agencies with whose views she was not in accord.

In 1640 we find this "troublesome female" arrived in Lynn, Massachusetts, where she received a land grant of four hundred acres. The following year she bought there a large estate called "Swanscut" that had previously belonged to Deputy Governour John Humphrey who had married a daughter of the Earl of Lincoln. For this she paid £1100, a price that seems to have strained her resources for the time as Lechford, writing in 1641, says "she is, good lady, almost undone by buying Master Humphrie's farm, Swampscot." Whether financially embarrassed by her purchase or not, which appears open to doubt, she nevertheless stocked the farm with cattle and put it under extensive culture. "Swampscot," according to all accounts was a pleasant place lying between the ocean cliffs and a river back of them, and Lady Deborah passed her time between here and Salem, in the latter town having a small house next door to that of the Reverend Hugh Peters. Though living mostly at Lynn, she belonged to the church at Salem, for Lechford says of her, "Lady Moody lives at Lynn, but is of Salem Church."

Being a person of consequence, Lady Deborah was held in great respect of her neighbours and the authorities until she ran foul of the inexorable New England theocracy, fell under ecclesiastical discipline, and was excommunicated for heresy. Lady Deborah evidently possessed a marked degree of magnetism and appears to have been a born leader, whether she was heading a company of colonists or setting forth religious doctrine. The annals of the Town of Lynn for 1642 record that at the Quarterly Court, on December 14th. of that year, "The Lady Deborah Moodie, Mrs. King, and the wife of John Tillton, were presented, for holdinge that the baptising of Infants is noe ordinance of God."

Mrs. King was a neighbour, and John Tillton afterwards removed with Lady Deborah to Gravesend and there became an officer of the town. Had Lady Deborah been living in the present day and generation, we may be

perfectly sure she would have been directing sundry
women's clubs, working with might and main in political
campaigns, and energising various sorts of uplift move-
ments; as it was, in seventeenth century New England
there was no scope for this "first American feminist" save
to plunge into doctrinal controversy, personally direct the
management of her lands, or lead a band of malcontent
colonists to start a new venture. Alluding to her forsak-
ing the religiously hostile atmosphere of Massachusetts
and setting out with her little following to find a place of
tolerance, Judge Benson compared her to Dido leading
a colony into a strange land.

Despite her differences with the ecclesiastical authorities in Massachusetts, Lady Moody apparently remained
on the most cordial terms with Governor Winthrop, and
he evidently entertained a sincere regard for her. When
she removed from Massachusetts, he wrote "the Lady
Moodye, a wise, and anciently religious woman, being
taken with the error of denying baptism to infants, was
dealt with by many of the elders and others, and admon-
ished by the church of Salem, whereof she was a member;
but persisting still, and to avoid further trouble, she removed to the Dutch, against the advice of all her friends."
From another source, a letter of the time anent one of her
followers is not so charitable in its implication; it says
"Rev. Mr. Walton of Marblehead is for Long Island
shortly, there to set down with my Lady Moodie, from
under civill and church watch among ye Dutch."

To avoid contention, and still more to avoid interference and persecution, Lady Moody deemed it expedient
to sell her farm at Lynn and move on elsewhere to a spot

where the ecclesiastical authorities were less aggressive in protecting their particular variety of religious liberty to the exclusion of all competing belief or teaching. Not tarrying long in Rhode Island or at New Haven—they were too near the scene of her recent disagreement to be beyond the reach of meddlesome annoyance—she and her companions kept on to the Colony of New Netherland and settled at Gravesend on the western end of Long Island. Their establishment there dates from 1643.

The grant to Lady Deborah and her associates comprised the whole of Coney Island and all of Gravesend and Sheepshead Bay. In December, 1645, a general patent for the whole town of Gravesend (exclusive of certain individual grants) was issued to Lady Moody, Sir Henry Moody (her son), Ensign George Baxter and Sergeant James Hubbard, their heirs and successors, authorising them to "build a town with such necessary fortifications as to them may seem expedient, . . . to have and enjoy free liberty of conscience, according to the manners and customs of Holland, without molestation, . . . and to establish courts and elect magistrates, to try all causes not exceeding 50 Holland guilders."

Lady Moody's house at Gravesend was a comfortable one for the time, substantially built, and as commodious as could be expected in an infant country. The dwelling was strongly fortified and served as a blockhouse or citadel in case of Indian attacks, which were not infrequent. In the spring of 1643 the colonists built a stockade around their houses, leaving their farm lands outside, and every man went to his work armed. Coney Island they used as a pasture for their cattle. From the outset, the Gravesend settlers endeavoured to deal fairly with the Indians, and even after Kieft's second patent they purchased the lands of Gravesend for "one blanket, one gun, one kettle," which, as things went according to the redskin view of valuation, was not a bad price. General conditions, however, were so unsettled that there was no security for anyone within a wide radius of Kieft's centre of disturbance. The worst Indian attack occurred in 1655 when the settlers, gathered around Lady Moody's house, had to hold out for a considerable time until help arrived from New Amsterdam. Lady Moody believed in taking no chances with the Indians and insisted on a constant state of watchful preparedness amongst her retainers and associates.

It was, perhaps, owing to the strain of perpetual vigilance that Lady Deborah felt enough dissatisfaction with her Long Island venture to induce her to write Governour Winthrop in the spring of 1644 asking him whether he would advise her to return to the Massachusetts Colony. Deputy-Governour John Endicott heard that Governour Winthrop had received such a letter from her ladyship and hastened to forestall such a calamity as her return by vigorously opposing any contemplated encouragement on Winthrop's part. Endicott evidently thought Lady Deborah a terror and preferred her room rather than her company.

She appears to have been held in wholesome awe by others as well as Endicott. Amongst her other possessions, she owned a large herd of swine that foraged on Coney Island. From the old records we learn that the crew of a certain English privateer, the *Seven Stars,* landed on the farm of Anthony Jansen Van Salee, in the bay, and stole his pumpkins. They were on the point of carrying away a lot of hogs from Coney Island but forebore when they discovered they belonged to Lady Moody.

Whatever intentions she may have entertained at one time of withdrawing from Long Island came to naught, for she remained there all the rest of her life. Apparently she was on the best of terms with Kieft's successor, Governour Stuyvesant, if we may judge from the tone of a letter written by Stuyvesant to Lady Deborah, in 1654, informing her of the appointment of commissioners to settle the boundaries between Gravesend, Anthony Jansen's land, and the land patented to Pennoyer. The letter is subscribed "Your honour's affectionate friend, P. Stuyvesant." Another incident that occurred near the same time also indicates Stuyvesant's confidence in the Chatelaine of Gravesend. The Gravesend settlers, who were mostly English, notwithstanding the fact that they held their lands under a patent from the Dutch on condition of allegiance to the States General, were always chafing under Dutch rule and eager to join in alliance with Connecticut and the other English settlements on Long Island. When war was going on between England and Holland, in 1653, the Gravesend colonists became more restless than ever and were plotting with the New England colonists to attack the Dutch when Cromwell, in 1654, made peace with Holland. This averted the New England attack on New Amsterdam. The Gravesend colonists, disappointed of their thrust at their Dutch neighbours, now became openly disaffected, denied the right of the Director-General to pass upon nominations, and appointed twelve men of their own selection to manage the affairs of the town. Ensign Baxter and Sergeant Hubbard they nominated magistrates. This nomination was obnoxious to Stuyvesant for both men had been openly and actively hostile to Dutch authority. In order to compose matters, Stuyvesant went in person to Gravesend in December and stayed at Lady Moody's house. She appears to have acted as peace-maker. "Her high standing and character amongst the settlers gave her great influence over them. Stuyvesant also had a great respect for her; for he confided to her the nomination of the magistrates for that and subsequent years, and her popularity with the Gravesend people reconciled them to this unusual procedure."

Although the town of Gravesend was never constituted either a patroonship or a manor, Lady Moody virtually enjoyed all the powers and prerogatives of a lord of the manor through sheer force of character and personal influence. Whether the Dutch disapproved of the religious attitude of Lady Moody and the Gravesend settlers or not, they never interfered with them. The town in general seems to have been affected with anabaptist views and to have had no settled church. In 1657, when Domine Megapolensis and Domine Drisius sent to the Classis at Amsterdam a report of the state of the churches in New Netherland, they speak of the inhabitants of Gravesend as being Mennonists—"yea," the account reads, "they, for the most part, reject infant baptism, the Sabbath, the office of preacher and the teachers of God's word; saying that through these have come all sorts of contention into the world. Whenever they meet together, the one or the other reads something for them."

Lady Moody's cordial relations with Governour Winthrop appear to have been enduring for in 1649 she wrote him asking to look after some personal matters for her in connexion with her affairs at Lynn. Her letter is as follows:—

"Worthi Sur,—My respective love to you remem(bered,) acknowliging my selfe for youre many kindness (es) & respecte to me much obliged to you. I have written divers times to you, but I doubt you have not received it; at present, being in hast, I can not inlarg my selfe, only my request is yᵗ you will be pleased, either by this bote, if in your wisdom you see not a conuenienter opertunitie, to send to me those things yᵗ Mr. Throgmortone brought for me, & I understand are with you, for I am in great need of yᵐ, together with Marke Lucars chest & other things. So with my respective love to you & youre wife, with Mrs. Lacke, remembred, hoping you & they, with youre children, are in helth, I rest, comitting you to yᵉ protection of yᵉ Allmighti. Pray remember my nesesiti in this thing.

DEBORAH MOODY."

William King purchased Lady Moody's plantation at Lynn, and a letter to her agent, in 1649, has on the back of it a list of things she desired sent to her at Gravesend. The list is an illuminating commentary on the domestic needs of the time in an establishment like that at Gravesend. Just why Lady Deborah wished these things from Massachusetts instead of getting them from New Amsterdam it is hard to say. The memorandum calls for:

"Two yards black Taffety
40 yeardes of broade dowlasse

THE HOUSE OF LADY DEBORAH MOODY

> 40 yeardes, at 4s. per yard, of Broadclothe
> of white justenn, 10 yards;
> of brown justenn, 10 yards;
> oune good greene Rugg
> oune paire of blankets
> of narrow teek for boulsters and pyllows 20 yards
> 8 seyeths for mowing (I pray let them be very good) ;
> of plow chains 3;
> & 2 peauter pots."

There is also a request for nails, saws, augurs, and other tools; shoes, skillets and other articles for domestic use, and one hundredweight of iron.

A deed in the Gravesend records, given by her son Sir Henry Moody (as he signed himself) conveyed land to John Johnson which had been "received from his deceased mother, Deborah Modye." This deed is dated May 11th., 1659, so that Lady Deborah must have died prior to this conveyance, but the exact time of her death is not known.

Her followers in the Gravesend colony seem to have intermarried with the neighbouring Dutch families so that the identity of the English settlement was eventually merged with that of the western Long Island population. Sir Henry Moody, Lady Deborah's son, subsequently left Gravesend and went to Virginia.

THE SCHENCK HOUSE
MILL ISLAND
BUILT IN 1656

J AN MARTENSE SCHENCK VAN NYDECK, born in Amersfoort, Holland, emigrated to the New Netherlands and, in 1656, built this house on Mill Island, which is now a part of Bergen Beach. The house is typically Dutch in every way, and shews all the characteristics common to the domestic Dutch architecture of the Hudson Valley, the west of Long Island, and northern New Jersey. In addition to its thoroughly Batavian outward aspect, it is interesting to note that tradition says the building was framed by a ship's carpenter, and an examination of the structure within tends to confirm this current report. One of the illustrations shews the framing of the timbers, and it is easy to see how the method resembles that of ship construction.

Although the house is apparently not large, at least so far as its external appearance goes, it, nevertheless, possesses that mysterious quality of elasticity shared by most of the Dutch dwellings. It is always amazing on entering houses of this type to see how much room there really is inside, and how much space can be contrived out of seemingly nothing. When we remember this, it is not hard to understand how large Dutch families were sheltered under a roof-tree that seemed of but modest extent.

The family of Schenck Van Nydeck was of ancient descent and their lineage has been traced back without

246

SCHENCK HOUSE, REAR VIEW, MILL ISLAND

SCHENCK HOUSE, BEDROOM WITH SHIP FRAMING, MILL ISLAND

a break to the 14th Century. They were Lords of Afferden, besides holding sundry other titles. General Peter Schenck Van Nydeck was born at Gosh in 1547. His son Martin was born in 1584. The said Martin was the father of Jan Martense Schenck, who emigrated to America.

Captain John Schenck, long before Jamaica Bay was ever thought of as a terminal for ocean liners, built a wharf on the end of Mill Island, and commanded a ship that plied between the New and the Old Netherlands. It was said by old residents of the flatlands, in Bergen Beach, that Captain Schenck was at one time a lieutenant of Captain Kidd's, and certain people called the house "The Pirate House". This name, however, seems to have been entirely undeserved, as there is no record of any member of the Schenck family having followed the calling of piracy, and there are no tales of Captain Kidd hiding money or treasures on this place. This may seem strange, for the spot was most convenient for men of Captain Kidd's later profession, and one can scarcely understand why he never made use of it.

It is not impossible that Captain Schenck may have engaged in privateering, as so many of his contemporaries did, without any loss of personal prestige or the respect of the community in which they lived. The line between privateering and piracy is sometimes very difficult to draw, nevertheless, many respectable sea captains took out letters of marque upon the slightest excuse and managed to do well unto themselves under this pretext. And it was rarely that any inconvenient questions were asked!

The heirs of Captain Schenck sold the place to Joris Martinse of Flatbush for £2,500. The new owner was master of the property when the Revolutionary War broke out. Apparently, he performed, or tried to perform, the difficult feat of carrying water on both shoulders. While outwardly not swerving from his allegiance to the King, he nevertheless contributed handsomely to the American cause, handsomely, that is, for those days, having given between $5,000 and $6,000.

Perhaps it was owing to this ambiguous attitude of Joris Martinse that Captain William Marriner stopped at his house when he made his famous Midnight Expedition in Flatbush. It was here that he captured Major Moncrieffe. Marriner, it should be remembered, was a prisoner on parole from the British Army, and his performance in breaking his parole by leading a guerilla expedition and making prisoner an officer to whom he was under obligations, can hardly be looked upon as an honourable and creditable performance, although at the time his exploit was acclaimed amongst the Whigs with much applause.

Nearby there is a little old mill, and it is said that when the British soldiers were hastening on their way along Long Island, the thrifty Dutch proprietors of the mill sold their red-coat visitors flour for $1.00 a pound.

The Martinse family eventually sold the property to General Philip S. Crooke, and after diverse vicissitudes of ownership, it passed into the hands of the Atlantic, Gulf and Pacific Company.

STATEN ISLAND

STATEN ISLAND

FROM the very outset of its colonisation, Staten Island has always been cosmopolitan in its make-up. Dutch, French Huguenots, Walloons and English all settled close together. Though they might gather into little racial coteries, nevertheless an ultimate blending of the different elements was inevitable.

The architecture of Staten Island reflects this fundamental cosmopolitanism. While there are old houses of distinctly Dutch type of derivation, and other old houses that are equally English in their inspiration, yet one cannot go to any one part of the island and say this neighbourhood is purely Dutch in its collective manifestation, or that neighbourhood is just as purely English. It is no unusual thing, indeed, to find old houses in which both English and Dutch characteristics are blended.

The history of Staten Island, from the earliest times, is filled with engaging incidents, and its natural scenery offers no less charming diversities than does that of Long Island, but we fail to discover in Staten Island that potent local consciousness that has made Long Island what it is. There is no place for it in the microcosm of Staten Island. The island's proximity to New York City, and the ready access to Manhattan, have had something, too, to do with this.

This does not mean to say that Staten Island is by any means lacking in individuality. It would be hard, indeed, to find any place where the individuality of the region

251

is more distinctly marked, but it is a complex individuality and, in our retrospect of Staten Island history and
Staten Island domestic architecture, we must be ready to
recognise and sympathetically appreciate this complex
quality which becomes the more fascinating the more
intimately we become acquainted with it.

When John Coleman, one of Hudson's party, was
investigating the island which his master named for the
States General of Holland, he was shot in the neck by
Indians and his comrades buried him at Coleman's Point
on Sandy Hook. Ever since that time to the end of the
Revolutionary War, and afterwards, Staten Island managed to occupy a position in the middle of the stage of
events. The Peach War and the Pig War, and sundry
other hostilities and commotions that William the Testy
provoked by his tactless irascibility, riveted Manhattan's
attention upon Staten Island during an eventful period
of early Colonial history. In 1640, the Director-General
had set up a still on Staten Island and put it under the
charge of William Hendricksen, so that, in all likelihood, it is the first place where spirits were made in
America. Perhaps Kieft's solicitude over this distilling
venture may have sharpened his touchiness about the
Indians.

Directly English rule was established, Governour
Francis Lòvelace shewed deep interest in the affairs of
Staten Island, then considered "the most commodiousest
seat and richest land" in America, and bought it again
and finally from the Indians with formalities that left no
doubt in their minds that they were parting with it, once

FOUNTAIN HOUSE, NEW DORP, WEST END, C. 1668

NICHOLAS BRITTIN HOUSE, NEW DORP

and for all, to the white man without reserving any claim whatsoever. It was doubtless a good thing to have the Indians a little farther away and their title extinguished, but if Lovelace had waited a little while he might have saved his money; the island must inevitably "have dropped into his hand as a ripe plum." In the very same year in which Lovelace completed his memorable purchase, 1670, Daniel Denton naïvely observed, "wherever the English came to settle, the hand of God mostly removed the Indians, either by wars among themselves, or some raging mortal disease."

Early in the period of English control, Long Island, Staten Island and Westchester were all classified as the three Ridings of Yorkshire. Suffolk was called the East Riding; King's County, part of Queen's and Staten Island made up the West Riding; and the remainder of Queen's and Westchester made the North Riding. In 1683, however, the Assembly abolished the *Ridings* and established *Counties* in their stead, directing that the county of Richmond should "conteyne all Staten Island, Shutter's Island, and the islands of meadow on the west side thereof." But long before this—in 1675, to be exact —a Court of Assizes held in New York ordered that "by reason of the separation by water, Staten Island shall have jurisdiction by itself, and have no further dependence on the Courts of Long Island, nor on its militia." Ever since then Staten Island has been an independent judicial district.

Prior to these legal enactments anent the status of the island in the Province of New York, and prior to Governour Lovelace's final re-purchase from the Indians, Captain Christopher Billopp had established New York's claim to the possession of Staten Island over the claims of New Jersey by sailing around it in less than twenty-four hours, and was rewarded therefor by a grant of land that afterwards became the Manor of Bentley. The presence of men like Captain Billopp living on the island, and the ease of crossing thence to New York City, as well as the fair aspect of the country itself, offered sufficient inducement to the Lovelace family to identify themselves closely with its affairs and fortunes and to acquire land there. Besides the lively interest shewn by the Governour, Sir Francis Lovelace, his brother, Thomas Lovelace, was sometime Sheriff of the County and his official signature is appended to many ancient documents connected with the conveyance of property.

It was this same Thomas Lovelace's son who died in 1671 and was buried with all the pomp and ceremony that would have marked the funeral of a person of his quality at home in England at this period. There is an old document that gives a detailed account of the obsequies. It is one of those choice bits of contemporary evidence that help us to realise the vivid contrasts that often occurred in the early Colonial days between the crude conditions of life in a new land and sundry cherished elegancies and refinements which those who could had brought with them. The description of the lying-in-state and the cortege is worth quoting in full:—

"The ffuneral Solemnities at the Interm^t of M^r. W^m. Lovelace at New Yorke in America 1671.

STATEN ISLAND

The manner of Exposing the Corps in the Roome before the Buriall

1. The Roome was very spacious and hung all about wth Mourning and Escootcheons thereupon of his Peternall Coate to the number of 30.

2. Round the sayd Roome were placed Turkey worke chayres richly wrought.

3. In the Middest of the Roome stood the Hearse with Sheete and Pall encompased with 8. of his Paternall Escotcheons.

4. At the head a Pall of deaths heads and bones richly embroidered hung over as a Canopy.

5. Over the middle of the Herse a rich Garland hung adornd with black and white Satten ribbands and an houre Glasse impending.

6. At the ffeete a sheild 4 foote square cotes of Armes quartered and gloriously gilt which together wth the Garland remaines as a monment in the Church to this day.

7. Round the hearse stood A black stand with Silver Candlestick wax Tap's and p'fumes burning night and day to the view of all people.

8. A Rich Cupbord of Plate worth 200^li

9. 4: Attendants night and day.

10. The Partall or entry to the Roome was curiously adorned wth pictures Statues and other fancies in carved worke.

The ffunerall Procession.

1. The Capt: of the dead.
2. The Minister.
3. An Esqr in mourning carrying the Sheild.
4. The 2: Preaching Ministers.
5. Two Maidens clothed in white silke carrying the Garland wth Cyprus Scarves and Gloves tyed with a whole peice with black and white Satten Ribband.

6. The Corps carryed by 6. Gentlemen Batchelers all in Mourning, with Skarves and Gloves.

7. The Pall held up by 6. virgins all in white Silke wth Cyprus Skarves and Gloves.

8. Tho: Lovelace Esq: father to the deceased and his Lady in close Mourning.

9. 4: Halbertes with velvet Coates and Badges thereon embroidered with his Creast of 40^{11} a Coate.

10. Coll: ffrancis Lovelace p'sent Governo^r of New Yorke and uncle to the deceaced in close Mourning single.

11. Capt: Dudley Lovelace uncle also to the deceased in like mourning single.

12. The Councell all in Mourning.

13. The Mace with Maior and Aldermen in their black Gownes.

14. The Principall Burgers of the Citty 2: and 2.

15. All the English and Dutch Women 2: and 2.

16. The cheife English and Dutch Men. 2 and 2.

17. All Masters of Shipps and Vessells.

18. All the other English and Dutch men. 2. and 2. to the number of 500. the greatest p't of them in black.

Wines sweet meats and Bisketts and such Services till 10. at night.

At the entrance of the ffort stood his Royall hignesse's Company of Guards with Colours furl'd Drums beating a ffunerall March and afterwards severall great Gunns fired thence.

At the Interm^t of the Corps 30. peices of Ordnance more fired."

At the time of the Revolutionary War, Staten Island was the first New York territory on which the British troops landed. The Loyalist sentiment there was particularly strong, and until peace was declared in 1783, many of the chief officers made their headquarters there at one time or another. There, in the Manor House of Bentley, Lord Howe had his memorable interview after the Battle of Long Island with Benjamin Franklin, John Adams and Edward Rutledge in the attempt to open the way for a speedy peace.

When peace came, at long last, after years of struggle, it was on Staten Island that Aaron Burr passed part of the closing period of his pathetically sinister life. From Staten Island Cornelius Vanderbilt started the ferry that laid the foundation of his fortune and paved the way to a career of amazing portent. On Staten Island Garibaldi came to dwell for a season of rest and refuge after exhausting struggles and perils borne for the sake of his beloved Italy.

Truly, the story of Staten Island is as varied as the character of the people who have made their home there from the earliest settlement by white men down to the present day. And that story is just as full of fascination as it is of astonishing variety.

THE MELYN PATROONSHIP OF STATEN
ISLAND

JUNE 19, 1642–1661

CORNELIS MELYN was one of those troubled, dramatic characters, plaything of a tempestuous fate, that flit now and again like meteors across the stage of early Colonial history only to disappear from the scene as suddenly as they came, leaving little or no trace of their course behind them.

He was a Belgian by birth and was apparently born to a position of some standing and substance, if we may judge from the scanty records of his youth and early manhood that have come down to us. He was baptised in Antwerp on the 17th. of September, 1600, and presumably first saw the light of day not long prior to that date. On the 13th. of November, 1606, guardians were appointed for him as both his parents had died only a short time before. From 1606 till January, 1613, he was at school. Then we next hear of him in 1618 when, so it is recorded, he gave notice that he was minded to travel and see foreign parts, an intention which, it is reasonable to suppose, he forthwith carried out. Further than this, we know that he was in Antwerp in 1626 for the necessary legal formalities attending the final settlement of his father's estate, that he afterwards moved to Holland and engaged in business there, and that he is referred to in the Van Rensselaer Bouwier Manuscripts.

In 1638 Kiliaen Van Rensselaer, the first Patroon, in

a letter to Director-General Kieft, mentions Melyn as a supercargo, and on various occasions seems to have employed him or to have been associated with him in different enterprises. It is not unlikely that Van Rensselaer's influence and prestige as one of the Lords Directors of the West India Company assisted Melyn to interest "those men of wealth and station who became connected with him in his colonisation schemes."

Melyn was himself a man of both means and position and, as subsequent events shewed, one whose personality had to be reckoned with in any undertaking with which he might be associated. So much for the antecedents, early career and character of the first Patroon of Staten Island.

In 1638 Melyn made a voyage to New Netherlands and formed such a favourable opinion of the country and the prospects it offered that he went back to Holland to fetch out his family. Having obtained permission from the Directors of the West India Company to take possession of a portion of Staten Island as Patroon, with all the customary privileges, and to settle colonists there, he set sail again for the New World in August, 1640, with his people, most of his private means, his cattle, goods, and all necessary equipment for extensive agriculture. He had gone but a little way on his journey when the ship was captured by the Dunkirk pirates and he was obliged to go back to Amsterdam.

Undaunted by this serious misfortune, he determined to pursue his efforts. His grant was renewed in February, 1641, and, aided by the West India Company, he sailed in the ship *Eyckenboom* with forty-one colonists, reaching New Amsterdam in August of that year. As was customary, and indeed obligatory, Melyn bought from the Indians the land assigned to him, thus securing a clear title, and, on the 19th. of January, 1642, Director General Kieft issued letters patent confirming the grant and title to all of Staten Island, save so much of it as was not already occupied by the farms or bouweries of David Pieterse De Vries.

De Vries, in his dealings with the Staten Island Indians, had pursued a policy of kindness, justice, conciliation and tactfulness, and this same policy Melyn also followed, although in Melyn's case—through no fault of his own, however—he did not always meet with such invariably successful results as his neighbour De Vries. Director Kieft, on the other hand, hot-headed, obstinate, and touchy to the extent of being a veritable official porcupine, was prone to construe every act of the Indians as an hostile demonstration and retaliate with violence. Consequently, during the whole of his tempestuous administration, his hands were embrued in Indian blood, the colony was kept in a constant state of nervous tension, turmoil and dread, and the colonists were subjected to many a sudden outrage that was really provoked by the chronically truculent attitude of "William the Testy."

For seventeen years Melyn held the Patroonship of Staten Island, and during nearly all of that time he was harassed by hardships, vexations, and a seemingly endless succession of misfortunes that long before would have worn out and discouraged any man with less tenacity of purpose.

On his arrival in his *colonie* he straightway set about

building houses, ploughing land, and doing everything to establish agriculture on a firm basis. All might have gone well with his undertaking in continued prosperity had not the erstwhile good feeling between Dutch and Indians been rudely ruptured just at this time through Kieft's hasty vindictiveness and habitual lack of tact, whereby the whole of New Netherlands was plunged in bloodshed. Although Melyn and his people were not molested as soon as some of the other settlers—perhaps because of their numbers and their settlement close together—in 1643 the Indians fell upon them with terrible fury, slew many of them, drove off or killed the cattle, and set fire to the houses, barns and crops, so that Melyn, with his wife and children, had to flee for their lives to New Amsterdam and stay there till 1647.

This Indian uprising was so widespread and of such alarming nature that Kieft felt obliged to summon all the people together and ask their advice and help. This general gathering, thereupon, chose from amongst themselves a representative body called "The Eight Men," of whom Melyn was one. Several days later, at Kieft's summons, the "Eight Men" met "to consider the critical condition of the country" and resolved to push the war vigorously against certain of the hostile tribes. They soon elected Melyn their president and, the following year, sent to the Amsterdam "Chamber of XIX," of the West India Company, a communication anent "the deplorable condition" existing.

In this letter, Kieft and his Council were severely taken to task and the Director-General himself came in for a measure of vituperation. However well deserved this censure may have been, it later provoked unbridled ill-feeling and proved a source of trouble to Melyn who was generally credited as the author. Kieft, it seems, was not aware of the contents of this letter until long afterwards, but from the outset he displayed animosity towards Melyn and badgered him with petty annoyances whenever he could find an excuse. In 1645 Melyn was charged with selling wine to the Indians, the next year on some trumped-up technicality he was ousted from a plot of land he had leased from the Company in the city, on the spot where Trinity Church now stands, and in divers other ways it became plain that he was the butt of Kieft's active dislike.

When Kieft publicly handed over the authority to his successor, Peter Stuyvesant, in May, 1647, Melyn and several of his associates in the "Eight" not only ignored the special opportunity obviously made for them to thank the outgoing Governour for his "capable conduct of affairs," but said quite plainly that they would *not* thank him because they had nothing to thank him for, and soon after Stuyvesant had taken the reins of government they lodged a formal complaint of Kieft's reckless administration. Melyn and Kuyter, who were foremost in presenting this complaint, urged that the members of Kieft's Council should be closely examined regarding the whole provincial policy from 1639 onwards, and that the results be submitted for review to the authorities in Holland.

Stuyvesant forthwith became alarmed and indignant. If Kieft's acts were to be called in question at the demand of the people, his own doings might later be subjected to the same judgement. In his opinion the whole thing was a piece of impertinence and unwarranted interference with "the Lord's anointed." If he countenanced the accusations and complaint, it would create a dangerous precedent, damaging to his own authority and that of his successors. He therefore sided with Kieft, while Melyn and Kuyter he regarded not as members of the board of "Eight Men" called into being by Kieft, but merely as private individuals. He convened a special Council meeting, did not await the advice of his Councillors, arbitrarily declared that it was treason to petition against one's magistrates, "whether there was cause or not," and summarily dismissed the memorial of the two "malignant" persons.

Stuyvesant furthermore ordered Melyn and Kuyter, instead of Kieft and his Council, to be questioned concerning the cause of the Indian War. The case was prejudged before it began and, on the 25th. of July, 1647, sentence was given. Stuyvesant, full of wrathful indignation at what he deemed unpardonable presumption, advocated that Melyn be done to death and his property confiscated. The more moderate views of the Council, however, at last prevailed and Melyn was sentenced to seven years' banishment, a fine of 300 guilders, and forfeiture of all benefits to which he might ordinarily be entitled from the Company. Kuyter got off with three years' banishment and a fine of 150 guilders. Despotic and obstinate in his excitement, Stuyvesant denied Melyn and Kuyter the right of appeal to the higher authorities in Holland and told Melyn:—"If I were persuaded that you would divulge our sentence, or bring it before their

High Mightinesses, I would have you hanged, at once, to the highest tree in New Netherland."

After this, naturally, there could be no peace between Melyn and Stuyvesant until the latter was compelled by his superiors to take a more reasonable attitude. Agreeably to their sentence of banishment, Melyn and Kuyter were sent away in the ship *Princess Amalia,* sailing for Holland on the 17th. of August, 1647. In the same ship sailed the former Director-General Kieft, homeward bound with a tidy fortune of 400,000 guilders aboard with him.

Driven out of her course into the Bristol Channel, on the 27th. of September the *Princess Amalia* struck a rock off the Welsh coast and went to pieces. In this peril Kieft's conscience smote him. He came to Melyn and Kuyter and said:—"Friends, I have been unjust to you, Can you forgive me?" Kieft and many others were drowned. Melyn and Kuyter clung to wreckage and were finally driven ashore. Fortunately, by dragging they recovered the chest with their papers, and with these they pursued their way to Amsterdam.

Arrived there, they ignored the West India Company and laid their case directly before the States General. Their cause they pleaded with so much success and such potent influence did they bring to bear that William, Prince of Orange, wrote Stuyvesant a letter telling him that Melyn and Kuyter had been given full permission to go back to New Netherland and he was not to molest them; the States General, by special act, suspended Stuyvesant's sentence and cited him to defend it at the Hague; and their High Mightinesses further added a clause confirming to Melyn and Kuyter full enjoyment of all the rights of colonists in New Netherland. The West India Company, chagrined at the wreck of their ship and at having the case carried over their heads, "greatly regretted that while so many fine men were lost, two rebellious bandits should survive to trouble the Company with their complaints," but they were powerless to oppose.

With the empowering documents, Melyn arrived at Manhattan in the winter of 1648–1649 and demanded "that the acts of their High Mightinesses should be read and explained by the 'Nine Men' to the commonalty who were assembled in church within Fort Amsterdam." Despite some noisy opposition, the mandamus and summons were duly read to the people and Melyn's position was publicly vindicated. After the reading Stuyvesant replied, "I honour the States and shall obey their commands. I shall send an attorney to sustain sentence." No further answer or comment would he vouchsafe. Van Dincklagen candidly admitted that the Council had erred in their former action towards Melyn, but all the rest of the Councillors maintained an obstinate silence.

This dramatic little episode, as may readily be imagined, did not make for future cordial relations between Melyn and Stuyvesant. As a matter of fact, the rest of Melyn's career as Patroon of Staten Island was filled by contentions and bickerings with the Director-General, and the latter never let slip an opportunity to embarrrass and annoy Melyn. Melyn was soon charged with distributing arms and ammunition amongst the Raritans and South River Tribes. Next, the report was circulated that he was egging on the Nyack Indians to attack Stuyvesant and thereupon the Council obligingly passed a resolution that four halberdiers should attend the Director-General as a bodyguard whenever he walked abroad.

Melyn refused to appear to answer to the absurd charges made against him, fortified himself in his colony on Staten Island and established a manorial court there. Here the Director-General, however inwardly raging he might be, dared not arrest nor molest Melyn in defiance of the explicit orders he had received from Holland.

In 1650 Melyn had induced Baron Van de Cappellen, one of the Committee of the States General, along with several Amsterdam merchants, to join his Staten Island venture at colonisation. Accordingly, a number of farmers and farm labourers, and a goodly supply of cattle and agricultural equipment were sent out in the *New Netherland's Fortune*. Delayed by rough weather, the ship was obliged to put in at Rhode Island for water and supplies to continue the journey to New Amsterdam. Stuyvesant made this stop at Rhode Island the excuse for another prosecution against Melyn, seized and confiscated the ship on its arrival upon the pretext that it belonged to the contumacious Patroon of Staten Island, and summoned Melyn to appear, which, of course, he did not do. Unfortunately for Stuyvesant the ship, which he sold, belonged to Van de Cappellen and his associates and when it appeared on a return trip to Holland, Van de Cappellen replevined it and, after a long law suit, the West India Company was compelled to make restitution and give statisfaction for Stuyvesant's indiscretion into which he had let his bumptious pig-headedness and spleen carry him.

The year 1655 saw a fresh outbreak of trouble with the Indians on Staten Island. This disturbance, known as the "Peach War," it seems scarcely necessary to say, was none of Melyn's making for he had consistently from the beginning advocated kindly and moderate measures with the Indians, and had punctiliously practised what he preached. Melyn and his ninety colonists, at that time cultivating eleven flourishing farms, were, however, the victims who suffered for the provocations furnished by others. The houses were burnt, the prosperous bouweries were laid waste, fifteen or sixteen persons were slain, and fifty-one carried into captivity. Melyn himself was obliged to pay a ransom of 1400 guilders in order that he and his wife, his son and his son-in-law might escape being burned alive in a fire that was already burning for them.

Two years later Staten Island and the parts of the country nearby were still feeling seriously the effects of the massacre of 1655, and the difficulties under which they suffered were not lightened by the mulish obstinacy and vindictiveness of Stuyvesant who let slip no opportuntiy to shew his ill-will. It is only fair to the last Dutch Governour to say that his peculiar mental bias and his conception of the duties and prerogatives of his office often led him into unreasonable positions and extreme actions which his instincts as a man and a gentleman could scarcely have countenanced. It was a case of conduct dislocated by warped notions of official obligations and a general lack of tact. But even though misunderstanding rather than malice may have prompted Stuyvesant's chronic attitude, it was equally hard to bear. Wearied with constant opposition and petty annoyances, and seeing no likelihood of improvement in relations, in 1657 Melyn left New Netherland, where he had experienced nought but official injustice and vexation, and moved to Connecticut where he took the oath of allegiance to the British Crown on the 7th. of April in New Haven.

On the 13th. of June, 1659, there was executed a deed by the terms of which Melyn surrendered to the West India Company the Patroonship of Staten Island for a consideration of 1500 guilders. This consideration, be it noted, was for the *right of lordship* as Patroon, which Melyn yielded up, and did not affect his property rights on the island. The West India Company thus acquired the right of lordship or *jus patronatus* for their corporation, and that was what the payment was for. The deed expressly states that the West India Company shall make "restitution of all such Sum or Sums of money, which were produced from certain his houseings & Lotts scituated & being upon ye Manhatans in New Amsterdam neer ye ffort (which were sold by Governour Stuyvesandt by Execution in behalf of Daniel Michiels master of ye Ship ye New Netherland's Fortune) shall be restored to him again in New Netherland by sd. Company & chamber for ye sd. Moneys or so much thereof as may yet be found to remain with ye sd. Company."

The document also stipulates "that he for ye future as a free Coloneer & inhabitant for himself & his Successors shall hold & possess as free & legal estate, ye lands houses & lotts, which he hath there in ye sd. Colony, & hath hitherto made use of & which he yet shall be able to improve (& by others not possessed) they shall enjoy ye Succession thereof & by will, writings, donation or gift, agreemt. or otherwise may dispose thereof, as according to ye Articles of Privileges & Exemptions granted to Patroons & Coloneers."

Although this sale of his rights as Patroon to the West India Company and the accompanying assurance of his actual property rights did not occur till 1659, as previously noted, he had removed to New Haven in 1657 and taken his oath of allegiance to the British Crown. Of his life at New Haven we know nothing, except that he was living there in 1662. Beyond that we have no record of him.

THE VANDERBILT HOUSE
PORT RICHMOND

THE initial appearance of the Vanderbilt family in the Province of New York, so far as public records are concerned, occurred in 1685. In that year the records shew that Aert Jansen van der Bilt—as the name was then spelled—had a substantial holding of land in Flatbush under a patent from Governour Dongan. It is not unlikely that the said Aert may have been preceded in the Province by either his father Jan or by an uncle.

In the same year there is record of an Aris van der Bilt who was also settled in Flatbush. Aris may have been a brother of Aert, but if not a brother was almost certainly a near relative. Besides the land he owned in Flatbush, Aris was likewise possessed of a considerable tract in Staten Island, presumably acquired in trade from the Indians.

Jacob van der Bilt, the son of Aris and his wife Hilitje, was born in January, 1692, and, in due time, took to wife one Neilje whose patronymic is not recorded in the van der Bilt records but who, in all likelihood, was the daughter of Dionys or Denys Nyssen, a carpenter in Flatbush who had married the relict of Nicholas Van Brunt. This widow Van Brunt was Helena Cortelyou, the daughter of Jacques Cortelyou, the immigrant. It is recorded that the children of Denys Nyssen and Helena took the names of Denys or Denyse and that the daughter Neilje married Jacob van der Bilt.

VANDERBILT HOUSE, STAPLETON, PORT RICHMOND

House in which Commodore Vanderbilt was born

GAMBREL-ROOFED HOUSE, OPPOSITE MORAVIAN CEMETERY, DONGAN HILLS

THE VANDERBILT HOUSE

To his son Jacob, Aris van der Bilt of Flatbush deeded his Staten Island holdings near the village of New Dorp, possibly as a wedding gift to establish the young couple on a base of their own. The establishment seems to have prospered, at least so far as progeny were concerned, for Jacob and Neilje had eleven children.

The Moravian settlement on Staten Island was close to the van der Bilt bouwerie and it was not long before the van der Bilts allied themselves with the followers of Count Zinzendorf whose visit, in 1741, gave marked impetus to the colony of religious enthusiasts. In 1762 we find Cornelius van der Bilt, the seventh son of Jacob and Neilje, joining in a petition to the central Moravian authorities at Bethlehem, in Pennsylvania, for permission to build a Moravian church on Staten Island. Permission was granted, the cornerstone of the new church was laid in July, 1763, and the van der Bilts seem to have borne their share in completing the undertaking.

Jacob van der Bilt, the fourth son of Jacob and Neilje, born in 1723, eventually married Mary Sprague, and the youngest child of Jacob the younger and Mary Sprague, born in August, 1764, was Cornelius, who in time became the father of the famous Commodore who was to become such an outstanding figure in the affairs of New York during the nineteenth century.

Cornelius van der Bilt, the son of Jacob and Mary Sprague, began to earn his living—he was then well under twenty—by ferrying the produce from his father's farm and the farms of neighbouring farmers across the bay to New York, then under British occupation. After the evacuation of New York by the British forces,

Cornelius began to run a ferry from Stapleton, on Staten Island, to Whitehall Landing in New York. This periagua ferry Cornelius seems to have run in a somewhat desultory fashion, as he appears to have done nearly everything else through life. He was a restless sort of person, blessed with little of the "stick-ative-ness" and determination that ensured his famous son's success.

Discouraged by the winters, when for days together he could not sail his periagua ferry-boat to New York for the ice in the bay, Cornelius bought a bit of farm land at Port Richmond. There he met, courted and married Phebe Hand. Phebe, born at Rahway, was the niece of Major-General Edward Hand who had been the Adjutant-General of the Continental Army. Cornelius and Phebe were married early in 1787, and the house shewn in the illustration was their home.

Phebe was in many respects a most remarkable woman and the sterling qualities of her character made up for the lack of sundry traits which her spouse might have possessed to his greater advantage. It was to qualities inherited from his mother that most of the Commodore's success in life was due. The story of Cornelius and Phebe van der Bilt, and their son Cornelius, the Commodore, has been so admirably and so fully told by Arthur D. Howden Smith in his "Commodore Vanderbilt" that it would be an impertinence to rehearse the details here.

Cornelius Vanderbilt—so he came eventually to spell the family name—the fourth child and second son of Cornelius and Phebe, was born on the 27th. of May, 1794. Arthur Howden Smith says of him:—"He was a lusty brat, and from infancy was notable for his stature, his wilfulness and his readiness to think for himself and go his own gait." From the outset he gave every evidence of having a good, clear mind, but he was not one of the sort that took kindly to school or book learning. He much preferred to be doing something more active and something that shewed more readily concrete results. In appearance he was "big-bodied, rangy, tow-headed, blue-eyed" and characteristically a Dutchman.

He was inventive, quick, resourceful and persevering and, above all, absolutely dependable, for he could always be relied upon to do exactly what he said he would do, even though for the time it might be to his disadvantage. His determination, his reliability and his aggressiveness came early into full evidence, both while he was working for his father and when he got a periagua for himself, by dint of industry and effort, and started to run a ferry to New York on his own account. He was also forceful in expression and years afterward, when he had become a prominent figure in the financial life of New York, the street brats of the city would run after him and listen to see if they could increase their stock of profane expletives by any novelties in swearing that might drop from his lips. He was a great and unconsciously picturesque figure, and for a full picture of a most fascinating and robust character the reader cannot do better than peruse Howden Smith's biography.

In connexion with the Commodore's later life, it is impossible to resist the temptation to relate an anecdote of his brother, Captain Jacob Hand Vanderbilt, commonly known to old Staten Islanders as "Captain Jake." Captain Jake was born in September, 1807, in the old house. By eighteen he was in command of a steamboat and, in many ways, was given an opportunity to share in his brother's prosperity. In short, he did well for himself and, with his ample means, he was free and generous in his hospitality. Incidentally, he was an ardent lover of fine horses and owned not a few of which anyone might well be proud. It was said by a narrator of local Staten Island history that "pretty much everyone on the road took the Captain's dust. Even Wall Street did it once, and this was how it came about and how the trouble was mended." Brother Cornelius had advised Jake to make a certain investment in stocks. The stocks failed to perform as expected, with the result that Captain Jake sustained a substantial loss. Strained relations followed and "Jake ceased his Sunday custom of dropping in on big brother for tea."

Not long afterwards, one afternoon when Captain Jake was coming back from New York on the ferry-boat to Staten Island, he saw a negro with a road cart and a span of exceptionally fine black horses. The Captain asked the negro where he was going with them. The darkey was rather non-committal and merely replied "Staten Island," whereupon the Captain, who had some of his more illustrious brother's habits of speech, told him to "Go to hell!"

To Captain Jake's great amazement, when he reached his house he found the darkey and the horses standing in front of his door. The darkey then handed the Captain an "olive branch" in the shape of a note from brother Cornelius saying that the horses were for him and winding up with the laconic advice "Don't be a damned fool; come around to the house and have tea."

Captain Jake rubbed his hands over the splendid coats of the horses, decided they were distinctly worth having, and merely observed "Well, they cost me $40,000." However, the breach was healed and Brother Jake and Brother Cornelius again had tea together in amity.

THE DONGAN MANOR OR MANOR OF CASSILTOWN

CASTLETON

ERECTED 1687: HOUSE BUILT, 1688

WHEN Governour Thomas Dongan arrived in the Province of New York, the people found him a genial, hospitable gentleman, generous and sociable and always anxious to be surrounded by numbers of his friends, not because he wished flattering attention but because he delighted in congenial society. He was given to travelling about and, it is said, rarely went anywhere without taking a party of his friends along with him.

From this travelling about in the Province and associating constantly with the agreeable people he found there, he conceived the idea of remaining more or less permanently, even though, in time, he might be supplanted by another governour sent out in his stead. With this in mind, the next step obviously was to acquire an estate suitable to his station.

On his tours of inspection he had found Staten Island a most agreeable spot and he decided in its favour for his own habitation. As head of the government and the source whence grants of land were made, he could not grant nor convey land to himself with any degree of legal propriety. The only way in which his end could be accomplished was to grant land to another person and then buy from him the land thus granted.

John Palmer was the man chosen to be the instrument

276

in thus realising the Governour's desires. He was not only a personal friend of Dongan's but he was, apart from that, a person of consequence and Ranger for Staten Island. He had likewise been appointed by Dongan one of the two first judges of the New York Court of Oyer and Terminer. Furthermore, he was a member of the Provincial Council.

Prior to the date when the manorial patent was granted, Palmer had gradually acquired by purchase a number of adjacent holdings in the neighbourhood of what is now West New Brighton. When these several percels of land, obtained by successive acquisition, together aggregated the desired area, the Governour issued a patent or manorial grant to John Palmer for the whole estate. This manorial grant bore date the 31st of March, 1687. It conferred all the customary rights and powers given the lords of manors and stipulated the usual obligations and responsibilities. This instrument, to which was attached the great seal of the Province, was afterwards commonly known as the Palmer or Dongan Patent. It was executed to John Palmer and Sarah, his wife.

On the 16th. of April next following, the said John Palmer and Sarah, his wife, conveyed all the land described in the patent to Thomas Dongan "for a competent summe of lawfull money" after an ownership of about a fortnight. In this way the Governour secured a valid title to the estate.

In the following year, 1688, Governour Dongan built his Manor House thereon and spent much of his time on Staten Island developing his land and managing his mill, which stood on part of the property not far from the house. This house was afterwards so thoroughly mutilated and modernised during the gingerbread and jigsaw period of domestic architecture that it is scarcely recognisable as a seventeenth century structure, part of the "modernisation" taking the form of an absurd portico with columns out of all scale with the rest of the building. Unfortunately there are no old sketches of the Manor House shewing it in its original condition so that it is necessary to use a good deal of imagination in visualising its pristine appearance.

Despite their former friendliness, Dongan experienced a great deal of annoyance and hostility from the people during the Leisler Rebellion because he was a Roman Catholic and the greater part of the population were seized with an absurd panic of dread that all Roman Catholics were plotting against their lives. This ridiculous hysteria soon passed by and order was restored, but not long after this Dongan was superseded in the governourship of the Province and eventually returned to England and then went to Ireland where he succeeded to the earldom of Limerick. His nephews were left in possession of Dongan Manor but, in the course of several generations, the descendants proved themselves quite worthless and the estate was dissipated, the lordship of the manor lapsing, or rather evaporating, through sheer inanition.

Edward Vaughan Dongan, the youngest son of Walter Dongan, was born in the Manor House. He held a commission as Lieutenant-Colonel in the Third Battalion of Skinner's Brigade, and was killed in the Morning Star

DONGAN'S HOUSE, ERECTED IN 1661.
Destroyed by fire Christmas, 1878

RUINS OF LATOURETTE HOUSE, DONGAN HILLS
From an old sketch
Once Colonel Simcoe's headquarters

Road, in Northfield, in August, 1777, at the age of twenty-nine. He was buried in Trinity churchyard, in New York City.

During the Revolutionary War John Bodine occupied the Manor House. In 1802 it was sold to Alexander Macomb.

THE AUSTEN HOUSE
CLIFTON
C. 1669

LOOKING out across the Narrows, and not more than 300 feet from the water's edge, stands the Austen House, at Clifton. It has the distinction of being one of the few old Staten Island houses that has escaped neglect, destruction or imbecile "improvement" absolutely destructive of identity. Exterior changes were made in the nineteenth century, but the general outward character was preserved; within, the seventeenth century structure is everywhere plainly visible.

The house was built about 1680, or earlier; it is said, indeed, to have been occupied in 1669. In 1670 David Lake came from England to Gravesend on Long Island. In 1679 he obtained a considerable grant of land on Staten Island whither he then removed, and from that time till the early years of the nineteenth century the Lake family occupied this house. During the Revolution Lord Howe made it his headquarters for some time and, it is said, after hostilities had ceased, he here discussed terms of peace with Benjamin Franklin.

Sir Henry Clinton, Baron Knyphausen and other officers are numbered amongst the guests and once, when Baron Riedesel was dining there, the house was surrounded by a party of the "Cowboys" who probably made off with some plunder in their usual manner. General Washington, Lafayette, "Mad" Anthony Wayne and General George Clinton were also, at one time or another, guests beneath the roof.

THE AUSTEN HOUSE, ON THE NARROWS, CLIFTON

THE AUSTEN HOUSE

About 1835, John H. Austen bought the house and it is still in the possession of a descendant. Mr. Austen was the grandson of Peter Townsend who made the famous West Point chain; a link of it is still preserved here. Once, when sailing with Commodore Vanderbilt, Mr. Austen asked him, "Have you ever noticed the delightful old house where I live at Clifton, Commodore?"

"Yes, yes, indeed, I have! Why, I used to visit there and spark the prettiest girl on Staten Island—in fact, the prettiest girl I ever saw! When I was a youngster I made the acquaintance of Sally Lake, who was undoubtedly the most beautiful girl anywhere about. Her parents lived in and owned the house you now live in, they being well off while I was poor. Sally's mother and elder sister objected to our going together, and when I asked the reason, they said, 'Corneel Vanderbilt, we want Sally to marry a man who can take care of her, and we don't propose to let her throw herself away on such a poor shack as you are'! That ended it; I gave Sally up and quit going there."

On a window pane are scratched the words

"Sall Lake
C. 1812"

C Stands for Cornelius, and "Corneel," holding and guiding Sally's hand, cut these words with a diamond ring on her finger.

THE PERINE HOUSE
DONGAN HILLS

THE old Perine House in Staten Island is an excellent example of the small domestic architecture for which the Dutch and Huguenot settlers in that part of New York were responsible. The original house seems to have been built by Captain Thomas Stillwell late in the seventeenth century. It is said that the original house burned early in the eighteenth century and was replaced by the present structure. About 1713 the "replacement" was, in all likelihood, a rebuilding and enlargement of what was left after the fire. The house, as it stands to-day, is a low, rambling structure, partly of wood and partly of stone, and obviously represents the construction of different dates. In any event, this dwelling and its predecessor—part of which is apparently incorporated in the existing building—have been continuously lived in since the seventeenth century.

Lieutenant Nicholas Stillwell came from Surrey to Manhattan by way of Virginia, arriving in 1645 or 1646. In 1644, he had sided with Clayborne in the rebellion in Virginia and hence was so distinctly a *persona non grata* in the Old Dominion that he found it expedient to remove to Dutch jurisdiction. Soon after his arrival at Manhattan, he established himself at Gravesend and later removed to Staten Island, where he died in 1671. He was one of the three officers commanding the troops in the Esopus War of 1663. Under Stuyvesant he was

THE PERINE HOUSE, DONGAN HILLS

Sheriff of Long Island, Magistrate of Gravesend from 1649–1663, and, in 1654, presided over the Court Martial for the trial of freebooters and pirates.

Removing from Gravesend to Staten Island about 1664, in 1667 he was made Constable of Staten Island, an office which carried with it the right to appoint two overseers who, with the Constable, constituted a court of petty jurisdiction. Nicholas Stillwell had four sons, Richard, Nicholas, Jeremiah and Thomas. Nicholas the younger seems to have remained in Gravesend and Jeremiah went to New Jersey; Richard and Thomas appeared in Staten Island. Our present concern is with Captain Thomas, the youngest.

In 1670 Thomas married Martha Billeau or Boileau, who seems to have been a daughter of Pierre Billeau or Boileau, one of the Walloon settlers at Old Town in 1661, who held a Dutch ground brief for land opposite the Valley of Iron Hill. The land adjacent on the East was granted to Captain Thomas Stillwell who afterwards, apparently, acquired the land originally held by Billeau. The 1685 survey mentions a confirmation by Governour Andros to Captain Thomas Stillwell in 1677.

At Thomas Stillwell's death, in 1704 or 1705, the property went to his three daughters, Ann, Rachel and Frances; the last named had married Nicholas Brittin. This Nicholas evidently acquired the interests of his two sisters-in-law for, at his death, in 1739 or 1740, he devised all this land to his daughters Martha and Rachel. Rachel later married one of the Dongans, a great nephew of Sir Thomas Dongan, the former Governour. All the heirs jointly conveyed the property to Walter Dongan, and Thomas Dongan, husband of Rachel Brittin and eldest son and heir of said Walter, in 1749 conveyed the house and land to Joseph Holmes, innkeeper.

From this we are justified in surmising that the house from this time (1749) was an hostelry, especially as a tradition in the Perine family coincides with this report. How long it remained a tavern, or under what name, we do not know. From Joseph Holmes, who bought it, and Sarah his wife, it descended to their daughter Ann, who married Edward Perine in 1758. Edward Perine was the son of Peter Perine whose father, Daniel, was the fourth son of Daniel Perrin, the *emigré;* the progenitor of the family in America, coming from the Isle of Jersey, in 1655, with Philip Carteret.

Edward Perine was a weaver and left an interesting pattern book, on the flyleaf of which is the legend,

> "Edward Perine his book,
> God gives him grace therein to look,
> And when the Bell for him doth Toll,
> The Lord of Heaven receive his sole.
> May 22, 1743."

In addition to patterns and directions for weaving, the book contains genealogical data. There are likewise recipes for homemade remedies for sundry diseases of man and beast. For example, one is "a cure for polevil. Tak wite oake bark and bile it rite strong and wash it with that." Incidentally there occur instructions for the "doctrine" of horses.

Connected with the Perine House are two stories that

have been handed down from generation to generation and become local traditions. One of them is this. An Irishman by the name of Arthur Nicholson, cornet in the seventeeth Light Dragoons, came to America with his troop at the outbreak of the Revolutionary War in 1775. Quartered on Staten Island, he fell in love with a Staten Island girl who, however, was blessed with many other beaux. These were gradually narrowed down to two, both of them military men, and as neither would surrender his claims to the favour of the lady it was decided to fight a duel in the forest. Nicholson came out best in the duel, his antagonist being so badly wounded that he never recovered. The girl on whose account this duel was fought died from shock when she had news of it. In all likelihood, the wounded officer was brought back to the Perine House to die, and this doubtless increased the unhappiness and shock to the young lady.

Another story is as follows. During the Revolutionary War, the British troops, of which there were so many on Staten Island, were quartered in the various houses of the neighbourhood. The Perine House at one time was so crowded with soldiers billeted upon the family, that the widow Perine and the children had only one room for their own use. As it was then the fashion for women to wear more or less conspicuous buckles on their shoes, those who wished to be in the fashion were extremely particular about this item of foot decoration. The metal of which the buckles were made was usually considered indicative of the social rank of the wearer. Plain folk used common metal; those of higher station wore silver.

It seems that Ann Perine possessed a pair of silver shoe-buckles which were the pride of her heart, so much so, that she wore them almost constantly, the skirts of the period being short enough to display this foot embellishment to great advantage. One morning it so happened a soldier came in for a drink of water and it at once became evident to Ann that his eyes were fixed on her shoe buckles. Something prompted her, when he left, to take off the valuable buckles and put on a common pair, and subsequent events proved that she was right.

Not long after dark the soldier came back and brazenly demanded her shoe buckles that he had seen on his first visit. She denied owning such treasures and thrust forward one foot to shew its decoration was of no value. The soldier replied that these were not the ones she wore in the morning but she stuck to her story that she had no others, and when he found that he gained nothing by argument he went to the candle and began to prime his gun, expecting to terrify her by this action. Just at this point, a neighbour passed by, heard the noise of contention and came in to find out what it was all about. Learning the cause of the trouble, he so upbraided the soldier for his lack of gallantry that the latter slunk out into the dark.

The history of the Perine House in the main has been uneventful. People who have been well known and borne a superior part in the life of the community have lived in the house, but the happenings connected with the structure itself have, as a rule, not been of an unusual nature. The extent of history connected with the house itself for the most part consists merely of such stories as have just been recounted.

The house is now the property of the Staten Island Historical Society which has its quarters there, and the fabric is carefully preserved both without and within.

THE KRUZER-PELTON HOUSE
THE COVE, WEST NEW BRIGHTON
1722

AT THE "Cove" at West New Brighton stands what is generally known as the Kruzer-Pelton house. It is reputed to have been built in 1722 by Joseph Rolph but, as it was later occupied by the Kruzers, a family of considerable means for the time, their name was attached to it. In 1839, Daniel Pelton, Senior, of New York bought the place, and since then it has perpetuated the names of both the Kruzer and Pelton occupants. It is also claimed that a member of the de Groot family was really the builder and that the place was actually the property of the de Groots till 1814.

Within comparatively recent years there have been additions and alterations, but the oldest part of the house still retains much of its ancient character. This part of the structure is long and low, and exhibits the typical peculiarities of the early Staten Island manner of building—see vignette on title page of this volume. There is only one storey, with an attic or half-storey above it. The dormers, which pierce the long, sloping roof were, in all likelihood, added at a later date when the growth of the family made it necessary to use the attic space for further bedrooms. The first part of the house erected has stone walls; the next part, added about 1776, has stone walls sheathed outside with weather-boarding; and a brick enlargement took place in 1832.

288

KRUZER-PELTON HOUSE, WEST NEW BRIGHTON

THE KRUZER-PELTON HOUSE

At the time of the Revolutionary War, the widow Kruzer, Kruser or Cruser—the name has been spelled in various ways at different times—lived in this house, and it is from that period that the building figures with some prominence in local history. During not a little of that time, General Cortlandt Skinner made the house his headquarters. As the Skinner and Kruzer families were on the best of terms, the latter were not bothered by the disorders of that troublous era, whatever their political convictions and leanings may have been.

Cortlandt Skinner was the last Attorney-General of New Jersey under the Crown and, both because of birth and the important civil post he held, was one of the most prominent personages of the neighbourhood. His mother and the mother of General Oliver De Lancey were both daughters of Stephen Van Cortlandt.

Unswerving in his allegiance to the Crown when the war broke, and being a man of strong convictions which he translated into action, he organised a brigade known as "Skinner's American Loyalists" and was most active in his support of the British cause. Living, as he did, at Perth Amboy, it was natural that he should transfer his activities to Staten Island where there was, from the first, a strong sentiment of loyalty to the Crown. Perth Amboy, too, was within too easy reach of the American forces, and too incapable of defence for it to be a desirable British outpost.

Many of the best and most substantial families in the Province of New York, however much they may have disapproved the measures of the British Ministry, remained loyal to their oath of allegiance, and felt it their

duty to support the Crown in the struggle that had been
precipitated partly by ministerial stupidity, partly by
obstinacy, hot-headedness and selfishness in certain
quarters on both sides. Writing nearly an hundred years
afterwards, Edward Floyd De Lancey very justly ob-
serves:—

"It is a common belief that the loyal inhabitants of
America, at the era of its first great Revolution, the truly
loyal, those who acted from principle, were the unhesitating
supporters of the British Government in its unjustifiable and
tyrannic invasions of the rights and liberties of its American
people. . . . The ideas of 'loyalty' and 'loyal men,' and
'rebellion' and 'rebels,' which had been current in the United
States since the Revolutionary War, were rudely shocked and
quite changed by the outbreak and subsequent crushing of the
civil war at the South. Americans then learned by experience
for the first time, and in a way never to be forgotten, that
'loyalty' was a virtue, that the supporters of 'the powers that
be' were worthy of honour, and that 'rebels' and 'rebellion'
were to be put down at any cost by the strong hand. A pre-
cisely similar view did very large masses of the people of the
British Colonies take when the war of the American Revolution broke out."

The Loyalists recognised the existence of wrongs quite
as keenly as did anyone else, but through the constitutional means indefeasibly theirs as British subjects, rather
than by armed resistance, they firmly hoped for the
redress of their grievances.

Impelled by loyalty of the sort just explained, it is not
to be wondered at that many able-bodied men should
volunteer their services under the Crown and, in many

cases, regiments of loyal Americans were enlisted, like those in Skinner's regiment, and saw active service throughout the entire contest.

For a long time there was a story current that Lord Stirling shot General Skinner at the Cove and that the latter died in the hall of the Kruzer-Pelton house. There is absolutely no foundation for this legend. General Skinner outlived the Revolutionary War for many years. Furthermore, there is no record that he was ever personally under fire during the whole war.

While Prince William Henry, afterwards King William IV, was in America—he was the youngest admiral in the British Navy—he was on one occasion the guest of General Skinner at the Kruzer-Pelton house. Here, also, came Major John André to enjoy Cortlandt Skinner's hospitality. The old house at the Cove, therefore, has very distinct associations with personages conspicuous in history during the Revolutionary period.

At the end of the war, Cortlandt Skinner went to live in England, where, in recognition of his services in America, he was put on half pay as a Brigadier-General. He died in 1799 at the age of seventy-two. His wife survived him, dying in Ireland, at Belvoir Park, near Belfast, in 1810. Cortlandt Skinner's son, Philip Kearney Skinner, was likewise an active Loyalist and bore a commission in the fourth battalion of his father's brigade. After the war, he remained in the British military service, serving in the Twenty-third Regiment of Foot. By successive promotions he reached the rank of Lieutenant-General in 1825. He died in London, April 9th., 1826.

When peace came at last, the Kruzer family remained in undisturbed possession of the old house at the Cove. Kruzer or Cruser, the "lightning calculator," who toured the country with P. T. Barnum's shew as an arithmetical phenomenon, was born there.

CHRISTOPHER HOUSE
WILLOW BROOK

THE Christopher House at Willow Brook was built partly of stone, partly of wood, in the typical old Dutch Colonial manner by Nicholas Christopher somewhere about the middle of the 18th Century, or, perhaps, a little earlier. At the time of the Revolutionary War, his son, Joseph, lived there.

Like other old Dutch houses of its type, it is long and low with one full storey and an attic. The roof is pierced by dormers, which, however, do not appear to be generally coeval with the building of the house. Most of the old Dutch houses of this type had no windows in the attic save those in the gable ends, the upper floor being used chiefly for the storage of household goods and farm products. It was only when the family expanded to such an extent that there were no longer sufficient accommodations below stairs that the upper storey was used for sleeping rooms. It was at such times that the dormer windows were cut into the roof.

At the time of the Revolutionary War, the house stood in a secluded spot, screened by weeping willows, and there was much heavy woodland in the near neighbourhood, so that it was in every way a suitable place of secret meeting for the local Committee of Safety. Furthermore, Joseph Christopher was an ardent Whig and a member of the Committee of Safety.

At the outbreak of the Revolution, there being no one to exercise the controlling power in the Province in lieu of the Royal Governours, who in most cases had remained loyal to the Crown, the Committee of Safety assumed the duties of controlling and regulating the affairs of the Province until State institutions were formed.

The first Provincial Congress of Massachusetts, in February, 1775, took measures towards appointing Committees of Safety in the various colonies, and defined the duties they were to fulfill. Amongst these duties was resistance to executing acts of Parliament, to muster the militia, and to collect war supplies and funds. The example of Massachusetts in this respect was quickly followed by the other Colonies, and Committees of Safety were appointed in all of them to assume the burden of local administration.

In view of the large number of Loyalists in both Staten Island and Long Island, and the lukewarmness of others who had not declared actively for either side, the Committee of Safety had to meet as secretly as possible, and for this purpose no house could have been more suitable, because of its secluded location, than the house in which Joseph Christopher lived. It is said that many persons, who were especially sought for one reason or another by the British troops, fled thither and found refuge. Many others also, it is said, were caught on the way and summarily dealt with.

CHRISTOPHER HOUSE, WILLOW BROOK

THE MANOR OF BENTLEY
NEAR TOTTENVILLE
ERECTED MAY 6, 1687: HOUSE BUILT CIRCA 1668

IN TOTTENVILLE, at the southern extremity of Staten Island, on a slope overlooking Raritan Bay, stands Bentley Manor House. It was once a goodly dwelling of stone, commodious and handsome judged by the local standards of its time, and a suitable dwelling for people of quality. In actual size it is little more than the ordinary stone farm house of the sort so frequently met with in Pennsylvania, New Jersey or Delaware. But for the date of its erection, about 1668, it was an unusually large and imposing abode.

Unfortunately, for many years past it has suffered neglect and is now in a semi-ruinous condition, occupied by tenants who have no interest either in its history or in its preservation. It is to be hoped, however, that its day of salvation is not far distant and that it may be rescued and preserved as a historic monument as it is fitting it should be.

The walls are still sound and the only thing needed to make it once again a building of note is careful and conscientious restoration.*

The first Lord of Bentley Manor, and the builder of the house, was Captain Christopher Billopp, sprung of a family that came from Coventry. Barnard Billopp, of Coventry, born in the latter half of the sixteenth century, at an early age enlisted in a cavalry regiment and was repeatedly promoted in recognition of his merit and bravery. Of his two sons, Christopher and James, the latter is said once to have saved the life of Queen Elizabeth who thereupon rewarded him with a commission in the Royal Navy but subsequently commuted the honour to a court appointment that was more to the liking of the recipient.

James Billopp's eldest child, a daughter, mastered by love of adventure and anticipating the feminist self-sufficiency of the present age, disguised herself and served as an officer in the army. When her disguise was at length detected, after several years of active service, tradition has it that James I was so pleased with her spirit that he ordered her military pay continued, notwithstanding she had been mustered out of the service.

Christopher Billopp, the brother of this independent and energetic lady, was a London merchant and, having married one of the court ladies, became a government contractor under Charles I, both he and his wife being high in the King's favour. It was the son of this Christopher the merchant, likewise named Christopher, who afterwards became Lord of the Manor of Bentley on Staten Island.

This last named Christopher, born in London about 1638, was destined for a naval career especially at the King's wish and under his patronage. In due time he was commissioned as Captain, making sundry voyages to distant parts and having not a few opportunities to emulate the daring of his venturesome military aunt. On one occasion, captured by Turkish pirates, he was beaten,

BENTLEY MANOR HOUSE, WEST FRONT, TOTTENVILLE

BENTLEY MANOR HOUSE, TOTTENVILLE, AS IT APPEARED IN 1844

wounded by them, and left for dead, but was fortunately picked up by an English ship and borne home.

It was in the spring of 1667 that the much-travelled Captain Christopher set sail for the western world in the little ship "Bentley" of two guns. He arrived in New York Harbour just on the eve of the settlement of Staten Island's territorial status. The island was claimed by both New York and New Jersey and finally, in order to end the dispute, the Duke of York decided that all islands lying in the harbour that could be circumnavigated in twenty-four hours should belong to New York, while others should go to New Jersey. It fell to the lot of Captain Billopp to effect the decision. He sailed around the bone of contention, completing the entire circuit of the island in a little over twenty-three hours. Hence Staten Island was adjudged to belong to New York. In grateful recognition of the service he had thus rendered, the Duke of York granted Billopp a tract of 1163 acres on the southern end of the erstwhile disputed territory. And this was the beginning of Bentley Manor.

Although the grant to Billopp was not erected a manor until the 6th of May, 1687, the letters patent bearing that date, the house was built about 1668 and is, therefore, one of the most ancient if not, indeed, the oldest dwelling now standing on Staten Island. It is also, incidentally, a visible memorial and witness of an important historic fact.

When he had built his house, naturally the next step for Captain Billopp was to get married. Soon after setting up his establishment, we find him taking to wife a sister of Thomas Farmar, the same Thomas Farmar who, in 1714, became a Judge of the Supreme Court of New Jersey.

When the Duke of York organised a company of infantry, in 1674, Billopp was commissioned a second lieutenant. In 1677, Sir Edmund Andros appointed him "commander and sub-collector of New York, on Delaware Bay and river."

While Billopp held the public offices just mentioned, some trouble arose and he was accused of having "misconducted himself" by making "extravagant speeches in public." Just what was the nature of these speeches we do not know, but in all likelihood they were of a political character. Governour Andros was exceedingly angered by them, recalled Billopp and revoked his military commission. The Duke approved the Governour's action and another was appointed to fill the lieutenancy.

Billopp then withdrew to his plantation on Staten Island, and nothing more is heard of him for several years. Then his name appears again as one of the signatories to a complaint against Governour Andros. As a result, the Duke sent an agent to investigate the charges and Andros was summoned back to England. Governour Brockholls succeeded Andros, and Sir Thomas Dongan succeeded Brockholls. Under Governour Dongan, Billopp's affairs seem to have run in a smoother channel. It was under Governour Dongan that the estate was created the Manor of Bentley.

Just what was the ultimate fate of Christopher Billopp, first Lord of Bentley Manor, or when he died, we do not know. Tradition has it that he set sail for England in his little ship, the Bentley, and was never heard of afterwards. He left a wife and, at least, one daughter. He had no male issue. The only ray of light is supplied by tombstones. The daughter, Eugenia Billopp, married her relative Thomas Farmar, the younger and, as a condition to his inheriting the estate, the widow of Captain Billopp required him to assume the name of Billopp. The inscription on one tombstone reads:—

"Here lies the body of Evjena the wife of Thomas Billop, aged 23 years. Dec'd March the 22nd, 1735."

The other stone informs us:—

"Here Lyes ye Body of Thomas Billopp, Esqr., Son of Thomas Farmar, Esqr. Deceased August ye 20, 1750, In ye 39th. Year of his Age."

If the date of Eugenia Billopp's tombstone be correct, she was born about 1712. If Christopher Billopp was lost at sea, as tradition says, his disappearance could not have been long prior to that date.

The son of Thomas (Farmar) Billopp and his wife Eugenia was Christopher Billopp, named for his grandfather. The date often given for his birth is 1737, but if the date on his mother's tombstone be correct, he must have been born in 1735 or earlier. This Christopher Billopp, later a Colonel in the King's Army, is described as

"a very tall, soldierly looking man, when in his prime. He was exceedingly proud, and his pride, at times, led him to the verge of haughtiness. Yet he was very kind-hearted, not only to those whom he considered his equals, but to his slaves, as well as to the poor people of the island. No one ever went from his door at the old Manor hungry. It was his custom to gather the people of the Island once a year on the lawn in front of his house and hold a 'harvest home.' He delighted to talk to them and offer advice for their welfare."

He is further pictured to us as fond of dress, scrupulously neat in his attire, given to courtly display, and passionately fond of horses, with a stable filled with the finest-bred animals in the land. He was most generous, delighted to entertain lavishly, and lived at the Manor House with great circumstance, maintaining his coach with liveried coachman and footmen.

His wife was a daughter of Judge Benjamin Seaman, and both Judge Seaman and Colonel Billopp were members of the New York Assembly. On the 23rd. of February, 1775, they both voted against sending delegates to the Continental Congress. Being a staunch Loyalist, upon the outbreak of hostilities Colonel Billopp organised and commanded the Staten Island Native Loyalists.

He was particularly obnoxious to the Whigs of New Jersey and twice they took him prisoner. After this first capture, Mrs. Billopp seems to have abandoned the Manor House for it was used for a time as a cavalry barracks. Devoting it to such a purpose naturally did not improve its condition, so that when Lord Howe decided to use it as a place of meeting with the committee from the Congress at Philadelphia, a good deal of house cleaning had to be done.

Lord Howe arrived on Staten Island the 12th. of July, 1776. He had spoken in favour of America in Parliament and had done all in his power on behalf of the Colonists. Now his one aim, so far as his instructions would permit him, was to conciliate the American leaders, pave the way for amicable negotiations and devise some means by which peace might be restored. After several fruitless attempts to open a channel of communication, he finally hit upon a plan. General Sullivan was a prisoner in the British lines. Him Lord Howe sent on parole as a messenger to Congress. When General Sullivan reached Philadelphia, John Adams called him a "decoy duck" and intimated that it would have been better had he been shot than sent on such an errand. Nevertheless, after hot debate it was decided to send Benjamin Franklin, John Adams and Edward Rutledge as a committee to treat with Lord Howe.

Meantime Lord Howe had done all he could to prepare a suitable reception. He had caused Bentley Manor House to be cleaned and set in order. The drawing room, which is to the right of the door as you enter the house, was made ready for the interview. It was "spread with green moss and decorated with boughs. A cold luncheon of ham, mutton, tongue, bread and claret" was set forth for the guests. Lord Howe was "a very grand person, indeed, being the King's first cousin, and a grandson of George I." His butler, likewise, was "a very grand and imposing personage," and we may be sure that nothing was omitted that might contribute to a fitting welcome.

When the three commissioners from Congress reached Perth Amboy on the 11th. of September, 1776, they found Lord Howe's own barge-awaiting them at the boat landing to row them across the Kill van Kull. When they reached the Staten Island side, Lord Howe himself was waiting at the water's edge to meet them and escort them to the Manor House. John Adams wrote:—"We walked up to the house between lines of grenadiers, looking fierce as the furies and making all the grimaces and motions of their muskets which (I suppose) military etiquette requires, but which we neither understood nor regarded."

The failure of this interview to produce any result is well known. Lord Howe had done all within his power to open the way to peace and he was genuinely chagrined at the barren outcome.

Colonel Billopp's other capture by the Perth Amboy Whigs was after this manner. The British authorities had prohibited communication between Staten Island and New Jersey, and Billopp was very rigid in enforcing this prohibition. One day, some watchers stationed in the steeple of St. Peter's Church in Perth Amboy saw Colonel Billopp going into his house. They ran to their boats, pushed rapidly across the Kill van Kull and made off with their captive before anyone knew what they were about.

"The British, then in possession of New York, had confined in irons several Americans who had been made prisoners, and to retaliate for this measure, Colonel Billopp was taken to the Burlington Gaol." Elias Boudinot's order committing him to custody reads:

"To the Keeper of the Common Gaol of the County of Burlington, greeting:—You are hereby commanded to receive into your custody the body of Col. Christopher Billopp, prisoner-of-war, herewith delivered to you, and having put irons on his hands and feet, you are to chain him down to the floor in a close room, in said gaol, and there to retain him, giving him bread and water only, for his food, until you receive further orders from me, or by the commissary of prisoners for the State of New Jersey, for the time being. Given under my hand, at Elizabethtown, this sixth day of Nov., 1779."

Colonel Billopp was exchanged, not long after this, and continued in active service till the end of the war.

Owing to Colonel Billopp's staunch loyalty to the Crown and his many activities in behalf of the British cause, he was included by name in the New York Act of Attainder. When this act became operative upon the conclusion of peace, Christopher Billopp and his family, along with many other expatriated Loyalists, went to live in Nova Scotia. On the 16th. of July, 1784, the commissioners sold to Thomas McFarren of New York "the Manor of Bentley, containing 850 acres for $4695.00, forfeited by the attainder of Christopher Billopp."

Note: Since the above was written, measures have been taken to restore and preserve the Manor House as an historic shrine.

INDEX

305

INDEX

INDEX

INDEX

Dongan—(*Continued*)

Manor (v. also *Cassiltown*), 276-279

Patent, 277

Rachel, 283

Governour Sir Thomas, 35, 86-88, 96, 120, 127, 227, 270, 276-279, 283, 298

Thomas, 284

Walter, 278, 284

Drinking, regulations, 14, 15

habits, 15

Drisius, Domine, 243

Drunkenness, 14

Drury Lane Theatre, 122

Dudley, Governour Thomas, 29

Duke, of Clarence, 123, 124, 174, 183, 196

of York, 297, 298

Dukes County, 76

Dunch, Edward, 236

family, 236

Walter, 236

Sir William, 236

Dunkirk Pirates, 259

Dutch, East India Co., 41

Reformed Church, 230

settlers, 251

West India Co., 165, 199, 204, 259, 261, 265, 266, 268

Dyer, Mary, 61

E

East Greenwich, 90, 130

Easthampton, 8, 10, 11, 17, 27, 45, 47, 48, 53, 54, 92, 218

East River, 180

Eaton, Governour Theophilus, 127

Manor, 19, 127

Eaton's Neck, 127

Ecclesiastical, organisation, 8

polity, 8, 10

"Eight Men," 261, 263

Elbertse, Elbert, 195

Elizabeth, Queen, 236, 296

Elizabethtown, 303

Endicott, Deputy-Governour John, 29, 241

Entail, 140

Erie Canal, 178, 179

Erskine, Sir William, 45, 117

Esopus War, 282

"Established Church," 12

Eyckenboom, The, 259

F

Fairfield, 127, 141

Fairs, Southampton, 21

Southold, 21

Fanaticism, 94, 97

Fanning, Lady Lydia, 104

Lord, 104

Farmer, Thomas, 297, 299

Farrett, James, 30, 35, 58, 59, 77, 78, 81

Farrington, Edward, 164

Feake, Hannah, 164, 170

Fenny, Compton, 74

Fenwick, Colonel George, 28

Field, Benjamin, 171

names, 113, 114

Susanna, 171

Fire Island, 105

Fish, Rev. John, 141

Fisher's Island, Manor of, 68-73

Fishing, customs, 5

Fiske, John, 221

"Five Towns," Dutch, 24

Flatbush, 24, 184, 185, 192, 198, 216, 248, 270, 271

Flatlands, 24, 190, 194

Fletcher, Governour Benjamin, 41, 89, 92, 98, 129

Floyd, Arrabella,

Betsey, 104, 105

David Richard, 140, 146

Elizabeth, 145

family, 107-114

house of, 107-114

Nicoll, 109

308

INDEX

INDEX

INDEX

INDEX

INDEX

313

INDEX

Platt, Isaac, 22
  Mary, 104
  Judge, 104
Plowman, 95
Plum Island, Manor of, 74, 75
Plymouth, 75
  Colony, 173
  Company, 58
Political sentiment, 25
Poplars, Lombardy, 175
Port Richmond, 270, 272
Port Royal, 135
Portsmouth, N. H., 162
Presbyterians, 25
  Church, Jamaica, 202
  Whigs, 110, 124
Prince, family, 173-176
  house, 173-176
  Thomas, 173
  William, 173-175
Princess Amalia, The, 264, 265
Privateering, 41-43
  privateers, 135, 218
Privy Council, 72
Profanity, 14
Progress, Long Island (Washington's), 216, 230, 231
Prospect Park, 184
Provincial Governours, 7
Punishments, bodily, 11
Puritans, 202
  authorities, 62
  outlook, 18
Puritanism, 8

Q

Quacks, 20
Quakerism, 10
Quakers, 9, 60, 61, 164-166
  aggressiveness, 9
  disabilities, 61, 62, 135
  Flushing, 25, 26
  opposition to, 9
  persecuted, 150, 170
  whipped, 92

Queen Anne, 69
Queens, County, 76, 146, 198, 253
—Village, Manor of, 20, 103, 119-126
Queen's Rangers, 151

R

Race-course, Newmarket, 23
  racing, 14, 15, 23
Racial divisions, 6
Ranger of Staten Island, 277
Rapalje, Engletie, 214
  Margrietje, 193
Raritans, Indians, 265
Raynham, Hall, 148-155
  Manor of, 148
Recipes, "Tangier Book," 102, 103
Religious liberty, 61, 169, 170, 200, 226
Republican Court, 161
Rhode Island, 135, 149, 240, 266
Richmond County, 76, 253
Ridings, Yorkshire in New York, 3, 9, 253
  East, 3, 9
  North, 3
  West, 3
Riedesel, Baron, 280
Roads, Long Island, 21, 224
  North Country, Middle, South Country, 22
Robbins Island, 58
Robinson, William, 61
Rolph, Joseph, 288
Roman Catholics, 9, 96, 169, 170
  Maryland, 169, 170
  Toleration, 169, 170
Rouse, Thomas, 59
Rowdyism, 94, 97
Royal Society, 70, 72
Rumford, Count, 123, 124
  Town of, 124
Rutledge, Edward, 257, 301

314

INDEX

315

INDEX

INDEX

317

INDEX